School Physical Education and Teacher Education

Setting a common international agenda for physical education, this book asks how physical education and physical education teacher education can be reconfigured together so that they are responsive to changes in today's fast-paced, diverse and uncertain global society.

It argues that only a revolutionary move away from national policy silos can reinvigorate physical education and lead to improved, equitable outcomes for children and youth, and both novice and veteran teachers. Drawing on developing success stories in diverse places, this book emphasizes three important strategies:

- international-comparative analyses, which facilitate cross-border knowledge generation, innovation, professional learning and continuous improvement;
- solid, dynamic partnerships between teacher education programmes and exemplary school physical education programmes; and
- knowledge-generating teams consisting of exemplary teachers and teacher educators.

Each chapter provides viable alternatives and rationales framed by unique national and local contexts. Significantly, these chapters announce that the work that lies ahead – and starts now – is a collective action project. It necessitates collaborative research and development among policy leaders, researchers, teacher education specialists, physical education teachers and, in some cases, school-age students.

This is essential reading for all researchers with an interest in physical education or teacher education, and an invaluable source of new perspectives for physical education students, pre-service and in-service teachers, and educational administrators and policymakers.

Ann MacPhail is a Physical Education Teacher Educator in the Department of Physical Education and Sport Sciences at the University of Limerick, Ireland.

Hal A. Lawson is Professor of Social Welfare and Educational Policy and Leadership at the University at Albany-SUNY, USA.

Routledge Studies in Physical Education and Youth Sport
Series Editor: David Kirk, *University of Strathclyde, UK*

The *Routledge Studies in Physical Education and Youth Sport* series is a forum for the discussion of the latest and most important ideas and issues in physical education, sport, and active leisure for young people across school, club and recreational settings. The series presents the work of the best well-established and emerging scholars from around the world, offering a truly international perspective on policy and practice. It aims to enhance our understanding of key challenges, to inform academic debate, and to have a high impact on both policy and practice, and is thus an essential resource for all serious students of physical education and youth sport.

Also available in this series

www.routledge.com/sport/series/RSPEYS

School Physical Education and Teacher Education

Collaborative Redesign for the Twenty-first Century

Edited by Ann MacPhail and
Hal A. Lawson

Routledge
Taylor & Francis Group

LONDON AND NEW YORK

First published 2020
by Routledge
2 Park Square, Milton Park, Abingdon, Oxon OX14 4RN

and by Routledge
52 Vanderbilt Avenue, New York, NY 10017

Routledge is an imprint of the Taylor & Francis Group, an informa business

British Library Cataloguing-in-Publication Data
A catalogue record for this book is available from the British Library

Library of Congress Cataloging-in-Publication Data
A catalog record has been requested for this book

ISBN: 978-0-367-35246-2 (hbk)
ISBN: 978-0-429-33018-6 (ebk)

Typeset in Goudy
by Wearset Ltd, Boldon, Tyne and Wear

Contents

Foreword

Doune Macdonald

This book is both ambitious and ground-breaking. Not only does it make the case for framing "grand challenges" in Physical Education (PE) and Physical Education Teacher Education (PETE), it articulates the challenges and offers solutions. "Grand challenges" are difficult, important and crystallizing problems which invite global and collaborative solutions. To my knowledge, Ann MacPhail and Hal Lawson are the first in our field to outline what are the grand challenges for PE and PETE and this contribution should not be underestimated. Powerful institutions of our time, such as the Gates Foundation, use grand challenges to seize people's imaginations and mobilize resources. Such is the potential for the 13 grand challenges outlined in this collection. In the words of Ann and Hal, the grand challenges serve as "a unifier and rallying mechanism" (p. 6) at a time when:

> There is a significant gap between recommended practices and policies and what happens in the day-to-day realities of schools. To address this, we need to stop working in isolation and work with, and learn from, each other, while remaining mindful of systematic differences visible nationally and internationally.
>
> (p. 9)

Before reading the book's grand challenges presented initially in Chapter 1, I encourage you to reflect for a moment on what you would see as the grand challenges of the field from your perspective. A curriculum that fails to connect with the future needs of young people? A lack of resources that limits what can be provided to support quality PE programmes? A failure to invest in teachers' professional learning and leadership? The grand challenges that Ann, Hal and their contributors present are a confluence of enduring problems globally with an eye to the impacts of globalization, diversity, neoliberal accountabilities and digital technologies. Yet, refreshingly, this book is not pessimistic nor weighed down with theoretical obfuscation. Each chapter's challenge is accompanied with highly considered ways to react, rethink, redesign and collaboratively research for collective action and optimal impact.

The book opens with Ann and Hal outlining the case and approach for "An international framework for strategic planning, proactive leadership and adaptive designs" (p. 2). A stimulus was Hal's 2018 edited book, *Redesigning Physical Education: An Equity Agenda in Which Every Child Matters*, which focuses on evidence-based (re)designing of curricula in nine countries with a closing tilt at our enduring entanglement with industrial age schooling models. This book takes an international-comparative framework drawing on well-established and emerging authors from across ten countries to promote cross-border learning, development, lesson-drawing, and knowledge generation.

This disruption to traditional ways of knowing and working are shared trademarks of Ann's and Hal's scholarship as is their demonstrable and enduring commitment to equity and excellence. Each grand challenge chapter represents a determination to value the richness that multiple perspectives – in roles, professions, disciplines, countries, languages, cultures, genders – can bring to defining and addressing a grand challenge. Some of the diverse writing teams reveal that they have not met face-to-face but nevertheless greatly valued the creative tension in their collaboration.

There is also a discipline to the text that you would expect from Ann and Hal. Each grand challenge chapter is informed by a SWOT (strengths, weakness, opportunities, threats) analysis, opens with perspectives on the challenge, explores alternative responses and closes with reflections on the collaboration, which is particularly poignant where the voices of teachers have been included. The initial articulation of the "grand challenges" was an exercise in "problem-setting" so insightfully identified by Hal over 30 years ago (see Lawson, 1984); an enduring concept from which these authors springboard. The reader is invited to recognize the contextual distinctiveness in how each grand challenge is approached but remain open to learning from other contexts and defining their own grand challenges.

"Adaptive leadership" is another strong conceptual tool that offers a powerful line of sight throughout the book. Adaptive leadership approaches challenges as complex problems requiring time and experimentation with colleagues from across organizational boundaries. In the collaboration, participants are encouraged to examine their values, relationships and approaches. Marked by shared responsibility and continuous learning (Heifetz *et al.*, 2009), adaptive leadership is the perfect corollary for mobilizing responses to grand challenges. In Chapter 15, Hal invokes "PE readers-as-leaders" to encourage those in the PE profession to continually learn from within and beyond the profession in order to position themselves as bold and informed leaders open to experimentation and change to address the turbulent and demanding contexts in which they may work.

As student and employer expectations of what constitutes a high quality teacher education put traditional practices under pressure, incorporating grand challenges into PETE programmes could address questions of programme relevance, develop twenty-first century skills (e.g. problem-solving, creativity), introduce the value of transdisciplinarity and inter-professional practice, and excite students to be lifelong leaders. Giving advanced undergraduate students a semester to collaboratively address a relevant grand challenge as a capstone in their programme could be a step-change for the field. There is substantial evidence for the educational value of learning through collaborative, authentic and risky tasks (Fung, 2017) and, by embedding grand challenges into our programmes, we could model career-long problem-setting and problem-solving. Likewise, PE academics' research has been criticized for its lack of programmatic coherence (e.g. Tinning, 2010). Grand challenges, possibly those outlined in the following chapters, could frame national and international research and doctoral programmes such that PE and PETE researchers generate substantial, longitudinal, and international data that inform evidence-based, quality experiences for our students.

An international-comparative approach to these deftly articulated grand challenges makes for a compelling and accessible book for all those in the PE field as well as those who work with them. The book instantiates the argument that shared problem-setting and problem-solving across traditional boundaries produces richer and more nuanced solutions. In Chapter 16, Ann outlines the significant contributions that could be made to young people's physical activity, sport and health-related needs through professional partnerships, including scholar-practitioners, research ecosystems, shared recognition and new ways of dissemination. Ann and Hal's vision for this book, captured in the subtitle *Collaborative Redesign for the Twenty-first Century* resonates with Richard Florida's (2002) text, *The Rise of the Creative Class*, a "class" that includes educators, scientists, and designers and others who value individuality (not individualism or conformity), meritocracy, diversity and openness. In many ways, creativity is at the heart of this edited collection that shares new ways of working for an optimistic future.

References

Florida, R. (2002). *The Rise of the Creative Class*. New York: Basic Books.

Fung, D. (2017). *A Connected Curriculum for Higher Education*. London: UCL Press.

Heifetz, R., Linsky, M., and Grashow, A. (2009). *The Practice of Adaptive Leadership: Tools and Tactics for Changing your Organization and the World*. Cambridge, MA: Harvard Business School Press.

Lawson, H. (1984) Problem-setting for physical education and sport. *Quest*, 36(1), 46–60.

Tinning, R. (2010). *Pedagogy and Human Movement: Theory, Practice, Research*. Abingdon: Routledge.

Grand challenges as catalysts for the collaborative redesign of physical education, teacher education, and research and development

Ann MacPhail and Hal A. Lawson

School Physical Education (PE) and companion Physical Education Teacher Education (PETE) programmes in higher education in diverse parts of the world share an important developmental trajectory. For example, they have been developed in response to the dominant model for a universal school in the host nation, which encourages ideas about "a one best PE system". Leaders emphasize "reforms" and "improvements" in existing programmes, practices, and policies. "Dis-connects" between PE and PETE are commonplace. Conflicts among PE teachers, even in the same school, are not unusual, at the same time that PETE faculty-researchers engage in international contests for the one best PE model for the universal model for a school. Above all, equitable opportunities and outcomes for all manner of children and youths remain elusive (Lawson, 2018), particularly in national, state/provincial, and local contexts in which elite sport performance dominates the PE agenda.

Meanwhile, an international research and development enterprise emphasizes standardization founded on commonalities and similarities involving PE, PETE, and their relations. Examples start with three international handbooks, which provide valuable reviews of theory, research, and practice. Like all such reviews, *The Routledge Handbook of Physical Education Pedagogies* (Ennis, 2017), *The Routledge Handbook of Primary Physical Education* (Griggs and Petrie, 2017), and *The Handbook of Physical Education* (Kirk *et al.*, 2006) emphasize retrospective accounts of progress indicators and collective achievements. These handbooks, like other international research and development literatures, are essential repositories for PE and PETE pedagogy. They summarize what American sociologist Dan Lortie (1975) called "the shared technical culture" for teachers and teacher educators, recommending optimal practices and policies for the important work of helping young people around the world adopt health-enhancing, physically active lifestyles.

However, these handbooks are selective in two important ways. They minimize the importance of national and state/provincial contexts, oftentimes offering the impression that the knowledge bases they summarize will travel easily across national and regional borders. At the same time, they convey the impression that societies, schools, communities, families, and young people are in a relatively stable state, enabling PE professionals worldwide to prioritize reforms and modest improvements in schools, teacher education programmes, and public policies. Put another way, these handbooks emphasize an inward-looking perspective. They risk promoting the assumption that today's PE programmes and schools, like PETE programmes and higher education institutions, will be more or less the same tomorrow.

An international framework for strategic planning, proactive leadership, and adaptive designs offers an important, timely alternative. It encourages PE and PETE professionals and other key stakeholders to perform regular assessments of strengths, weaknesses, opportunities and threats. In shorthand, these strategies are called SWOT assessments. Twin SWOT assessments are recommended: (1) ones directed at the internal environments, i.e. intra-professional strengths, weaknesses, opportunities, and threats; and (2) ones directed toward external environments, i.e. local, state/provincial, national, and international fixtures, challenges, and changes. While some of this SWOT work can be framed as futures-responsive, it also has the potential to yield programme and policy catalysts which may shape more desirable futures for PE, PETE, teachers, children and youths, and schools and communities.

All SWOT assessments yield important knowledge regarding the unique features and developmental trajectories of nations, world regions, states and provinces, and local contexts. Nevertheless, the multifaceted process of globalization is a homogenizing force. It helps to explain cross-border commonalities and similarities alongside unique characteristics. Toward this end, the field of international and comparative education is founded in part on the advantages gained by cross-national studies focused on commonalities, similarities, and differences. It emphasizes manifest needs, vexing problems, and promising solutions.

Drawing on this international-comparative perspective, this book presents the results of a specialized SWOT analysis. *Grand Challenges* are identified and described in the following chapters, illuminating dramatic and somewhat variable changes underway in nations around the world. While modest reforms and incremental improvements in PE and PETE may be fit for purpose, these grand challenges also may necessitate the strategic redesign of PE, PETE, and their relations (Lawson, 2018). Either way, teachers and teacher educators confront inescapable questions regarding how best to respond (e.g. via reform and improvement strategies) as well as whether and how to assume leadership for bold redesign strategies. Each chapter provides viable alternatives and rationales, albeit framed and limited by particular national and local contexts.

Significantly, these chapters announce that the work that lies ahead – and starts now – is a collective action project. It necessitates collaborative research and development among policy leaders, researchers, teacher education specialists, PE teachers, and, in some cases, school-age students. No wonder: each grand challenge is an adaptive problem without easy answers (Heifetz *et al.*, 2009). In other words, the work that lies ahead is not merely implementation of what may be considered as optimal practice models and strategies. It also involves strategic innovation and bold redesign in schools and community education systems, which are like moving targets because their leaders also are wrestling with adaptive problems caused by emergent grand challenges.

Whether in school systems, PE, or PETE, responsive research and development initiatives outstrip the expertise of one or a few authorities. Thus, it is timely and important to marshal the talents and expertise of international experts, especially eminent physical education teacher educators, expert PE teachers and policy stakeholders. Team-based writing is a practical necessity because addressing internationally-relevant grand challenges requires collective action, albeit with important reminders. For example, contextual uniqueness rules out the idea of a singular generalizable solution.

In other words, while professionals everywhere may confront the same or comparable grand challenges, the context matters. The implication is that singular "one size fits all" solutions no longer are good currency. To wit: continuous quality improvement strategies are fit for purpose in some contexts, while bold redesign is needed in others.

This book provides a framework for all such understanding. More than social analysis, it offers practical strategies and innovative policy proposals for practising and prospective teachers and teacher educators. This new rationale can be hailed as "unity with diversity" founded on international-comparative analysis.

The importance of an international-comparative framework

This book is a sequel to *Redesigning Physical Education* (Lawson, 2018) which also offers an international-comparative perspective. Framed by an American-style analysis in the initial chapters, teams of authors representing mostly English-speaking, Euro-centric nations provided developmental treatises of reform, improvement and redesign initiatives in their host nations. One of the benefits from the book is enhanced understanding of international commonalities, similarities, and uniqueness; and particularly what leaders have done in response to emergent needs and challenges, while striving to create a more desirable future.

Changing contexts

The timing is right for more such collaborative, international-comparative analyses. The context for schools, higher education institutions that serve as organizational homes for PETE programmes, and policy is changing rapidly and dramatically. In contrast to relatively stable nations with firm boundaries, today's global societies change rapidly and even dramatically. For example, unprecedented numbers of people continue to cross borders, bringing diverse languages and cultural traditions from sender nations to receiving nations that provide new homes. Meanwhile, successful technological innovations and new policy designs in one nation are being evaluated to determine their import and transferability for a host nation – and with special interest in how emergent models and strategies developed elsewhere hold promise for emergent and persistent challenges in the host nation.

Cross-border learning, development, lesson-drawing, and knowledge generation

All such international-comparative analysis undertaken with the possibility of cross-border transfer of innovative institutional designs, policies, and practices is ripe with uncertainty, complexity, and risk. Few innovations developed in one nation transfer easily and effectively to others because the national, regional, and local contexts differ, and each nation's somewhat unique social institutional designs matter.

On the other hand, a particular nation's developing success story is noteworthy as leaders address one or more vexing problems that also challenge other nations. Although the direct technology transfer is not feasible or advisable, there is much to be learned from international-comparative analysis. In fact, new knowledge developed in one nation has practical import for other nations, which raises an important practical question. How can its potential be realized and maximized?

Schön and Rein (1995) developed the idea of "lesson-drawing" to describe this cross-border, knowledge-sharing and learning-rich process. It is founded on several ideas which also are foundational for this book. For example, diverse nations oftentimes confront identical and comparable challenges – as indicated in the structure of this book. While myriad forces and factors are at play as proposed solutions are crafted, implemented, and evaluated in a host nation, there is much to be learned and gained as this process unfolds. Kurt Lewin's (1952) framework for an action-oriented science has particular relevance. Assuming he was correct when he claimed that one of the best ways to understand any phenomenon is by attempting to change it in its naturally-occurring context(s), it follows that PE- and PETE-focused innovations developed to address a grand challenge in one nation have import for others.

Drawing on Lewin, failed, partially effective, and successful innovations provide insights into the phenomenon of interest – a special grand challenge. More specifically, they enhance agenda-setting, also known as problem-setting (Lawson, 1984), focused on the grand challenge. Experiences in one nation recommend alternative ways to frame the needs, opportunities and problems in other nations, perhaps nominating a special language or discourse system. Here, comparative social analysis paves the way for strategic social action across borders and in context-sensitive ways.

This priority for nation-specific, contextual sensitivity derives from disciplines known variously as international-comparative studies, globalization studies, and sustainable development studies. In contrast to rough-cut, early twentieth century frameworks founded on flawed assumptions regarding international commonalities and important similarities, international-comparative research and development, operating under several names, is more nuanced. For example, the idea of Regional Development Studies emphasizes nations' social geographic, demographic, and economic development features, including claims that nations in particular parts of the world have enough in common to be considered, studied, and perhaps improved together. At the same time, inherited classifications such as post-industrial nations, industrialized nations, and developing nations continue to be applied in particular regions of the world.

Framing and addressing international grand challenges: key assumptions

This book is structured to enable Physical Educationists and paediatric Kinesiology specialists to draw on salient frameworks and strategies derived from international-comparative analyses and regional development studies as they strive to make progress in meeting physical activity, sport, and health-related needs of children and youths worldwide. The main assumptions need to be made explicit in order to prevent misunderstanding and facilitate strategic, collective action in particular nations.

- As globalization advances, physical educationists and paediatric Kinesiology specialists in diverse parts of the world must address emergent and future needs and priorities, herein called Grand Challenges.
- Although these grand challenges play out somewhat uniquely in host national contexts, salient commonalities and similarities recommend the generic inventory presented in this book.
- Although a particular grand challenge may not be evident or prioritized at this time, the steady march of globalization predicts its eventual emergence with needs for strategic action.
- Educators, broadly defined to include educational policy leaders, are already wrestling with some of the same grand challenges, and their efforts are manifested in innovations in schools and education systems overall.
- The foundational efforts of Physical Educationists and paediatric Kinesiology specialists to address one or more grand challenges in particular parts of the world offer important lessons for colleagues in diverse nations worldwide.
- Lesson-drawing from real-world efforts in particular nations to address one or more Grand Challenges is not to be interpreted as imperialism, a thinly-veiled colonial initiative, or yet another homogenizing influence of globalization.
- Every model or strategy developed to address one or more of the Grand Challenges depends on firm partnerships involving teachers, teacher educators and other professors, and public policy leaders because every constituency influences and is influenced by the overall system.
- No present-day PE school programme model or teacher education counterpart appears to be fit for purpose to address all of the Grand Challenges.

- International research and development networks formed around models and strategies for addressing the Grand Challenges signal an important strategy whose time has come.
- Books like this one are important catalysts for improvement and redesign because they highlight shared and comparable grand challenges and offer lessons to teachers, teacher educators, policy leaders, and others with regard to how best to meet the needs of diverse young people worldwide.

Shared grand challenges as a unifier and rallying mechanism

The idea of "grand challenges" unites the chapters and provides a unique focus for the book. The assumption is that the challenges confronting PE and PETE are manifest in some form in nearly every nation.

However, the authors of each chapter are exposed to and work in very different systems of PE and PETE. They describe, explain and justify their work in ways that invariably are context-dependent. Two implications follow. The priorities and action strategies they identify and describe may not be transportable. However, authors' descriptions regarding how they established and named their respective agendas (Lawson, 1984), including how and why they opted for particular strategies, offer rich learning and professional development opportunities for teachers, teacher educators, and other professionals interested in school PE programmes.

The basic idea for important grand challenges has been tried and tested in two other professions. As the twenty-first century dawned, engineering used the grand challenges idea as a stimulus for proactive improvements and proposals for bold redesign. The American social work profession followed suit in 2014. Significantly, both professions continue to be animated by members' and leaders' shared focus on grand challenges, and also policy proposals.

The identification and development of the grand challenges chapters illustrates the generative, creative potential of this concept. While some specific grand challenges suggested to authors at the start of the writing project remain, authors have reframed some and added others. This developmental progression gives expression to this book's idea of collective action to achieve a collective impact. Courageous conversations are implicit in each chapter and the book overall, and it is here where the voice of the practitioner community is invaluable.

Colonialism is an ever-present danger in every international-comparative analysis, particularly ones that provide possible solutions and recommended innovations. To guard against the risks and dangers, the grand challenge chapters in this book are jointly authored by international teams. This strategy provides a rich, unique international perspective on each of the grand challenges, and it sets the stage for policy and practice lesson-drawing across national borders as well as innovation design and transfer.

Introducing the grand challenges

The authors and editors have agreed on 13 grand challenges with due recognition that they are not the only ones. These grand challenges are representative of what professionals in diverse nations worldwide would discover and prioritize if they initiated SWOT analyses. "Representative" does not mean or imply identical language and framing because agenda setting typically varies as a function of the host nation, public policy trajectories, institutional designs, and educational expectations and aspirations (Lawson, 1984). The grand challenges are presented in the following sequence.

> Chapter 2: The aims and outcomes challenge: preparing physical education teacher educators and teachers for twenty-first century redesign imperatives and accountability requirements.
> Chapter 3: The standards-based curricular reform challenge: shared responsibility through networking.
> Chapter 4: The alignment and coherence challenge: developing university–school partnerships for the simultaneous improvement and redesign of school programmes and teacher education.
> Chapter 5: The innovation challenge: maintaining programme standards and developing cohesion while developing and testing alternative designs in new kinds of schools.
> Chapter 6: The interdisciplinary challenge: preparing teacher educators and teachers to span knowledge, organizational and international boundaries.
> Chapter 7: The professional socialization challenge: teacher education for a preferable future for physical education.
> Chapter 8: Cultural competence challenge: readying schools and university programmes for student, teacher, and faculty diversity.
> Chapter 9: The digital age challenge: preparing physical and health educators to understand and support "online" youth.
> Chapter 10: The physical education school curriculum challenge: the shared construction, implementation and enactment of school physical education curriculum.
> Chapter 11: The research and development challenge: better aligning teachers' and teacher educators' needs, priorities, and demands.
> Chapter 12: The evidence-based decision-making challenge: developing research-supported, data-informed, structures and strategies in schools and teacher education programmes.
> Chapter 13: The professional development challenge: achieving desirable outcomes for students, teachers, and teacher educators.
> Chapter 14: The public policy challenge: preparing and supporting teacher educators and teachers as change agents and policy entrepreneurs.

In response to the subsequent discussions that arise across the 13 grand challenges, the editors each provide a response in the two closing chapters;

Chapter 15: Learning to plan and planning to learn during turbulent times. Chapter 16: Developing commitments and capacity to learn with, and from, each other.

The layout of each grand challenge chapter

Each chapter briefly introduces the specific grand challenge, including any special circumstances that the authors believed surrounded what they were being asked to do. This introduction may include assumptions each author brings to the grand challenge.

Some chapters explore alternative responses to the grand challenge. Diverse views are important because they reflect everyday reality. The choices and practical decisions authors describe encourage the reader to place herself or himself in the same position, considering the alternatives as generative ideas for future enactment. As important as the "message" that arises from each chapter is the process experienced by each author team as they joined forces to consider and address a specific grand challenge. For some authors, this may have been the first time they had operated in a space shared by others with different perspectives, experiences and vision with respect to a specific challenge. The priority assigned to the views, voices, experiences, and preferences of practising teachers is a special asset. The international literature overall frequently omits them – at a significant cost to the knowledge base for the profession.

The idea of team approaches to grand challenges is timely and important. To acknowledge this important part of the grand challenge process, some author teams include a short epilogue at the end of the chapter to capture the conversation around the construction of their chapter. This reinforces the practical experiential development perspective, where authors reflect on how they (collectively) processed and addressed the grand challenge. This approach enables diverse readers to gain a shared understanding. They learn something about the reality of working together, with an aligned discourse around addressing challenges with a view to benefiting the collective good, i.e. "us", rather than the individual.

Each chapter concludes with proposing a collaborative (across jurisdictions and stakeholders), relevant future research agenda, specific to the grand challenge, with the potential to impact PE and PETE policy and practice internationally. Where appropriate, author teams suggest the roles of specific stakeholders in contributing to the research agenda.

Recommended perspective for readers

If it is safe to assume that the grand challenges identified, described, and addressed in an international-comparative framework have some measure of international relevance, this book provides a jump-start and a preliminary guide for SWOT assessments undertaken locally. This work is not easy. The challenge is to strike a justifiable balance between global challenges and both the desirability of, and necessity for, more nuanced, national, state/provincial, and local policy, practice and research development.

International consensus is not a priority or a realistic outcome. The main aim for all SWOT assessments is to jump-start reactive and proactive planning, interrupting presentism rooted in the perceived inevitability and effectiveness of the status quo.

Viewed in this way, this book should appeal to leadership-oriented individuals, groups, and teams, particularly in schools and their higher education partners. Beyond these typical stakeholder groups, the challenges presented in this book are relevant to many national and international organizations. For example, the International Association for Physical Education in Higher Education (AIESEP) shares a common interest in physical education, physical activity and sport pedagogy across the lifespan. The National Association for Kinesiology in Higher Education (NAKHE) wishes to foster leadership in kinesiology management and policy related to teaching, scholarship and service in higher education.

At a micro-level, the number of physical education, health and sport pedagogy Special Interest Groups (SIGs) attached to national organizations is sizeable and continues to grow. There are many collective spaces where members working in partnership within and across organizations can be nurtured and supported. This in turn, should encourage the growth of international networks of practitioners and scholars as well as illustrate the need for a unifying understanding and agenda on how best to advocate for, and enact, a collaborative redesign of school PE and PETE.

The bottom line remains and can no longer be ignored and denied. There is a significant gap between recommended practices and policies and what happens in the day-to-day realities of schools. To address this, we need to stop working in isolation and work with, and learn from, each other, while remaining mindful of systematic differences visible nationally and internationally. Diversity is an asset when it is framed by common purpose, and particularly when the voices and views of practising teachers, teacher educators, and paediatric specialists are joined and heeded. Such a collective action project allows for a shared understanding on why we have set such an agenda and encourages enactment through ongoing learning and capacity building. Ultimately, we serve young people around the world and, as we do, we also make our professional work easier and better.

References

Ennis, C. (ed.) (2017). *Routledge Handbook of Physical Education Pedagogies.* Oxon: Routledge.

Griggs, G. and Petrie, K. (2017). *The Routledge Handbook of Primary Physical Education.* Oxon: Routledge.

Heifetz, R., Linsky, M. and Grashow, A. (2009). *The Practice of Adaptive Leadership: Tools and Tactics for Changing your Organization and the World.* Cambridge, MA: Harvard Business School Press.

Kirk, D., Macdonald, D. and O'Sullivan, M. (2006). *The Handbook of Physical Education.* Sage: London.

Lawson, H. (2018). *Redesigning Physical Education. An Equity Agenda in Which Every Child Matters.* Oxon: Routledge.

Lawson, H. (1984). Problem-setting for physical education and sport. *Quest*, 36(1), 46–60.

Lewin, K. (1952). *Selected Theoretical Papers.* London: Tavistock Publications.

Lortie, D. (1975). *Schoolteacher: A Sociological Analysis.* Chicago: University of Chicago Press.

Schön, D. and Rein, M. (1995). *Frame Reflection: Toward the Resolution of Intractable Policy Controversies.* New York: Basic Books.

Chapter 2

The aims and outcomes challenge

Preparing physical education teacher educators and teachers for twenty-first century redesign imperatives and accountability requirements

Lisette Burrows, Mary O'Sullivan, Ger Halbert and Emily Scott

Introduction

Global, national and local shifts in political, cultural, economic and educational discourses mean Physical Education (PE) teachers and teacher educators must understand, adapt and respond to a bewildering array of challenges and do so frequently. One of these challenges is the dual-edged, perennial one of clarifying the aims and outcomes of PE and PE teacher education (PETE). Beyond these two programmes are the formidable challenges of gaining agreement among PE teachers and PE teacher educators.

The challenge is at once local, national, and international. As MacPhail and Lawson (2020) signal in the opening chapter, while easy answers are elusive, experiences in one nation (can) recommend alternative ways to frame the needs, opportunities and problems in other nations. Local solutions to local problems will almost always work best, and many initiatives embraced in Ireland and New Zealand have a distinctly home-grown flavour to them. In so saying, as will become evident below, there are shared governmental pressures in both countries and shared struggles around meeting and/or challenging those pressures across these two nations.

Our writing/thinking team comprises an academic and a teacher from New Zealand, a teacher educator and researcher from Ireland and a policymaker with a senior administrative role in Ireland's National Council for Curriculum and Assessment. Each brings a set of assumptions, knowledge and expertise garnered from their assorted roles and their particular geographic and career locales. It is the different stories we each bring that fuel our collaborative attempt to think through the challenge of preparing teacher educators and teachers for twenty-first century redesign imperatives and accountability requirements.

Lisette arrived at this challenge as a tertiary physical educator of 25 plus years of experience. Her research has predominantly dealt with issues of social justice and diversity in relation to school-based PE.

Mary is at the end of her career as a teacher educator and researcher for over 35 years. She has worked in PETE in Ireland, the United States and Canada with a commitment to building teachers' capacities as leaders, innovators and advocates for PE.

Ger has taught HPE for over 30 years and has been a key influencer of policy in Ireland's PE curriculum for schools in her role with the National Council for Curriculum and Assessment.

Emily has taught secondary school HPE in New Zealand over a 20 year period. Recently, she has undertaken postgraduate study in the area of primary school HPE where she is exploring variations on the theme of what matters in HPE.

Ireland and New Zealand are clearly different contexts so we began our collaborative journey with a context-specific brainstorm of some of the key issues (large scale and closer to home) confronting Irish PE and New Zealand PE that we believe have resonance for a global context. We were struck by the parallels. Issues that featured prominently were (i) catering to diverse student populations; (ii) planning for, and assessment of, learning; (iii) meeting accountability requirements; (iv) addressing student wellbeing; (v) dealing with outside providers of physical activity/sport; (vi) juggling competing agendas as to the aims of PE; (vii) negotiating extra-curricula demands; and (viii) grappling with the specialist versus generalist PE teacher debate at primary school level. Each and all of these could have served as foci for this chapter. Framed by this extensive menu of alternatives, we have selected three anchors for the work that best meets our brief to prepare teacher educators and teachers for twenty-first century redesign imperatives and accountability requirements. These are challenges identified in both contexts, and challenges that our reading and collated professional expertise suggest may resonate with those experienced in other nations. These are, in no particular order: (1) justifying and advocating for the place of PE in schools; (2) how do we know what is learned and how to share that learning; and (3) dealing with diversity.

Our orientation toward these three challenges is undoubtedly framed and informed by our biographies. In so saying, our collaborative conversations and the learnings from our journey together has produced shared and richer understandings than those we could have achieved alone. To craft our discussion, we draw on excerpts from our conversations and interweave research and theoretical resources drawn from PE academics throughout. We begin each section by articulating the dimensions of the challenge. We pose our collective questions and reflections on this challenge for teachers, schools, PETE and policymakers, and conclude each section with our musings about potential ways forward. Our approach exemplifies what can be learned when engaged in a collaborative and deliberative process.

Anchor 1: justifying and advocating for PE in schools

The question of what counts as worthwhile knowledge, skills, attitudes and values in PE is an enduring one. Writers of successive international handbooks (e.g. Kirk, MacDonald and O'Sullivan, 2006; Kirk, 2009; Griggs and Petrie, 2017) and attendees at world summits (e.g. World Summit on PE, 1999 and Second World Summit on PE, 2005) have puzzled over it. Indeed, the current text can be regarded as another attempt to re-think, justify, rationalize the place, purpose and potential of PE in schools, albeit one that takes this challenge further by emphasizing the relationship between stakeholders in school PE's re-design. The challenge relates to broad and weighty issues about what is worth doing and why in terms of curriculum, yet it has a more personal angle to it. It is difficult to teach, to maintain even a modicum of enthusiasm for your subject, if you are not entirely sure what is special about it. It is also challenging to be, or become, what Hellison and Templin (1991) would refer to as a "reflective physical educator" without a solid platform from which to consider one's practice. Furthermore, in an increasingly crowded curriculum, with multiple internal and external demands on teaching time and emphases (Burrows et al., 2013), being ready and able to justify and advocate for the place of PE both within and outside of schools is fundamental. While we neither imagine nor desire a universalized response to this question, we nevertheless maintain that having some kind of philosophical position regarding what is worth learning and why in school-based PE is crucial to advance and/or maintain any version of quality PE. We regard this challenge as important for schools and teachers, PETE and policymakers.

Across our respective contexts, PE has been, and is, justified in multiple ways. At times, PE is regarded as a vehicle for enhancing student fitness (Alfrey and Gard, 2019) or developing motor skills for anticipated future engagement in sport (Bailey et al., 2009). At other times, PE is harnessed to public health agendas, whether these be reducing obesity rates (Kirk, 2006) or strengthening student wellbeing in a more holistic sense. Latterly, PE and its derivatives (play and physical activity) are regularly drawn on as means for achievement of socially desired outcomes, including emotional intelligence and ethical behaviour.

The shifting and ever-expansive justifications for PE's presence in the school curriculum are in one sense understandable. As educational scholars have been saying for years, school subjects are necessarily shaped by broader socio-political and economic agendas (Goodson, 2013). In so saying, the vagaries of governmental agendas should not necessarily interfere with the formulation of a clear, if dynamic, set of core beliefs that can serve as a platform from which to launch PE programmes that are meaningful, relevant and connected to the increasingly diverse needs and interests of young people.

Speaking and planning from a philosophical stance is not simply a rhetorical gesture. Being able to do so solves several other challenges PE teachers face in the current climate. Three are especially noteworthy. First, a clear philosophical position permits teachers and school principals to make decisions about what and who enters the school gates in support of the PE programme. If the local cricket club wants to deliver sessions to students, the question becomes, "Does the cricket club's intent match, embellish or detract from the core purpose of a PE programme?" If the Police wish to instigate a "keeping ourselves safe" programme with primary school students in PE time, how does that align with the "What is worth doing and why?" deliberations? Second, grounding practice in a clear philosophical commitment permits engaged and vibrant professional discussions with colleagues. When ongoing professional development resourcing is minimal, and/or focussed on "tips and tricks" for teaching different activities, opportunities to have meaningful conversations about why we do what we do and with what effects are golden. Third, being clear about what one believes and why is integral to developing and maintaining a sense of identity as a PE teacher. In the face of career instability (e.g. part-time roles), innumerable demands on one's time (e.g. recruited to coach extra-curricula sports teams; administrative burdens) and conundrums about the status of PE as a viable school subject, retaining a sense of what it means to belong to the PE profession would seem crucial. Nearly 20 years ago, Woods' (1990) life history work with retired teachers led her to claim "a teacher's self, in part at least, both finds expression in, and gives expression to a curriculum area" (Woods, 1990, p. 145). We suggest that little has changed in this regard. What teachers prioritize and do influences and is influenced by who they are – their social identities.

For teacher educators, committing to the notion that being able to justify and advocate for PE's role in schools as a non-negotiable professional capacity would mean that time, space and place would be given in initial PETE for pre-service teachers to talk and write about what drives their commitment to school-based PE. Comfortable spaces for sharing and interrogating values and beliefs about PE, opportunities to compare these with "established" scholarly positions and high stakes encouragement (e.g. via accreditation) to see the development and expression of a philosophy of PE as a fundamental precursor to good practice would constitute a strong and deliberate starting place.

As we signalled earlier, we see little reason to demand adherence to any universal, generic set of claims for PE's role in a young person's overall education, despite current trends to advance a range of best models (Casey, 2014). Rather, what seems to be needed at policy level is a broad, yet compelling, statement regarding the importance of PE that leaves some room for individual teachers and schools to make and re-make sense of this in relation to their specific contexts, needs, interests and aspirations of their students. The Ministry of Education (2007) in New Zealand has taken this route, broadly stating the aims of the curriculum area, clarifying broad principles and values that underpin it, but permitting teachers in diverse locales to develop programmes and philosophies premised on their unique circumstances. In terms of PETE, this requires the fostering of thinking, reflective, critically aware teachers who are able and willing to develop professional judgements regarding what should be done (curriculum and pedagogy) premised on solid understandings of their own contexts and their own personal commitments to the value of their subject area and the needs of their students.

Our necessarily brief canvas of the reasons why a philosophical stance is important yields few concrete answers. Indeed, perhaps that is the point. A global re-think of the purpose and potential of PE in the twenty-first century may not be needed, but local, partial, lived and contextualized re-thinking certainly is. And all such reconstructions necessitate learning, particularly teachers' continuing professional development (CPD). As Ger shares:

> Many teachers appear to get "lost" in the frenetic business of school and seem to lose sight of why they became teachers and, in particular, PE teachers. More needs to be done in CPD at both national and school level to allow teachers to reflect on their educational values, where these values came from, how they sit in their current practice, to "review/renew" their vows about what is important for them in their teaching for their students.

Anchor 2: how do we know what is learned and how to share that learning?

PE teachers report frequently on the marginalization of PE and on it not being a core contributor to the educational objectives of secondary schooling (Kretchmar, 2006). They lament the lack of expectations for student learning by parents or school administrators and that PE is neither recognized nor rewarded in any formal certificate of student learning (Sheehy, 2011).

The global focus on teacher accountability and on expectations that teachers provide evidence of student learning has provided opportunities (formal profiles of student achievements in PE) for teachers to remedy the latter, although not all are happy with these developments (MacPhail and Murphy, 2017). National policy, as reflected in curriculum and assessment initiatives, has impacted education practices in New Zealand and Ireland. While high stakes assessment has been a feature of these educational systems, recent policy developments demonstrate a shift from rote learning and summative high stakes examinations (i.e. *assessment of learning*) to the inclusion of formative assessment processes and a priority on classroom based *assessment for learning*. In these developments, the student is positioned at the core of the learning experience and student voice reflected in curriculum design, pedagogy, and assessment practices.

This policy context has created greater accountability for student learning and teacher requirements around gathering evidence of learning. This increased focus on what students are learning in PE, and on gathering evidence of that learning, has generated a greater emphasis on teachers' planning for meaningful learning and assessment strategies. The 2018 International Association for PE in Higher Education (AIESEP) Special Seminar on Assessment in PE reflected the "growing research interest in PE assessment, the complexities PE teachers meet in planning and carrying out assessment, and the increasing emphasis placed on accountability within education at large" (AIESEP, 2018). The differences in approach to PE assessment were evident in the scholarly presentations. The USA has invested in generating standardized, authentic and meaningful assessments for, and of, learning, while European and Australian presenters focused more on principles to guide the assessment capacities of PE teachers in assessing students in their contexts. Both approaches present significant professional development challenges for PE.

In both countries, PE teachers are expected to contribute to the core learning objectives of secondary school education. In Ireland, schools and teachers are provided with a greater degree of autonomy in how they plan content and assessments to align with, and support, students achieving learning outcomes and key skills. National level assessment guidelines (NCCA, 2018a) set out specific assessment activities to be completed. The focus has been on the alignment of learning outcomes, with teaching processes and assessment *for* learning. While teachers have the autonomy to plan for PE they must include evidence of student learning. They must demonstrate students' achievements of specific learning statements and key skills.

This policy focus on assessment *for* learning has created a major challenge for teachers and the educational system in general. The emphasis is on continuous assessment of student learning: (i) on formative teacher and peer feedback in support of student learning; (ii) on greater student responsibility for their learning; (iii) on high expectations for learning from teachers; and (iv) on clear teacher feedback to students and parents on what is going well and how they can improve.

Teachers need significant support to build their assessment capabilities (Hay and Penny, 2012) in order to facilitate genuine engagement by learners in assessment processes. These assessment capabilities (Black and William, 2018) include: (i) clarity of learning intentions and criteria for success; (ii) engineering of effective classroom discussions, questions, and debates as to learning intentions; (iii) providing feedback that moves student learning forward; (iv) activating students as peer resources for learning; and (v) motivating students as owners of their own learning. Traditionally, teachers have felt most confident in planning for subject matter content (i.e. designing motivational drills and progressions for engagement in a range of physical activities). The focus has now shifted to engaging with students around what to teach and how best to set up learning activities and assessments that provide evidence of student learning outcomes (see Chapter 3). This is a significant change in practice. A related key challenge is the ability of the educational systems to support teachers in developing these assessment capabilities and in shifting their mindset to learning as a central focus on their planning, assessment and practice.

International research on assessment in PE is not encouraging. Apparently, teachers do not prioritize assessment of learning and have limited understanding of the benefits deriving from it (Leirhaug, 2018). The reviews of literature have noted few examples of peer and self-assessment in contemporary practices, and very little critical reflection on the teachers' role or responsibility for assessment (López-Pastor *et al.*, 2013). It is hard to know if they are failing to recognize or reject the opportunity for greater school and teacher autonomy to plan for PE as they see fit and to provide evidence of that learning (MacPhail and Murphy, 2017).

The challenge for teacher educators is in redesigning PETE programmes to address assessment for and of learning. In addition, teacher educators partner with national Professional Development Programmes to provide sustainable school- and teacher-led communities of practice models to motivate and support teachers to take on the opportunities and challenges that assessment-focused policy developments have created for PE teachers. The creation of the assessment culture that provides students, teachers and parents with examples of student learning in PE can be a catalyst for collaboration among the stakeholders (teachers, schools, teacher education, national curriculum and assessment units) in developing teachers' assessment capabilities around students' authentic engagement and design of their learning assessments. This opportunity holds the potential to position PE as an equitable contributor to the student's educational development and a core aspect of student learning.

There is a need for the creation of practical examples of feasible and meaningful assessments. Facilitating and sustaining communities of PE teachers to create and pilot assessments for learning, aligned with national learning outcomes, will be a key policy imperative for government professional development agencies, teacher accreditation bodies, and PETE departments. Creating opportunities for preservice teachers to design learning assessments, and to research their impact on their own practice, will allow for a new generation of teachers to bring much needed expertise into the system. Professional qualifications and promotions must reward those teachers who make contributions to this knowledge base and to the creation of assessment artefacts, with opportunities to be advocates and mentors to other professionals in the field. Partnerships between national agencies, teachers, and teacher educators in building assessment resource banks, along with an evidence base for these assessments, can support the assessment competence, including diagnostic competence that this focus on student learning and assessment for learning has created for PE.

Anchor 3: dealing with diversity

Dealing with diversity in all its guises emerged as a shared preoccupation across our conversations. First, in both Ireland and New Zealand, an emphasis on student wellbeing and PE's contributory role regarding this is evident. Wellbeing is a woolly term (Liamputtong *et al.*, 2012), defined differently in each context. Its presence as a new area of learning in Ireland's second level education (NCCA 2018b) and its position as an underlying concept for New Zealand's Health and PE curriculum (Ministry of Education, 2007) points to a broader remit for PE, regardless of how it may be configured in both countries. Moving beyond PE for fitness, motor skill development and/or social development to PE's contribution (for example) to fostering resilience, a sense of purpose and belonging to a community permits, and indeed requires, a broader set of disciplinary and professional tools. Psychology, sociology, geography, gender studies and political studies, to name a few, are at least as important as physiology and biomechanics as conceptual resources when tasked with enhancing the wellbeing of differently located young people with vastly different life experiences and aspirations (Leahy *et al.*, 2016).

The diversity of the student population has increased the demands of the teacher "role" and is another challenge resonating across both nations. Teachers' work is shaped by time-poor parents struggling to house and feed their children and trends toward shift work and flexible hours in employment. The changes in societal values, including a decline in volunteerism and variable living arrangements, shape teachers' work contexts. A burgeoning "pay to play sport" mentality, escalating concerns about young people's physical activity and diet, and a proliferation of students who are "anxious" are additional sociocultural factors impacting PE teachers' capacity to teach in ways they are familiar with. The volume of administrative and reporting tasks undertaken by teachers also complicates and diversifies teachers' roles beyond what many are familiar or confident with.

An increased acknowledgement of the diversity of students, a mandate to cater for this diversity and a declared commitment to redressing inequities between and across groups is something worth celebrating in any educational climate. In turn, questions arise for schools and PETE regarding the resources (human and material) needed to support this ever-increasing diversity.

In contrast to the students in their care, PETE recruits are anecdotally a startlingly non-diverse population. Our collective experience suggests that many aspiring teachers arrive with largely uplifting experiences of school-based PE and/or sport, from family and cultural backgrounds that emphasize the value of mainstream education and are devoid of deep understanding of how that privilege shapes their engagement in a profession they love. There are therefore challenges in recruiting a diverse cohort to the teaching profession. There is a further challenge of how to ensure a predominantly non-diverse group has time and opportunity to begin to understand the different world views/experiences of others. Together with this dual issue of recruitment and diversity "education", there is the additional challenge for PETE regarding how time for the practicalities of teaching may be wedded with the desire to provide the opportunity to richly engage with alternative worlds.

For policy leaders there are issues around matching policy rhetoric with practice-related reality. In New Zealand, there are clear and embedded expectations that all teachers will respect and celebrate the diverse traditions, backgrounds and experiences of their students. Policies redress gaps between Pakeha (non-Māori) and indigenous (Māori) students' achievements. Teachers understand, and are committed to, working with content and teaching/learning strategies that may yield enhanced learning for marginalized learners. The resource and understanding needed to do this, however, is not always apace with the enthusi-asm to meet the needs of diverse learners. Ongoing professional development to support the aspirational goals of government on how to most effectively address diversity is needed.

Teachers can facilitate the likelihood that their teaching will "reach" a broader array of children and young people. A basic premise of quality pedagogy is to know your students, e.g. what and who motivates them, what bothers them, what excites them and what do they bring with them to class each day. Many cur-riculum documents advocate for student-centred learning. However, this is not conceivable without a working knowledge of how and what students think and experience. Finding ways to explore student understandings and draw on these in pedagogical decisions is vital.

There are no simple responses to the question of how to deal with an increas-ingly diverse student population. What is obvious across Ireland and New Zealand contexts is that monocultural ways of knowing and practice are not (and perhaps never have been) workable or viable if there is a genuine desire to embrace differ-ence. For schools, teachers, PETE institutions and policymakers, a genuine will to understand the "other" is paramount. So too is the capacity to respond to the diverse needs and interests once these are understood.

Conclusion

As we signalled in our opening discussion, constant change is the new "normal" for physical educators across both Ireland and New Zealand. Change, whether related to policy directions, teacher accountabilities or the status of PE as a school subject, will always yield fresh challenges for teachers, teacher educators and policy creators. The three challenges we have identified here exhibit surpris-ingly similar dimensions across Irish and New Zealand contexts. Our considera-tion of these has also unearthed several shared aspirations for what could help in moving beyond the identification of challenges to potential solutions.

Partnerships between national educational agencies, PE teachers and PETE researchers have already demonstrated the potential in supporting teacher and student learning in PE. In New Zealand, the Ministry of Education funds a "Teaching & Learning Research Initiative", encouraging groups of teachers and academic researchers to work together on projects to enhance a specific aspect of teaching and learning in local contexts. Opportunities to work collaboratively in ways that are genuinely respectful of the different knowledge sets and capacities that teachers and researchers bring to any education challenge are rare. Work-ing collaboratively would afford time and resources for educators to work in a sustained and generative fashion on the challenges we have identified in this chapter. For example, practical exemplars of feasible and meaningful assessments aligned with national learning outcomes could be generated and shared. Rich, detailed and grounded "stories" of schools "living" their unique philosophies of PE could be crafted, as could the sharing of case studies of schools that have been able to meaningfully address the challenges of working with diverse student populations. The Irish Teaching Council encourages teachers' engagement with research, facilitates a Research Forum, Research Webinars, and funds collaborative research projects by teachers and teacher educators.

We conclude with a narrative on the reality of redesign imperatives and accountability requirements from the viewpoint of Emily, who is currently immersed in a collaborative research project with primary school PE teachers:

> I have been struck by the "voice" of the practitioner. It is often an articulate, passionate and well-considered voice. It is sometimes hesitant and lacking in confidence and authority. It can also be a tired and frustrated voice. Importantly, it is always tempered by everyday realities that some who are not so close tend to forget. "Where will I fit an extra lesson of PE when our school is already (over)committed to providing extra reading, writing and mathematics programmes to our students who are recorded as at risk of not achieving?" "How am I supposed to manage the five children in my class who have high-level behaviour challenges and the three who desperately need learning support but don't get it?" "Where are the balls and why don't I have a key to the cupboard? How can I deliver the lesson without the equipment?" "Our children desperately need more opportunities to move and play. The benefits are obvious. We owe it to them to deliver the breadth of the curriculum.
>
> (Emily)

Even a brief narrative like that expressed above points to the importance of genuine and ongoing collaboration across PETE, policymakers and PE spaces in schools in supporting teacher, teacher educator, policymaker and student learning. Addressing the philosophical and pragmatic realities of work in these spheres, and pooling resources to work together on strategic innovation and redesign projects is a challenge, yet one worth facing.

References

AIESEP (2018). Future Directions in PE Assessment. Fonty's University, Eindhoven, Netherlands. 18–20 October 2018. Programme and presentations available at https://fontys.nl/Sportfolio/Evenementen/AIESEP-Specialist-Seminar.htm

Alfrey, L. and Gard, M. (2019). Figuring out the prevalence of fitness testing in PE: A figurational analysis. *European PE Review*, 25(1), 187–202. https://doi.org/10.1177%2F1356336X17715361

Bailey, R., Armour, K., Kirk, D., Jess, M., Pickup, I., Sandford, R. and BERA PE and Sport Pedagogy Special Interest Group (2009). The educational benefits claimed for PE and school sport: an academic review. *Research Papers in Education*, 24(1), 1–27.

Black, P. and William, D. (2018). Classroom assessment and pedagogy. *Assessment in Education: Principles, Policy & Practice*, 25(6), 1–25. DOI:10.1080/0969594X.2018.1441807

Burrows, L., Petrie, K. and Cosgriff, M. (2013). Health invaders in New Zealand Primary Schools. *Waikato Journal of Education*, 18(2), 12–24.

Casey, A. (2014). Models-based practice: great white hope or white elephant? *Physical Education and Sport Pedagogy*, 19(1), 18–34.

Griggs, G., and Petrie, P. (eds) (2017). *The Routledge Handbook of PE Pedagogies*. Oxon: Routledge.

Goodson, I. (2013). *School Subjects and Curriculum Change*. London: Routledge.

Hay, P. and Penny, D. (2012). *Assessment in PE*. London; Routledge. Ebook: https://doi. org/10.4324/9780203133163

Hellison, D. and Templin, T. (1991). *A Reflective Approach to Teaching PE*. Champaign, IL: Human Kinetics Books.

Kirk, D. (2006). The "obesity crisis" and school PE. *Sport, Education and Society*, 11(2), 121–133. DOI: 10.1080/13573320600640660

Kirk, D. (2009). *PE Futures*. London: Routledge.

Kirk, D., MacDonald, D. and O'Sullivan, M. (2006). *The Handbook of PE*. Sage: London.

Kretchmar, S. (2006). Life on easy street: the persistent need for embodied hopes and down-to-earth games. *Quest*, 58, 345–354.

Leahy, D., Burrows, L., McCuaig, L., Wright, J. and Penney, D. (2016) *School Health Education in Changing Times: Curriculum, Pedagogies and Partnerships*. London: Routledge.

Leirhaug, P. (2018). Assessment for learning: The Holy Grail? Mini keynote at *Future Directions in PE Assessment* (AIESEP Specialist Seminar). Fonty's University, Eindhoven, the Netherlands. 18–20 October 2018. Available at https://fontys.nl/Sportfolio/Evenementen/AIESEP-Specialist-Seminar.htm

Liamputtong, P., Fanany, R. and Verrinder, G. (2012). Health, illness, and wellbeing: an introduction. In P. Liamputtong, R. Fanany and G. Verrinder (eds) *Health, Illness and Wellbeing: Perspectives and Social Determinants*. South Melbourne, Victoria: Oxford University Press, pp. 1–17.

López-Pastor, V.M., Kirk, D., Lorente-Catalán, E., MacPhail, A. and Macdonald, D. (2013) Alternative assessment in PE: a review of international literature. *Sport, Education and Society*, 18(1), 57–76.

MacPhail, A. and Lawson, H. (2020). *School Physical Education and Teacher Education*. Oxon: Routledge.

MacPhail, A. and Murphy, F. (2017). Too much freedom and autonomy in the enactment of assessment? Assessment in PE in Ireland. *Irish Educational Studies*, 36(2), 237–252. DOI: 10.1080/03323315.2017.1327365

Ministry of Education (2007). *The New Zealand Curriculum*. Wellington: Learning Media.

NCCA (2018a). *PE Curriculum Specification: Leaving Certificate Ordinary and Higher Level*. Dublin: Government of Ireland. Available at https://curriculumonline.ie/Senior-cycle

NCCA (2018b). *PE Framework: Senior Cycle*. Dublin: Government of Ireland. Available at https://curriculumonline.ie/Senior-cycle/Senior-Cycle-Subjects/Physical-Education-Framework

Sheehy, D. (2011). Addressing parents' perceptions in the marginalization of PE. *Journal of PE, Recreation & Dance*, 82(7), 42–56. DOI: 10.1080/07303084.2011.10598657

Woods, P. (1990). *Teacher Skills and Strategies*. Basingstoke: The Falmer Press.

Chapter 3

The standards-based curricular reform challenge

Shared responsibility through networking

Deborah Tannehill, Peter Iserbyt and Lori S. Dunn

We identify and describe in this chapter the grand challenge of standards-based curricular reform that confront physical education (PE) teachers and physical education teacher education (PETE) faculty internationally. As we engaged in discussion, reviewed international literature, and brainstormed ideas, we identified core issues at the forefront of much of the international PETE discourse. These issues need to be explored prior to tackling the standards-based grand challenge. Four such issues are explored as we progress through the chapter: (1) evidence of students achieving standards; (2) barriers teachers face in teaching students to achieve standards; (3) the role of PETE in preparing teachers to teach to, and facilitate, student achievement of standards: and (4) lack of formal accountability.

Education systems design

When examining education systems internationally we find they have much in common, from shared core values, policies, and structures to the problems and challenges they encounter. Similarly, as countries endeavour to overcome these issues, in many instances, they are selecting like solutions and reform agendas.

From a global comparative perspective, the work of Anderson-Levitt (2003) has been particularly insightful. She highlights commonalities, similarities, and differences. She also discusses the global tensions in educational reform and the contradictions they display. These same contradictions confront all nation-specific education systems, and educators must grapple with them as they strive to provide a strong education for all young people.

In the case of sport pedagogy, the focus is on meeting physical activity, sport, and health-related needs of children and youth worldwide. In the same vein, Lawson (2018), in his recent book *Redesigning Physical Education*, takes the view that education systems design offers a planning framework for teachers and teacher educators in the current global society.

To clarify, a system might be viewed as a general set of elements connected to form a whole. For example, PE teachers, school programmes, PETE faculty and PETE programmes are components in the same system. All elements in the system influence one another, which suggests that understanding all parts of the system, and their interactions, is critical. All systems in turn are governed by a set of policies that are essential for the effective running of these systems. Policies might be considered formal statements that are issue- or system-specific and developed to reflect objectives that guide practice. We argue that all education systems (e.g. individual schools, school districts) are built on a systems design, albeit one that is not functioning well in all instances.

Common standards and assessment are frequently identified as a central piece of systems design. Standards are mandatory actions/rules designed to give formal policies support and direction. Consensus on what are considered acceptable standards can be contentious, and these standards are context-specific. Framed in this way, we question how any system that is educating children from different cultures and educational opportunities can serve diverse learners in the same way, emphasizing the same goals and curricula, and yet manage to achieve similar results.

Other challenges to this notion of a common systems design have been posed by Gordon *et al.* (2016) and Pope (2014). They share insight on how standards implementation has caused a two-tier hierarchy of academic areas with subject status determined through this hierarchy. More fundamentally, Kirk *et al.* (2018) question whether a holistic approach to education through standards is the most appropriate choice, given that teachers enact learning outcomes differently and a common standards approach limits student voices and choices.

Despite similarities among world education systems, schools inevitably reflect their own national culture. These cultural differences and the practical implications of such must be acknowledged. Consequently, it is a challenge to compare international education systems when considering how they are set up from a bureaucratic perspective.

For instance, in the United States, education remains primarily the responsibility of state and local government despite federal government efforts to standardize the curriculum through introduction of what is known as the "Common Core", which prioritizes maths and English. Alternatively, oversight for education policy in Ireland is, at the national level, by the Department of Education and Skills (DES), which is advised on curriculum and assessment issues related to early childhood, primary and secondary education by the National Council of Curriculum and Assessment (NCCA).

In Flanders, which is the northern part of Belgium, the Flemish government develops the standards for education which are adopted and operationalized in curricula developed by one of three education networks (Flemish community network, subsidized public network, and the subsidized private network) according to their pedagogical and philosophical view on schools and society as a whole. Schools, with oversight by the Inspectorate of Education, integrate the standards as operationalized by the educational networks in their school work plan, taking into account local infrastructure, staff members, and student population.

No one set of standards

Despite bureaucratic issues, provinces, states and nations around the world have developed standards to guide teaching and learning. Paradoxically, there is no common agreement on what the term "standards" means, let alone a common set of standards to guide what students should know and be able to do.

The term "standards" thus needs to be defined. Standards stipulate what students should know and be able to do as a result of participating in a PE curriculum. In other parts of the world, such standards are synonymous with "key concepts" and "key processes" (England), "content descriptions" (Australia), "learning outcomes" (Ireland, Turkey, and across the European Union), "attainment targets" (Flanders), and "achievement objectives" (New Zealand) (MacPhail, 2014).

As we examine PE standards internationally, we find that all countries do not share the same goals for students and their respective standards vary. For example, the European Physical Education Association (EUPEA) Physical Education Survey (2010–2011) reported that for the 22 countries/education sectors in Europe, exercise, health, physical activity, and social and personal development were most frequently cited as the aims of PE. However, even for these countries, how standards are interpreted results in PE programme variability. Even when the same goals are prioritized, differences in how to achieve and evaluate them vary.

Issues regarding national curricula are inescapable. According to Hardman *et al.* (2014), national curricula are prescribed in 79 per cent of nations. Only Canada, the United States, and Oceania have devolved systems where educational authority is passed on to provinces or states.

Many countries publish sets of benchmarking standards provided by governmental agencies, non-governmental national, and/or professional organizations (e.g. Society of Health and Physical Education – SHAPE America; European Physical Education Association). These organizations provide information on expectations for student learning, and may also provide guidelines for PETE programmes.

Three case examples illustrate the complexity of the standards-based challenge; the USA, Ireland and Flanders.

United States

In 1995, the National Association for Sport and Physical Education (NASPE) released PE content standards. These standards were based on the document *Outcomes of Quality Physical Education Programs* (NASPE, 1992), which included a definition of a physically educated person, i.e. what each student should know, do, value and experience.

Later, in their third iteration of the national standards, SHAPE America (2014), formerly NASPE, focused on developing measurable outcomes for these standards, aiming to empower physical educators to help students become physically literate individuals. A physically literate person is someone who has the knowledge, skills, and confidence to enjoy a lifetime of healthful physical activity (SHAPE, 2014, p. 1). Although each US state has educational autonomy, many states adopted the national standards, as did the International Council for Health, Physical Education, Recreation, Sport, and Dance (ICHPERSD).

Ireland

In 2009, Ireland adopted a learning outcomes approach to curriculum design (Coolahan, 2017). It spanned both primary (ages 5–11) and secondary (ages 12–18) curricula. At both levels, students take part in curricular options based on specific learning outcomes that guide teaching and learning.

One option for those aged 12 to 14 years is based on key skills taught through a whole-school approach that integrates these key skills into all content areas (National Council for Curriculum and Assessment, 2011). To supplement this, PE learning outcomes are specific to adventure activities, aquatics, athletics, dance, invasion games, net and fielding games, gymnastics, and health-related activity. For those aged 15 to 18 years, one option is a framework that provides clear learning outcomes of what students are expected to achieve in terms of knowledge, understanding, skills, and attitudes. Each of the five key skills is embedded in the learning outcomes through various PE curriculum models; adventure education, health-related physical activity, sport education, teaching games for understanding, contemporary issues, and personal and social responsibility.

Flanders

In Flanders, the government introduced standards in both elementary and secondary education in the 1990s. Authors of these standards recognized the importance of developing motor competencies, a safe and healthy lifestyle, and a positive self-image and social functioning (De Martelaer *et al.*, 2014).

While these domains have endured, the specific standards have been revised. Currently, there are 45 standards for elementary PE (ages 6–12). For secondary PE there are three two-year cycles with standards defined per two-year cycle; 35 standards in the first cycle (ages 13–14), 30 in the second (ages 15–16), and 25 in the third (ages 17–18).

These three case examples demonstrate that a standards-based approach to curriculum development requires teachers to select activities based on their contribution to meeting the standards. This structured approach contrasts with curricular goal development and activity selection based on teacher preference or tradition (see Chapter 7). Flexibility remains as standards do not identify the content to be taught, nor do they identify how the content will be delivered (Lund and Tannehill, 2015). They identify what has been deemed important for students to experience, know and be able to do.

Such a grand view of standards is deceptively simple. Four issues present a different picture.

Issue 1: evidence of students achieving standards

There is little research documenting student achievement of standards internationally. Hastie's (2017) review provides a useful summary of the evidence base of the extent to which the US national PE content standards have been achieved. His two conclusions have international relevance: (1) there is a dearth of evidence directly accounting for the achievement of the standards, and (2) fewer than half of the students participating in PE realize performance expectations. No one knows what, if anything, will be prioritized and done to bridge this gap.

In both Flanders and Ireland there is no clear evidence on whether the standards for PE are being met. Although the Inspectorate of Education of the Flemish government inspects every school every six years, it does not systematically collect and publish proof of student performance related to the PE standards. It should be noted, however, that the attainment targets (i.e. standards) in Flanders were created as an instrument to warrant the minimal quality of education in all schools. They are not conceived as standards to be met by every individual student but rather goals for everyone in a particular student population (Simons *et al.*, 2016). Limited evidence points to a discrepancy between the pronounced and actual realized school PE standards in Flanders (Daems and Leysen, 1995; Huts *et al.*, 2005).

In the Irish system, whole-school evaluation (WSE), a process of external evaluation of the work of a school, is designed to monitor and assess the quality, economy, efficiency, and effectiveness of the education system. At the secondary level, subject inspection is an established approach to evaluating individual subjects and is an integral part of WSE. Sometimes the inspection has a subject or curriculum focus. At other times, WSE concentrates on a range of different lessons across a wide range of subjects. Feedback is provided to the school community at the end of these inspections and a printed report is published on the DES website.

One assumption of teaching to standards merits special attention in PE. Assessment procedures should be aligned with those standards. Unfortunately, a major concern in PE is the lack of practical, valid, and reliable tools to assess students meeting the standards (Rink, 2013).

For example, in the US, the first valid assessment packages, called "PE metrics", were released in 2010 by AAHPERD. The current, third edition of PE metrics (SHAPE, 2019) offers a cognitive and motor skill assessment package aligned with the standards. Unfortunately, questions remain about whether they are practical for use in a school context, whether teachers know about them and employ them, and whether PETE faculty refer to them in their PETE programmes.

Issue 2: barriers teachers face in teaching students to achieve standards

A key question to consider is whether the contexts in which PE teachers work allows them to successfully teach to the standards. For example, MacPhail and

Hartley (2016) and Hastie (2017) identified working conditions and other mitigating factors that impact PE teachers' practice, including standards-based teaching.

Flanders provides a case example. Here, insufficient curricular time allocation, inadequate facilities, financial constraints, a lack of properly qualified personnel, and low status are among the problems facing PE teachers (De Knop *et al.*, 2004). Forty per cent of schools have no gym, resulting in PE being taught in inappropriate rooms or buildings (e.g. school cafeterias, chapels) (Agion, 2013).

Furthermore, unlike secondary schools, in 30 per cent of primary schools PE is taught by non-specialist teachers, which has been linked to lower levels of student physical activity and performance (see, for example, McKenzie *et al.*, 1993).

A compounding issue in Ireland is that secondary PE teachers are required to gain a teaching qualification in a second school subject. Iannucci and MacPhail (2017) found that teaching becomes more complex with the expectation of taking on two distinctly different roles simultaneously, with role conflict and prioritization key challenges.

The situation in the US is not much better. Recent discussions with PE teachers in the state of Washington resulted in identification of obstacles that inhibit teachers' work. Barriers included a lack of administrative oversight in teachers teaching toward standards, large class sizes, high numbers of students with special needs who require one-on-one support to meet the content standards, limited adult support to accommodate differentiated assessments, and lack of technology support in the gymnasium. One teacher noted that, "there are too many standards for the students to realistically learn in the time they have, so we resort to breadth over depth, just covering as much as we can rather than teaching a concept long enough for them to learn it" (personal communication).

We suggest that the above barriers, issues, and expectations teachers face when teaching PE impact the quality of their teaching and the outcomes they are able to achieve. As Rink (2013, p. 410) noted,

> it is difficult to hold teachers accountable for more than minimum expectations for learning when teachers do not have the time needed to teach for those expectations and when we have little information on how much time it takes for students to become competent in an outcome.

Issue 3: the role of PETE in preparing teachers to teach to, and facilitate students, achieving the standards

International snapshots of educational standards suggest that they tend to be rich in content and designed to require students to be active learners who can think critically, solve problems, and learn content that has application to their own needs and interests beyond school (Schleicher, 2018). This is a special kind of learning in PE. It suggests that teachers be equipped to do things differently, develop innovative and exciting pedagogies, and work as a teacher collective to engage young people in exciting and challenging ways that assist them to persevere in their own learning (see Chapter 8).

As Feimen-Nemser (2001, p. 1013) proposed for all manner of educators, "if we want schools to produce more powerful learning on the part of students we have to offer more powerful learning opportunities for teachers". This implies that teacher educators must design meaningful and sustained learning opportunities that prepare pre-service teachers (PSTs) to learn how to teach young people to reach educational outcomes.

What is happening internationally in the preparation of teachers to teach toward student achievement of standards? This does not seem to be a line of PE research that has been undertaken specifically, although research is abundant regarding what we know about good teaching (e.g. Ward, 2014).

To explore whether, and how, PETE faculty prepare PSTs for standards-based pedagogy, the authors of this chapter held informal conversations with several teacher educators at numerous institutions in the US, Flanders and Ireland in an attempt to gain insight into current practices in preparing teachers to teach toward student outcomes. We identified a set of themes that were repeatedly mentioned by a number of these colleagues as "key" aspects of their programme, intentionally chosen to enable teaching toward students achieving learning outcomes. Key factors included "living the curriculum", having a shared vision, instructional alignment of programmes and teaching practice, the progressive nature of teacher education, PSTs' application of theory to practice, modelling effective practice, and teaching toward standards. While research does not yet support the importance of these factors in preparing teachers to teach to standards, the teacher educators with whom we spoke believed these pedagogies were successful in doing so.

One innovative example demonstrates how teachers and teacher educators can be upskilled to meet the challenge of standards-based curricular reform while engaging with a national body. In this instance we see a national education body funding a collaborative "train the trainer" initiative between one PETE programme and a group of PE teachers. This collective group of educators explore how to most effectively plan for, and teach, a new national curriculum framed by six PE curriculum models (e.g. Sport Education, Contemporary Issues, Personal and Social Responsibility). Using specifically-developed planning templates that align learning outcomes, assessments, and learning experiences/teaching strategies, teachers design and trial various units of learning in their own schools coming back to the larger group to discuss implications for both PE teachers and PETE faculty. At this point, PETE faculty endeavour to incorporate these new strategies into their teacher education programme while the teachers engage with sharing their learning with other teachers through workshops sponsored by their national PE organization.

Another issue directly linked to the preparation of teachers is whether demonstrating proficiency in teaching to the standards is a requirement for graduation from PETE programmes. Again, we found no evidence to suggest that providing such achievement is expected. In Flanders, teachers graduating from all subject areas need to meet ten generic teacher education standards. Although two standards refer to learning processes and subject matter expertise, the PST does not need to offer proof of meeting subject-specific (i.e. PE) standards, but needs to be able to plan and implement practices that would lead to meeting these.

In the US, the national standards for Initial Physical Education Teacher Education (SHAPE, 2017) refer to alignment between teacher practices and content standards for students. Standard 3 (Planning and Implementation) states that, "Physical education candidates apply content and foundational knowledge to plan and implement developmentally appropriate learning experiences aligned with local, state and/or SHAPE America's National Standards and Grade-Level Outcomes for K-12 Physical Education..." (SHAPE, 2017, p. 3). As such, PETE students are assessed on their ability to plan and implement appropriate objectives that align with the SHAPE national standards and grade-level outcomes for K12.

It seems that PETE programmes in both Flanders and the US at best require PSTs to plan and implement practices that align with PE standards. Whether these practices, or others within the various programmes, are successful in helping students meet the standards is not assessed. One could therefore rightfully ask whether teachers graduating from these programmes are sufficiently prepared to teach to subject-specific standards and whether they will be successful in helping PSTs to be successful in teaching toward the standards.

Issue 4: lack of formal accountability mechanisms

In the US, every school receives funding for PE without minimal formal accountability on how that funding has enhanced PE provision. A limited number of states have a formal assessment and evaluation system that holds school districts, schools, and teachers accountable for students achieving standards. According to the 2010 Shape of the Nation Report (NASPE, 2010), 48 US states (92 per cent) had developed content standards that reflect those set either locally or nationally. However, only 34 states (67 per cent) require local districts to comply or align with these standards and only 19 states (37 per cent) mandate some form of student assessment in PE. In most cases, administration of the assessments is left to the individual school districts and only five states (10 per cent) forward the assessment data to their respective state Department of Education.

In Flanders, apart from regular inspection by the Inspectorate of Education, there are no formal accountability measures in place to ensure students meet the standards. Based on written documents and administration, the Inspectorate of Education judges whether the standards are integrated in the school curriculum and met at the school level. They do not assess whether individual students meet them. Also, for teachers to become tenured, they need to pass an assessment coordinated by their school principal or school board, which in general does not include assessment of students meeting the standards.

Development of some form of accountability can prevent programme erosion and act as a tool for advocacy. No stakeholder in the education community wants to be perceived as low-performing in a content area of a school programme, and they will do what is needed to improve their status. For PE, this could lead to more programme time, equipment, and support for professional development (Rink, 2013). Although some critics have argued that increased accountability for meeting standards will cause a narrowing of the curriculum (i.e. teaching to the test), it does increase the probability that those minimal expectations will be achieved (Rink, 2013). The South Carolina Physical Education Assessment Program (Rink and Mitchell, 2003; Rink and Stewart, 2003) demonstrated that low-performing schools only started to make changes when accountability (i.e. mandatory assessments) was put in place. This finding supports the need for some level of accountability to produce changes on a larger scale.

The grand challenge: shared responsibility through networking

The more we engaged in writing this chapter the more we have come to believe that the four issues we pose collectively reflect the true grand challenge. We kept asking ourselves, if we are going to learn from one another at both the school PE and PETE level, do we not need to work through all four issues, sharing insights and strategies that demonstrate promise? In other words, students achieving standards might be viewed as the central concern, with each of the issues orbiting around it in bidirectional ways. Since all countries are at different stages in the process of standards-based reform they are orbiting from different issues and at variable speeds, which makes a shared discourse difficult (Figure 3.1).

If we are to see progress made in meeting the challenges of standards-based curricular reform on an international level, networking is the key to beginning this dialogue and learning process. Aligning all stakeholders (i.e. teachers, teacher educators, and researchers) internationally through school-university partnerships (see Chapters 4 and 12), professional development initiatives (see Chapter 13), or international teaching, research and development networks are one means of achieving this. As suggested in Chapter 1, the idea of "lesson drawing" as a means for cross-border knowledge sharing is crucial if we are to gain insight from one another to solve the challenges faced in implementing standards-based reform.

The International Association for Physical Education in Higher Education (AIESEP) aims to bring together scholars in PE, physical activity and sport pedagogy worldwide to share knowledge and engage in quality research. Partnered with the European Physical Education Association (EUPEA), an umbrella organization for national PE associations in Europe, the two organizations we argue are an arena in which to locate this discourse and standards-based reform issues and research. Our suggestion is formation of a Special Interest Group (SIG) focused on standards-based reform led by a partnership of PE teachers, PETE faculty, policy leaders, and curriculum bodies. This SIG would engage in research

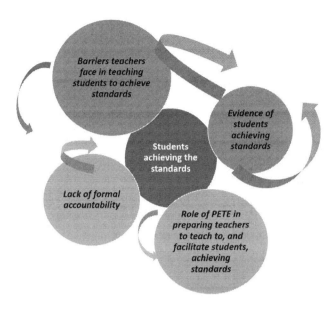

Figure 3.1 Issues faced in implementing standards-based reform.

endeavours, workshops, and lectures highlighting progress made by various coun-tries as they navigate and achieve success at steps along their standards reform journey. Following practices of other SIGs, meetings would rotate to different international locations and across professional meetings in order to engage all stakeholders.

An outcome of such collaborative international discourse might be (i) identifi-cation of effective practices in school PE and teacher education; (ii) development of assessment tools and practices to assess student achievement of standards; (iii) initiating research endeavours exploring aspects of the four issues shared in this chapter; (iv) trialling of accountability mechanisms focused on ensuring all stu-dents are on track to meet standards; and (v) proposing strong policy to ensure teachers are provided an environment where they can facilitate students achiev-ing standards. This type of experience allows all stakeholders to engage, share their perspectives, guide and support one another's initiatives, while working within their own countries to adapt and apply "lessons learned". Taking *shared* responsibility for finding solutions on how best to negotiate the four challenges facing PE standards-based curricular reform is critical.

References

Agion, B.E. (2013). De schoolgebouwenmonitor 2013. Indicatoren voor de kwaliteit van de schoolgebouwen in Vlaanderen. Consulted on March 19 via www.agion.be/sites/default/files/images/D_eindrapport_monitor2013_finaal.pdf

Anderson-Levitt, K. (ed.) (2003). *Local Meanings, Global Schooling: Anthropology and World Culture Theory*. New York: Palgrave Macmillan.

Coolahan, J., Drudy, S., Hogan, P. and McGuiness, S. (2017). *Towards A Better Future: A Review of the Irish School System*. Irish Primary Principals Network and the National Association of Principals.

Daems, F. and Leysen, A. (1995). Leve de school? Weg met de school? Attitudes en verwachtingen inzake onderwijs in Vlaanderen [Attitudes and expectations regarding education in Flanders]. *Tijdschrift voor onderwijsrecht en onderwijsbeleid*, pp. 348–363.

De Knop, P., Theeboom, M., Huts, K., Van Hoecke, J. and De Martelaer, K. (2004). The quality of school physical education in Flemish secondary schools. *European Physical Education Review*, 10(1), 21–40.

De Martelaer, K., Seghers, J., Cardon, G., Haerens, L., De Boever, E. and Cloes, M. (2014). Physical education stimulating a healthy lifestyle and critical sports consumption in Belgium. In M.K. Chin and C.R. Edginton (eds), *Physical Education and Health Global Perspectives and Best Practice*. Urbana, IL: Sagamore, pp. 43–56.

Feimen-Nemser, S. (2001). From preparation to practice: designing a continuum to strengthen and sustain teaching. *Teachers College Record*, 103(6), 1013–1055.

Gordon, B., Dyson, B., Cowen, J., McKenzie, A. and Shulruf, B. (2016). Teachers' perceptions of physical education in Aotearoa/New Zealand primary schools. *New Zealand Journal of Educational Studies*, 51(1), 99–111.

Hardman, K., Murphy, C., Routen, A. and Tones, S. (2014). *Worldwide Survey of School Physical Education, Final Report, 2013*. Paris: United Nations Educational, Scientific and Cultural Organization (UNESCO).

Hastie, P.A. (2017). Revisiting the national physical education content standards: what do we really know about our achievement of the physically educated/literate person? *Journal of Teaching in Physical Education*, 36(1), 3–19.

Huts, K., De Knop, P. and Theeboom, M. (2005). The social quality of school physical education in Flanders. *Sport, Education and Society*, 10(2), 257–275.

Iannucci, C. and MacPhail, A. (2017). The effects of individual dispositions and workplace factors on the lives and careers of physical education teachers: twelve years on from graduation. *Sport, Education and Society*. Available at: doi:10.1080/13573322.2017.1307175

Kirk, D., Bardid, F., Lamb, C.A., Millar, J.D. and Teraoka, E. (2018). Redesigning physical education in Scotland. In H.A. Lawson (ed.), *Redesigning Physical Education: An Equity Agenda in Which Every Child Matters*. London and New York: Routledge.

Lawson, H.A. (ed.) (2018). *Redesigning Physical Education: An Equity Agenda in Which Every Child Matters*. London and New York: Routledge.

Lund, J., and Tannehill, D. (2014). *Standards-based Curriculum Development in Physical Education*, 3rd ed. Burlington, MA: Jones and Bartlett Publishers.

MacPhail, A. (2014). International perspectives on the implementation of standards. In J. Lund and D. Tannehill (eds), *Standards-based Curriculum Development for Physical Education*, 3rd edn. Burlington: MA: Jones and Bartlett Publishers, 21–35.

MacPhail, A., and Hartley, T. (2016). Linking teacher socialization research with a PETE: insights from beginning and experienced teachers. *Journal of Teaching in Physical Education*, 35(1), 169–180.

McKenzie, T., Sallis, J., Faucette, N., Roby, J. and Kolody, B. (1993). Effects of a curriculum and inservice program on the quantity and quality of elementary physical education classes. *Research Quarterly for Exercise and Sport*, 64(2), 178–187. Available at: doi:10.1080/02701367.1993.10608795.

National Association for Sport and Physical Education (1992). *Outcomes of Quality Physical Education Programs*. Reston, VA: Author.

National Association for Sport and Physical Education (1995). *Moving into the Future: National Standards for Physical Education*, 1st edn. Reston, VA: Author.

National Association for Sport and Physical Education and American Heart Association (2010). *Shape of the Nation Report: Status of Physical Education in the USA*. Reston VA: National Association for Sport and Physical Education.

National Council for Curriculum and Assessment (2011). *Towards a framework for Junior Cycle: Innovation and Identity*. Dublin: NCCA.

Pope, C.C. (2014). The jagged edge and the changing shape of health and physical education in Aotearoa New Zealand. *Physical Education and Sport Pedagogy*, 19(5), 500–511.

Rink, J.E. (2013). Measuring teacher effectiveness in physical education. *Research Quarterly for Exercise and Sport*, 84(4), 407–418.

Rink, J. and Mitchell, M. (eds) (2003). State level assessment in physical education: the South Carolina experience [Monograph]. *Journal of Teaching in Physical Education*, 22(5).

Rink, J. and Stewart, S. (2003). Insights and reflections on a state assessment program. *Journal of Teaching in Physical Education*, 22(5), 573–588.

Schleicher, A. (2018). What makes high-performing school systems different? *World Class: How to Build a 21st-Century School System*. Paris: OECD Publishing.

Simons, M., Kelchtermans, G., Leysen, J. and Vandenbroek, M. (2016). Attainment targets in action. Mapping the operation, effects and future use of a Flemish educational policy instrument. Laboratory for Education and Society & Centre for Educational Policy and Innovation & Teacher Training, KU Leuven. Retrieved on 19 March 2019. Available at: www.vlaanderen.be/nl/publicaties/detail/attainment-targets-in-action-mapping-the-operation-effects-and-future-use-of-a-flemish-educational-policy-instrument

Society of Health and Physical Educators (2014). *National Standards & Grade-level Outcomes for K-12 Physical Education*. Champaign, IL: Human Kinetics.

Society of Health and Physical Educators (2017). *2017 National Standards for Initial Physical Education Teacher Education*. Champaign, IL: Human Kinetics.

Society of Health and Physical Educators (2019). *PE Metrics – 3rd edition. Assessing Student Performance using the National Standards & Grade-level Outcomes for K-12 Physical Education* Champaign, IL: Human Kinetics.

Ward, P. (2014). A response to the conversations on effective teaching in physical education. *Research Quarterly for Exercise and Sport*, 85(2), 293–296.

Chapter 4

The alignment and coherence challenge

Developing university–school partnerships for the simultaneous improvement and redesign of school programmes and teacher education

Jo Harris, Marc Cloes and Kerry Wilson

Introduction

Given the changing nature of schools within fast-changing, diverse and global societies, it is timely to review Physical Education (PE) and Physical Education Teacher Education (PETE) provision to determine if they are "fit for purpose". There is a strong rationale for reviewing and reconfiguring PE and PETE together, ensuring that they are aligned and coherent. For example: changing PETE and not PE would lead to real-world experiences "washing out" the effects of innovative professional preparation. Changing PE and not PETE would result in beginner teachers requiring additional professional development.

Others have offered the same improvement platform. In 1998, Goodlad called for simultaneous renewal of university–school relationships to create dynamic, interactive partnerships. More recently, Lawson (2018) has made a strong case for a critical, collective review of PE and PETE in order to work towards evidence-based policy and research-informed practice.

Although this work is unlikely to be easy or completed quickly, the systematic reproduction of existing PE and PETE cannot be permitted to continue. As the saying goes, nothing changes until something changes.

Challenges within PE and PETE are evident in every nation. They have the potential to drive the development of a common purpose, particularly better outcomes for teachers, and ultimately for students. Lawson's (2018) international-comparative analysis of PE, and its relationship with PETE, provides one scaffold. He proffers that gaps between ideal and achieved outcomes, shortfalls and conflicts should be catalysts for agenda-setting or problem-solving. He prompts theoretically sound, evidence-based redesign which moves the profession towards nuanced, customized forms of PE that better meet the needs of diverse young people. He urges the profession to build new futures for PE based on the claim that "Active healthy lifestyles established during childhood are life-enriching and, if they continue, they are life-extending and perhaps life-saving" (Lawson, 2018, p. xii).

We share Lawson's strong belief in the potential of PE to enhance students' lives and his vision for a bright and better future if the profession is able to think and act differently and collectively. However, we also acknowledge a number of challenges. The PE profession's renowned resistance to change is a major challenge (Kirk, 2010), and others are identified in the ensuing analysis.

Our author team represents two nations (England and Belgium). We work in varying contexts with different roles – teaching, teacher education and research. Nevertheless, we are experiencing identical comparable challenges in PE and PETE, which helps to explain why we reached agreement on a common strategy. We are advocates for the bridging of the gap between school-based PE and university-based PETE programmes (see also Chapter 11). We propose partnerships for simultaneous improvement and renewal because they are considered a best practice framework given that PE and PETE programmes are mutually constitutive.

We also know from research and development and from our team's partnership experience that alignment (i.e. consistent or compatible structures) and coherence (i.e. shared meanings and common understandings) are essential, yet these concepts have not previously been prioritized.

Overall, our team approaches this grand partnership challenge as an "adaptive problem without easy answers" (Heifetz *et al.*, 2009). We outline issues mutually influencing PE and PETE, describe the limitations associated with a lack of alignment and coherence between PE and PETE, and offer a range of viable actions to address this challenge. At the same time, we respect the limitations of a single, generalizable solution, given the variation and complexity of different national and local contexts.

Issues within and between PE and PETE

Our starting point is a shared understanding of issues within PE and PETE. We recognize that issues faced by one adversely affect the other. We proceed with a collective vision for PE and PETE to work together to address these issues and ultimately improve student outcomes.

Issues within PE

A long-standing issue for PE is that it can come across to students and their parents as lacking coordination and piecemeal, especially in its current activity-oriented form. Consequently, learning within PE (particularly in domains other than the physical) is not always recognized, which does little to enhance the status and value of the subject (Harris, 2018). This sub-optimal situation is not helped by parents infrequently meeting PE teachers during formal parents' evenings/consultations, resulting in them having limited understanding of what takes place in PE and why. Our experience is that this lack of understanding is also evident amongst non-PE teaching colleagues, including school principals and senior management who observe few, if any, PE lessons.

An associated issue arises in primary schools in Belgium and England. More often than not, PE is cancelled when time is required for other school activities.

Another ongoing, associated issue in PE in England is the shift towards it being outsourced to non-qualified teachers such as coaches and instructors, particularly in primary schools (Griggs and Randall, 2018). Whilst this is not the case in Belgium where specialist PE teachers remain in both primary and secondary schools, some outsourcing opportunities allow external coaches/instructors to teach curriculum PE, without the close collaboration necessary to ensure high quality PE provision that meets the needs of the students. The second author views the trend towards externalization of the curriculum (i.e. PE being delivered by "outsiders" such as non-profit organizations and private companies) in Belgium as a risk to the subject and profession.

A further issue is a trend towards a reduction in PE time in secondary schools in England due to exam pressure, additional curriculum time for other subjects, and staffing cuts (Youth Sport Trust, 2018). The third author reports that many secondary schools in the region in which she teaches have reduced PE time for 14–16 year olds.

A related issue is that, as PE is not a required subject within the English Baccalaureate, the number of students being offered, and opting for, PE examination courses in England has reduced. As a consequence, secondary school PE teachers are being required to teach other subjects. The additional planning and marking associated with this workload has caused some PE teachers to reduce their involvement in the extra-curricular programme.

The third author also reports that many PE teachers have additional pastoral responsibilities. Examples include reviewing and tracking student evidence and liaising closely with colleagues and parents to help ensure that all students in their tutor group make good progress in their learning. No wonder that some PE teachers struggle to maintain a work–life balance.

Adverse effects of PE issues on PETE

Limited understanding of PE and the learning associated with it has undoubtedly contributed to the confusion between PE, physical activity and sport, and PE's relatively low status and value in comparison with other subjects. This confusion has undoubtedly contributed to the reduction in PE time in many schools and the subject being partially outsourced to non-qualified teachers. An example of the adverse effect of these issues on PETE in the UK is that pre-service primary generalist teachers teach little or no PE during PETE and their PE subject and pedagogical knowledge are not developed by experienced teachers of PE in placement schools (Griggs and Randall, 2018; Randall *et al.*, 2016).

Issues within PETE

A long-standing problem in England and other countries such as Ireland and the USA (MacPhail *et al.*, 2018; Richards *et al.*, 2018) is the lack of PE specialists in primary schools, and primary school generalist teachers not being adequately trained to teach PE (Harris *et al.*, 2012; Tsangaridou, 2012). This is in stark contrast to countries such as Scotland and Belgium where specialists teach PE in primary schools (Kirk *et al.*, 2018; De Knop *et al.*, 2005).

Another PETE issue is how to address and challenge the acculturation effect of socialization (see Chapter 7) which occurs through pre-PETE interactions with influential agents such as parents, teachers and sports coaches (Templin and Richards, 2014). Primarily through what Lortie (1975) termed the "apprenticeship of observation", individuals develop strong, deeply rooted beliefs, expectations and values associated with PE, which Lawson (1983) referred to as individuals' subjective warrants.

Our experience of pre-service teachers in England and Belgium is that they commence their teacher education with a limited and narrow perception of PE, predominantly based on their own sporting experiences (see Chapter 7). Exposing and confronting pre-service teachers' subjective warrants remains a challenge for PETE, especially when there is conflict with the beliefs, expectations and values advocated within the PETE programme.

A further and related PETE issue is what to include in the content of PETE, given the various forms PE can take, e.g. (i) the multi-activity curriculum; (ii) approaches associated with physical literacy, fundamental movement skills and health-based PE; and (iii) models-based approaches such as Teaching Games for Understanding, Sport Education, Teaching Personal and Social Responsibility, SPARK (Sports, Play and Active Recreation for Kids) and Cooperative Learning (Green *et al.*, 2018; Lawson, 2018).

This issue is important in Belgium where the second author reports that many PE teachers continue to adopt direct instruction and a technical approach in their teaching. This encourages and expects students to perform drills to learn basic skills before moving on to tasks that aim to make sense of the activity (Frédéric *et al.*, 2009). A further impending issue for PETE in Belgium is preparing PE teachers for the curriculum subject of "Physical Education" becoming "Physical and Health Education" teachers. The second author predicts that this will represent somewhat of a revolution for many PE teachers who will need to adopt an increased focus on the transferability of skills from their subject to students' lives (Cloes, 2017a). To add to the problem, this change also coincides with an additional impending change in Belgium requiring all teacher education providers to work together for the first time.

Adverse effects of PETE issues on PE

Just as PE adversely affects PETE, so might PETE adversely impact school PE. For example, the inadequacy of primary school generalist teachers' preparation to teach PE results in them lacking the confidence and competence to teach the subject well, which inevitably leads to impoverished experiences of PE for many young learners. This has led to a call by Harris (2018) for PE specialists in primary schools in England, in line with the situation in Scotland (Kirk *et al.*, 2018) and Belgium (De Knop *et al.*, 2005).

Although Belgium already has PE specialists in primary and secondary schools, the second author considers that there is a need for increased collaboration between these specialists and their non-PE colleagues to help create an effective whole school approach to promoting healthy, active lifestyles (Cloes, 2017b; De Martelaer *et al.*, 2014).

Also, PETE needs to go way beyond exposing pre-service teachers to a series of activities, approaches and models of PE in order to ensure that the design of future PE curricula in schools addresses issues with the inherited multi-activity form of PE (as highlighted by Kirk, 2010) and forms the "cornerstones" of physical activity promotion (as recommended by Tappe and Burgeson, 2004). The PE profession needs to avoid the danger of replacing the multi-activity form of PE with a similarly disjointed and ad hoc collection of approaches and models-based practice.

The pervasiveness of the alignment and coherence challenge

The alignment and coherence challenge is grand in the sense that it is important and widespread on an international scale. It is frequently evidenced when pre-service teachers undertake teaching practice in placement schools. Predictably, the content of the PE curriculum and the way it is taught contrasts with that advocated within the university component of their teacher education programme.

Indeed, we are aware of situations in which pre-service teachers have been told by teachers in their placement schools that they must ignore nearly everything that they have learnt in the "ivory tower" of the university and instead learn what PE is like in the "real world". Situations like these clearly demonstrate limited consistency and compatibility between PE and PETE, and they help to explain why and how a lack of shared meanings and common purposes conspire against pre-service teachers adopting innovative orientations with the potential to transform PE in schools.

Harris's (2014) research provides further evidence of the alignment and coherence challenge. In her study, pre-service teachers were asked at the beginning of their PETE programme about their knowledge of how active children should be and their views on the learning that could take place in schools generally, and in PE in particular, to promote active lifestyles. Later in the PETE programme, the same pre-service teachers were asked about their views on the health-related programmes they had experienced during their teaching placements. Most had experienced health-related PE programmes which they considered ineffective in promoting healthy, active lifestyles amongst young people and which were at variance with their perceptions of the learning associated with this area of work.

Harris (2014) concluded that PETE was not adequately preparing future PE teachers to promote active lifestyles, nor did it address issues in health-related learning such as young people's views of PE and their conceptions about health, fitness and activity. Overall, these findings indicate, once again, that PETE and PE can be very much "at odds" with each other. This discrepancy prompted Harris and her colleagues to re-think the approach to health-related learning within PETE, while reconsidering continuing professional development (see Chapter 13).

The confusion caused by a lack of alignment and coherence experienced during PETE can be further exacerbated when newly qualified teachers take up their first teaching post. This is especially challenging if newly qualified teachers are in school environments that do not encourage them to be creative and experimental, but instead expect them to fall in line and deliver what is already on offer. The authors are aware of newly qualified PE teachers, in response to them challenging ongoing habits and routines, receiving negative feedback from established PE colleagues. The negative feedback often takes the form of comments such as "It will not work", "It is too complicated" or "It takes too much time", when changes to policies and practices are suggested. Some experienced teachers reject new ideas as these ideas require them shifting outside of their comfort zone, as well as change often involving additional work.

That said, the authors understand that in-service teachers have many demands on their time and recognize that they have insufficient opportunities for meaningful professional development focusing on collaboration, interaction and practice (see Chapter 13). The consequence of all of this for many beginning teachers is that they become accustomed to custodial teacher orientations and abandon their innovative perspective, which partly explains why the influence of PETE is deemed to be lost or marginalized (Blankenship and Coleman, 2009). A further exacerbating influence on early career PE teachers that we have experienced or witnessed is the effect of whole school pressures (e.g. those relating to time-consuming data and tracking processes), extensive extra-curricular PE expectations, and additional administrative, managerial and/or pastoral roles. These can serve to hinder teachers' pedagogical development and their drive, confidence and energy to challenge the status quo.

United we stand, divided we fall

Given that disconnects between PE and PETE are commonplace and problematic, uniting to collectively re-configure PE and PETE makes good sense to help them be "fit for purpose" and better able to respond to current and future challenges (see Chapter 11). One possible way of improving the alignment and coherence between PE and PETE is to ensure that partnership schools (which host pre-service teachers on teaching practices) are conversant with, understand and share the research-informed, evidence-based messages, approaches and models communicated and demonstrated during the university-based component of the teacher education programme (see Chapter 12). This can be achieved through shared training sessions between university and school staff and/or through joint PETE sessions in which pre-service and experienced partnership school teachers experience, share and discuss research-informed, evidence-based messages, approaches and models. Such sessions have been experienced by the lead author in primary and secondary PETE settings and have resulted in enhanced, authentic experiences for pre-service teachers and much-needed, relevant continuing professional development for experienced teachers. They have also triggered professional, pedagogical dialogue between pre-service teachers, university and school staff about the desire for change and how to achieve this, given the complexity and pragmatics involved.

Another way of improving PE–PETE alignment and coherence is for PETE providers to intentionally seek out and work with schools whose PE staff are conducive to a new vision of PE. This could lead to the creation of "flagship schools" working closely with the university on research-based practice and practice-based research, which would accelerate the process of improvement and re-design of PE and PETE. The expectation that higher education PETE providers in England work in close partnership with schools in the design, delivery and assessment of their teacher education programmes (Ofsted, 2018) helps this become a reality. In such instances, providers are prompted to advance their PETE programmes through, for example, partnership committees and subject advisory groups comprising forward-thinking teachers.

Teachers in these flagship schools can be encouraged and supported to undertake Master's and doctoral study (see Chapter 11) and/or to be involved in research projects focusing on transformative, needs-led PE. An example of the latter is the Promoting Active Lifestyles (PAL) research project (Harris *et al.*, 2016) which developed from previous research demonstrating the inadequacy of health-related aspects of PETE. This aligns with Lawson's (2018) view that a field that claims the ability to be a key influence on students' lifestyles should feel obliged to deliver on this immense potential.

The PAL project involved pre-service and experienced teachers from partnership schools being invited to work collaboratively (as a community of practice) with the aim of increasing students' activity levels within the school setting. A flexible approach to achieving this was encouraged to cater for a diverse range of school contexts, populations and budgets. Collectively, the pre-service and experienced teachers who volunteered to be involved created and developed resources around key PAL principles (whole school and PE-specific) and PAL paradoxes, with the support of university teacher educators/researchers.

Examples of whole-school PAL principles were (i) review the school's extra-curricular PE programme and consider how appealing/accessible it is for *all* students, and (ii) discuss the promotion of active lifestyles, including the "one hour a day" physical activity for health guideline, with all staff, governors, students and parents. The PE-specific PAL principles included (i) identify low active students and provide them with support/guidance/information and targeted/

bespoke activity sessions; and (ii) assess learning and progress in PE in active ways (e.g. show, demonstrate, shadow) (Harris *et al.*, 2016).

Examples of the PAL paradoxes included (i) PE lessons offer much needed, regular opportunities to be active, yet activity levels in PE are generally low; and (ii) PE teachers often claim to use fitness testing to promote activity yet many students dislike and learn little from fitness testing. Pre-service and experienced teachers' adoption of freely selected PAL principles ultimately led to positive changes to their philosophies and pedagogies associated with promoting active lifestyles (Harris *et al.*, 2016). Furthermore, some of the teachers have gone on to use the PAL paradox resources to influence the philosophies and pedagogies of colleagues in their own and neighbouring schools, supported by emerging communities of practice.

This type of research represents an innovative research and development PE–PETE partnership. It involves pre-service and experienced teachers and researchers collaborating, co-generating knowledge and improving practice and policy in the process, as advocated by Greenhalgh and colleagues (2016).

PE–PETE alignment and coherence also can be improved through university and school staff deliberately addressing the acculturation aspect of occupational socialization in the form of pre-service teachers' beliefs, expectations and values associated with PE (see Chapter 7). We are aware of PETE providers who strategically and explicitly focus on this at various stages of the teacher education process. For example, the first and second authors have experience of working with individuals over an extended period of time (up to five years) during which they study for a Master's degree incorporating PETE. This arrangement permits regular debate of key educational concepts and increases the potential for long-term influence.

We also know of university PETE staff undertaking doctoral study on the influences of PETE on pre-service and early career teachers' subjective warrants. This has led to the redesign of PETE in the lead author's institution to increase pre-service teachers' awareness of the beliefs, expectations and values they bring to PETE, where these emanate from, and how they affect their ability to acknowledge, evaluate, teach and create different forms of PE for young people. This ongoing development holds promise for helping pre-service teachers reflect on their past and how it influences their present and future.

A further opportunity to enhance alignment and coherence between PE and PETE arises through the requirement of initial teacher training providers in England to support teachers during their early years of teaching, particularly the first year (Ofsted, 2018). This is usually provided through numerous forms of professional development such as seminars, workshops, conferences, newsletters, resources and communication via email and social media platforms. These offer opportunities to further develop teachers' skills of, for example, curriculum design based on evidence-based practice. This has the potential to lead to future PE curricula that represent more than a collection of activities, approaches and models and that prioritize and clarify the diverse learning in PE and its contribution to students' lives.

Post-PETE support for beginning teachers can help them through the challenges of entering and becoming established within the profession whilst retaining their desire to assess and meet the needs of the children they teach. This may reduce the impact of organizational socialization, characterized by learning the ropes of the job and conforming to institutional norms in order to feel accepted (Templin and Schempp, 1989). It can also help smooth the often-rocky transition for new teachers who may feel marginalized and experience role conflict and reality shock (Blankenship and Coleman, 2009; Iannucci and MacPhail, 2018). The first and second authors have experience of providing professional development on specific topics and issues identified by early career teachers as particular areas of need. This may assist new teachers in redefining the context in which they teach and encourage them to feel empowered to share their ideas, experiences and opinions including, where necessary, challenging institutional norms, drawing on what they have learned from PETE.

Conclusion

Peter Drucker's (2008) question, "If we hadn't inherited it, would we do it this way?" provides much food for thought in terms of PE and PETE. A glib response is that "we wouldn't start from here" but, given where we are, and to contribute to policy and practice lesson-drawing, we propose the following future research agenda to improve PE–PETE alignment and coherence.

- Exploring and confronting the influence of acculturation during PETE.
- PETE working with partnership schools whose PE staff are conducive to a vision of PE that meets the needs of today's learners.
- Co-designing PETE and PE with visionary partnership schools and their learners.
- Ensuring that partnership schools involved in PETE are willing and able to contribute to a PETE programme which develops PE teachers who can design, teach and assess needs-led PE curricula.
- Working with PE staff in partnership schools on research focusing on needs-led PE.
- Supporting early career PE teachers through the challenges of organizational socialization.

We believe that the above research agenda has the potential to impact PE and PETE policy and practice internationally (see Chapter 14) and thus contributes to the call for collective action in the quest for beneficial impact prioritizing children's physical activity, sport and health-related needs.

Having said this, we recognize that our proposed viable solutions are framed, and thereby limited, by the particular national and local contexts within which we live and work. Nevertheless, we recognize that PE's vast potential to enhance children's lives across all nations and contexts relies on teachers' readiness and ability to confront and cope with issues within the field. We also recognize the value of sharing good practice in supporting beginning teachers to address such issues in order to provide the customized learning experiences their students need and deserve.

PE teachers and teacher educators are key policy actors in terms of what they prioritize, do and achieve. Rather than ignore or be overwhelmed by this responsibility, we urge that they unite to improve student outcomes. We also endorse the prudent and pragmatic advice to think big (or globally) and to act small (or locally) in this regard and to start now, as enhancing the quality of children's lives is surely what we are all about.

Epilogue

Constructing this paper proved an interesting challenge. The authors had never worked together previously as a group, and time and work commitments did not permit us meeting to discuss the content of the chapter. In fact, two authors have never met each other.

We are nevertheless familiar with each other's professional spaces, in that two of us have similar teacher education roles, albeit in universities in different countries, and we have had many professional discussions over the years relating to teacher education and health-related physical education. The teacher author is also familiar with the teacher education space as she undertook her teacher education at the university in England where the lead author works. She also has extensive experience as a teacher educator in her role as an experienced mentor within the same university in England's teacher education partnership programme. Our shared understanding of each other's roles and responsibilities in developing future generations of PE teachers helped us to collectively and comprehensively address the topic of this chapter, and to feel that we could each make significant individual contributions from our own standpoints.

References

Blankenship, B. and Coleman, M.M. (2009). An examination of "washout" and workplace conditions of beginning physical education teachers. *The Physical Educator*, 66(2), 97–111.

Cloes, M. (2017a). Preparing physically educated citizens in physical education. Expectations and practices. *Retos*, 31, 245–251. http://recyt.fecyt.es/index.php/retos/article/view/53497/32304

Cloes, M. (2017b). *Health and physical education from a European perspective*. Paper presented at the 22nd Annual ECSS Congress "Sport Science in a Metropolitan Area". Essen, Germany. Available at: http://hdl.handle.net/2268/212658

De Knop, P., Theeboom, M., Huts, K., De Martelaer, K. and Cloes, M. (2005). The state of school physical education in Belgium. In: U. Pühse and M. Gerber (eds), *International Comparison of Physical Education. Concepts. Problems. Prospects.* Oxford: Meyer & Meyer Sport, pp. 104–131. Available at: http://hdl.handle.net/2268/13513

De Martelaer, K., Seghers, J., Cardon, G., Haerens, L., De Boever, E. and Cloes, M. (2014). Physical education stimulating a healthy lifestyle and critical sports consumption in Belgium. In: M.K. Chin and C.R. Edginton (eds), *Physical Education and Health Global Perspectives and Best Practice*. Urbana, IL: Sagamore, pp. 43–56. Available at: http://hdl.handle.net/2268/167069

Drucker, P.F. (2008). *The Essential Drucker: The Best Sixty Years of Peter Drucker's Essential Writings on Management*. New York: Collins Business Essentials.

Frédéric, O., Gribomont, J. and Cloes, M. (2009). Comparaison des stratégies d'enseignement du basket-ball en milieu scolaire et en milieu sportif. *eJRIEPS*, 16, 6–21.

Green, K., Cale, L. and Harris, J. (2018). Re-imagination and re-design in physical education. Implicit and explicit models in England and Wales. In: H.A. Lawson (ed.), *Redesigning Physical Education. An Equity Agenda in Which Every Child Matters*. London: Routledge, pp. 156–170.

Greenhalgh, T., Jackson, C., Shaw, S. and Janamiam, T. (2016). Achieving research impact through co-creation in community-based health services: literature review and case study. *The Millbank Quarterly*, 94(2), 393–429.

Griggs, G. and Randall, V. (2018). Primary physical education subject leadership: along the road from in-house solutions to outsourcing. *Education 3–13, International Journal of Primary, Elementary and Early Years Education*. doi:10.1080/03004279.2018.1520277

Harris, J. (2014). Physical education teacher education students' knowledge, perceptions and experiences of promoting healthy, active lifestyles in secondary schools. *Physical Education and Sport Pedagogy*, 19(5), 466–480.

Harris, J. (2018). The case for physical education becoming a core subject in the national curriculum. *Physical Education Matters*, 13(2), 9–12.

Harris, J., Cale, L. and Musson, H. (2012). The predicament of primary physical education: a consequence of "insufficient" ITT and "ineffective" CPD? *Physical Education and Sport Pedagogy*, 17(4), 367–381.

Harris, J., Cale, L., Casey, A., Tyne, A. and Samarai, B. (2016). Promoting active lifestyles in schools: the PAL project. *Physical Education Matters*, 11(3), 52–53.

Heifetz, R., Linsky, M. and Grashow, A. (2009). *The Practice of Adaptive Leadership: Tools and Tactics for Changing your Organization and the World*. Cambridge, MA: Harvard Business School Press.

Iannucci, C. and MacPhail, A. (2018). One teacher's experience of teaching physical education and another school subject: An inter-role conflict? *Research Quarterly for Exercise and Sport*, 89(2), 235–245.

Kirk, D. (2010). *Physical Education Futures*. Oxon: Routledge.

Kirk, D., Bardid, F., Lamb, C.A., Millar, J.D. and Teraoka, E. (2018). Redesigning physical education in Scotland. In H.A. Lawson (ed.), *Redesigning Physical Education. An Equity Agenda in Which Every Child Matters*. London: Routledge, pp. 145–155.

Lawson, H.A. (1983). Toward a model of teacher socialisation in physical education: entry into schools, teachers' role orientations, and longevity in teaching. *Journal of Teaching in Physical Education*, 3(1), 3–15.

Lawson, H.A. (ed.) (2018). *Redesigning Physical Education. An Equity Agenda in Which Every Child Matters*. London: Routledge.

Lortie, D. (1975). *Schoolteacher: A Sociological Study*. Chicago: University of Chicago Press.

MacPhail, A., O'Sullivan, M., Tannehill, D. and Parker, M. (2018). Re-designing physical education in Ireland: Significant redesign over modest reforms? In H.A. Lawson (ed.),

Redesigning Physical Education. An Equity Agenda in Which Every Child Matters. Abingdon, Oxon: Routledge, pp. 171–181.

Office for Standards in Education (Ofsted) (2018). *Initial Teacher Education Inspection Handbook*. London: Ofsted.

Randall, V., Richardson, A., Swaithes, W. and Adams, S. (2016). *Generation Next: The Preparation of Pre-service Teachers in Primary Physical Education*. Winchester: University of Winchester.

Richards, K.A.R., Templin, T.J., Woods, A.M. and Graber, K.C. (2018). Re-designing physical education in the United States: a second look. In H.A. Lawson (ed.), *Redesigning Physical Education. An Equity Agenda in Which Every Child Matters*. Abingdon, Oxon: Routledge, pp. 123–133.

Tappe, M.K. and Burgeson, C.R. (2004). Physical education: a cornerstone for physically active lifestyles. *Journal of Teaching in Physical Education*, 23(4), 281–299.

Templin, T.J. and Richards, K.A.R. (2014). C.H. McCloy Lecture: Reflections on socialisation into physical education – an intergenerational perspective. *Research Quarterly for Exercise and Sport*, 85(4), 431–445.

Templin, T.J. and Schempp, P.G. (eds) (1989). *Socialisation into Physical Education: Learning to Teach*. Canada: Benchmark Press.

Tsangaridou, N. (2012). Educating primary teachers to teach physical education. *European Physical Education Review*, 18, 275–286.

Youth Sport Trust (2018). *Survey of Secondary PE*. Loughborough: Youth Sport Trust. Available at: www.youthsporttrust.org/sec-survey

Chapter 5

The innovation challenge

Maintaining programme standards and developing cohesion while developing and testing alternative designs in new kinds of schools

Phillip Ward, Melissa Parker and Diane Barnes

We begin by noting that our discussions occur within the context of government control of education. While much of what we discuss is grounded in the context of the United States, we draw on lessons from other countries to inform our writing. Given that educational change largely exists within the context of government control of education, and given that there have been few changes to that organizational framework in the US, our position relative to the grand challenge is that any changes must come from within the existing system. Such changes should be cognizant of the inclusion of physical education (PE) with the existing educational practices of this era. In this context, we take the position to not hypothesize about abstract or utopian views of what PE might be, but rather what PE can be within the existing system and how it can be both a part of, and also effect changes within, such a system.

In considering this grand challenge, we examine five proposals. All can be cultivated in the education system, while contributing to it. All represent feasible changes within reach of teachers and teacher educators. The five proposals overlap, as indicated by shared components. For example, our proposals are designed to: (a) be situated within state and national standards for PE in an age of accountability; (b) strengthen collaboration within school districts; (c) reconnect with health education to present a greater presence in policy discussions and practice than currently done; (d) become a part of the social-emotional learning movement; and (e) contribute to the Whole School, Whole Community, Whole Child movement (Centers for Disease Control, 2019).

There is another way to evaluate these proposals, and our analytical progression provides guidance. These proposals provide increasingly comprehensive forms of engagement, and the progression we provide implicates increasing degrees of influence and impact.

Proposal one: meeting the standards for PE in an age of accountability

This proposal is grounded in the belief that in an educational policy environment defined by teacher accountability, PE teachers must complete the tasks for which they are employed. In the case of the US, these tasks are defined by states and districts. Although employed by school districts, PE teachers are for the most part public sector or governmental workers. They are licensed and monitored by governments, and tasked by laws requiring them to teach to the standards for their subject area.

For example, the current accountability movement in education is structured by governmental policies, and it is focused on teachers demonstrating that their students have met the standards for the specific subject areas and grade levels (Ward, 2016). Teaching effectiveness is defined in performance-based terms. The spotlight is on teachers who produce student learning gains (Ward, 2016).

As such, there is a pressing need in the US and worldwide for teachers of PE to provide evidence that their students learn the content of school PE defined by the respective state standards. This should include the standards for school PE and also provide evidence of objectives beyond the state standards tailored to the local contextual needs of the students and the philosophy of the teacher. Such evidence must be the kind that is accessible and understandable to administrators, parents and policymakers.

In short, teachers must demonstrate that they make a difference in the lives of children. It is not sufficient to simply engage in the practice of PE as has been the case for much of the twentieth century and the first decade of the twenty-first century in the US. Evidence in the form of indicators or benchmarks of what teachers have accomplished in terms of student learning is required.

Proposal two: strengthening collaboration within districts and local education authorities

We ground this proposal in the belief that professional growth as a teacher is enhanced by collaboration, and that the right kind of collaboration has multiple effects. These collaboration effects are described in terms of culture, professional learning, and politics.

Collaboration as culture

Merriam-Webster's dictionary (2019) defines culture "as the set of shared attitudes, values, goals, and practices that characterize an institution or organization." We have often witnessed teachers sitting in a new initiative session where they are asked to engage in yet another activity designed to improve an educational function of the district. The consequences of frequent changes in direction include initiative fatigue, confusion, distrust and demoralization (Fullan and Quinn, 2016). These represent the very outcomes that collaboration as culture seeks to avoid. A critical feature of Merriam-Webster's definition of collaboration is the term "shared". Shared outcomes are neither short term and are rarely completed (Fullan and Quinn, 2016). That is, culture is seen as a process in the sense that it is ongoing. Culture will produce products, but culture itself is not a destination.

Collaboration can be taught and it must be reinforced over time. Fullan and Quinn (2016) note that collaboration in schools must have consistency and specificity relative to the shared purpose. They ask their teachers to discuss publicly what they do with each other and with others as evidence that they are all moving in the same direction. We also note that it is of importance that such collaborations are directed by experts.

Collaboration as learning

Our use of the term "learning" refers to teachers learning about: (a) their profession, including refining their understandings of curriculum and pedagogies; (b) their students; (c) their school; and (d) the shared understandings of attitudes, values, goals and practices. Viewing teachers as decision makers who share in the responsibility of the teaching and learning culture requires recognizing that they have a shared professional knowledge. This professional knowledge draws on a number of knowledge bases as well as teachers' craft knowledge. The task of teaching requires knowledge translation by teachers to create and operationalize their attitudes, values, goals and practices. Professional development that supports collaborative teacher learning should be based on teacher identified need (see Chapter 13). The characteristics of collaborative learning include ongoing and sustained efforts, supported by administration, occurring within communities, treating teachers as active learners, facilitated with care, and with a focus on improving student learning (Parker and Patton, 2017). The outcome of this type of teacher learning is teachers who have the capacity to help students learn.

Collaboration as politics

It is important that administrators, including principals, curriculum and professional development directors, engage in the process of collaboration. The mechanism for this engagement is advocacy, best approached from a number of perspectives including the sharing of information about activities that occur in schools through face-to-face meetings, using infographics to convey sound bites of information, and invitations to visit other gymnasiums as examples of what can be achieved. Such activities serve to familiarize administrators with the individuals, goals, and practices of PE in their district. Such engagement should be intentional, sequenced, and frequent. Similarly, parents should be informed of the work of PE teachers.

Among the specific messages that can be conveyed are that PE teachers are professionals with a defined knowledge base, standards for teaching, and that as teachers they are expected to prepare their students to meet designated state or national outcomes. In this context, it is reasonable to argue that PE teachers have a place in school improvement, emphasizing that the work they undertake in their classrooms, school, and community contributes to the overall educational mission of the school. In short, engaging in the politics of collaboration is evidenced by the value of the profession held by its practitioners.

The outcome of such efforts should be that when administrators and parents have to make decisions about the role of PE (e.g. hours devoted to teaching, fiscal support, teacher employment, professional support including support for collaboration) they do so from an informed perspective. This advocacy responsibility requires teachers to engage with adaptive competence (see Chapter 13) in a level of politics to push the agenda of collaboration. In short, teachers have a moral responsibility to contribute to improving the setting of education for children, and that cannot be defined solely by what they do in the classroom.

Proposal three: reconnect with health education to present a greater presence in policy discussions and practice

In this proposal we argue that educating teachers in both health and PE would serve several agendas. It provides teachers with a second certification area and this strengthens their value to school management. It also allows the teacher to integrate the subject areas. From a local policy perspective, many schools and school districts look for candidates with dual licences in health and PE to work in "Wellness" departments.

For example, in one district with which we are familiar, middle school "health and physical education" is taught every other day and "health" is taught on the intermediate days. The same teacher teaches both subjects and is able to know students well and make strong connections across the two subject matters. Having teachers educated in health and PE allows them to appreciate and advocate for the broader picture of wellness. In short, for employment security, local and national policy perspectives recommend educating teachers in both health and PE. This dual approach has many advantages.

Nevertheless, there are choices to be made as to how this might be operationalized in PETE. Some states (e.g. Michigan) have legislated a single health and PE degree. Elsewhere, some PETE programmes have combined health and PE into one degree. The strength of this legislative and programmatic effort is the recognition of the rationales discussed above. The challenge is that future teachers must be educated in "health and physical education" in the same number of professional credit hours formerly used for just "physical education". For governments and teacher education programmes, a critical consideration is the cost and time to graduation coupled with the challenge of meeting the teacher licensure standards for health and PE in a limited time.

The previous considerations relative to reconnecting health and PE represent teacher education approaches focused on the education of teachers. Australia provides an important case example for an alternative approach. Rather than treating health and PE as related, but separate, an integrated curriculum grounded in five propositions and based on their futures forecasting analysis has been created (Macdonald *et al.*, 2018). First is a focus on the *educative purposes* of a combined health and PE curriculum. Macdonald *et al.* (2018, p. 202), quoting the Australian Curriculum, Assessment and Reporting Authority, report that the health and physical education curriculum ensure, "ongoing developmentally appropriate opportunities to create, apply and evaluate knowledge, develop their understanding, and practise and refine the skills necessary to maintain their own and others' health and wellbeing and participation in physical education". This represents a focus on a knowledge, skills, and decision-making aspect of the curriculum.

Second is a focus on a *strengths-based approach* in the curriculum. The Australian curriculum draws on the salutogenic model of health promotion (Antonovsky, 1996); an orientation toward developing the strengths of the individual. This represents a significant departure from a deficiency or risk-based approach used by many curriculums. Third, the Australian health and PE curriculum emphasizes *purposeful, relevant and fun movement experiences* where students develop competence and confidence (Macdonald *et al.*, 2018). In discussing the meaning of this proposition, Macdonald (2019) noted that in interpreting the "relevant" focus, this may mean that individual pursuits rather than sports may be emphasized. This represents an important consideration in meeting the longer term needs of students.

Fourth, the curriculum focuses on *health literacy*. Health literacy is the extent to which individuals have the capacity to access and understand basic health information and services needed to make appropriate health decisions. Health literacy represents a connecting rod to larger public health issues that are addressed in school curricula. Finally, the curriculum focuses on engaging students in a critical inquiry approach. The approach requires students studying the curriculum to research, analyse, apply, and critique knowledge in health and PE. This last approach emphasizes that critical thinking is a foundational requirement for students in Australian schools (Macdonald *et al.*, 2018).

The Australian curriculum has many merits, but chief among them are: (a) the focus on integrating health and PE, and (b) the strengths-based focus. These represents significant departures from typical approaches in health and PE and place the child rather than the subject matter front and centre of educational objectives.

Proposal four: become a part of the social-emotional learning movement

In this proposal we argue that teachers of PE (and health) need to engage with the social and emotional learning (SEL) agenda rapidly reappearing on the educational landscape. Renewed interest in SEL has arisen from evidence that it contributes positively to both mental and social health outcomes and academic achievement (National Association of State Boards of Education, 2013). Two decades ago, in an effort to align school programming, the Collaborative for Academic, Social, and Emotional Learning (CASEL) defined SEL as "the process through which children and adults understand and manage emotions, set and achieve positive goals, feel and show empathy for others, establish and maintain positive relationships, and make responsible decisions" (CASEL, n.d.). This model is gaining international traction.

The CASEL model identifies five SEL competencies: self-awareness, social awareness, responsible decision-making, self-management, and relationship skills. Self-awareness refers to students knowing their strengths and limitations within a well-grounded growth mindset. Social awareness includes effectively managing stress, controlling impulses, and motivating one's self to set and achieve goals. Social awareness incorporates understanding the perspectives of others and empathizing with them. Responsible decision-making comprises making constructive choices about personal behaviour and social interactions based on ethical standards, safety, and social norms. The ability to regulate one's emotions, thoughts, and behaviours effectively in different situations reflects constructs related to self-management. Communicating clearly, listening well, cooperating with others, resisting inappropriate social pressure, negotiating conflict constructively, and seeking and offering help when needed defines relationship skills. Two things are striking about these constructs. First, PE is a ripe environment for their development; and second, in some PE contexts, teachers report: "we already do this".

PE and health education offer a natural environment for SEL teaching and learning, feasibly contending that SEL may be the backbone of a PE programme (Gagnon, 2016). Movement is a powerful learning form; it is emotional and interactive. Uniquely, the movement environment holds the potential for interaction, communication, responsibility, decision-making, goal setting, leadership, and self-direction. It is an environment that "allows kids to show more of themselves" (Hellison, 2003, p. 7). Noddings (1992) indicated the importance of the connectedness of physical activity and the holistic development of children, stating:

> ... play self is only one part of the self. We must be concerned also with the emotional, spiritual, and intellectual self, and clearly these are not discrete. We separate and label them for convenience in discussion, but it may be a mistake to separate them sharply in curriculum.
>
> (Noddings, 1992, p. 48)

Many would argue that various national and state PE and PETE standards, competencies, or outcomes reflecting personal and social responsibility (e.g. Gutiérrez-Gracía and Martinez-Alvarez, 2019; NCCA, 2017; SHAPE America, 2014; Scottish Government, 2009) already address SEL guidelines. Yet, SEL benefits do not automatically accrue as a result of participation in PE and standards are the foundation; not the end point. There is the need to conceptualize what SEL constructs mean and what the skills to achieve the constructs look like in the real world of children and youth in PE, without sacrificing the unique psychomotor learning that PE has to offer. While PE provides opportunities to develop SEL skills, intentional pedagogies or the development of learning experiences directly related to SEL are needed. Current curricular and instructional models in

PE clearly underscore SEL learning, e.g. personal and social responsibility, cooperative learning, and adventure-based learning, but SEL is broader than existing models. It is a curriculum within a curriculum. We argue that, if embedded deliberately in PE programming, regardless of model, there is a shift from "doing" SEL to transforming learning for students (Bartlett, 2019).

SEL represents a change in "deep culture of physical education" (Hellison, 2003, p. viii); thus, pre-service and in-service PETE has a responsibility, in very direct ways, to assist teachers in learning how to embed SEL into their teaching; exposure and rhetoric are not sufficient. One example of embedding this learning in pre-service PETE is planned and progressive re-visitation of SEL constructs, often using Hellison's (2003) Teaching Personal and Social Responsibility (TPSR) model throughout the programme. Although accomplished in myriad ways, many programmes have pre-service teachers initially "live" the TPSR curriculum during a physical activity content class, i.e. badminton – not as a single lesson, but for the entire semester. Second, drawing on their experiences of "living the curriculum", in a later course, students explore the theoretical assumptions underlying TPSR, prompting consideration of PE not just as a venue for the "physical self", but as an environment supporting holistic development. Lastly, students plan and teach units of learning using TPSR during their student teaching experiences and teach in one after-school programme using SEL constructs conceptualized from a perspective other than TPSR. In this manner, learning to teach SEL is scaffolded throughout the PETE experience.

SEL as a value added construct may be a boundary spanner for PE because it is used by multiple subject areas. Viewed in this way, it is a whole school approach positioning the child at the centre of the pedagogical encounter. As such, it allows PE to come to the table as a fully contributing member of the educational endeavour of the whole child, transcending subject areas.

Proposal five: contribute to the whole school, whole community, whole child model

The principal public policy dealing with health promotion in school settings in the USA has been the coordinated school health programme. In 2014, the Association for Supervision and Curriculum Development (ASCD) and the Centers for Disease Control and Prevention (CDC) developed and introduced the Whole School, Whole Community, Whole Child (WSCC) model. The model is grounded in five tenets:

- Each student enters school *healthy*, learns about, and practices a healthy lifestyle.
- Each student learns in an environment that is physically and emotionally *safe* for students and adults.
- Each student is actively *engaged* in learning and is connected to the school and broader community.

- Each student has access to personalized learning and is *supported* by qualified, caring adults.
- Each student is *challenged* academically and prepared for success in college or further study and for employment and participation in a global environment.

These tenets reflect the core nature of the collaboration between two agencies, one professional and the other governmental, in aligning and integrating health and education policies, practices, and resources in promoting the whole child. The model has ten components: (a) health education, (b) PE and physical activity, (c) nutrition environment and services, (d) health services, (e) counselling, (f) psychological and social services, (g) social and emotional climate, (h) physical environment, (i) employee wellness, and (j) family engagement and community involvement.

The WSCC model, much like the new Junior Cycle Wellbeing Framework (NCCA, 2017) in Ireland, or the Health and Wellbeing aspect of the Scottish Curriculum for Excellence (Scottish Government, 2009), has the potential to serve as a framework to develop school-wide collaboration that places the child at the centre of schooling, emphasizing a school-wide and community-based approach to supporting the child. These models recognize that academic achievement and health are mutually interdependent (Klobe *et al.*, 2015; Michael *et al.*, 2015). Healthier students are ready to learn and academically ready students are better able to access information and make informed decisions (Klobe *et al.*, 2015; Michael *et al.*, 2015). The WSCC model focuses the efforts of schools and communities on supporting the development of a whole child outcome described as "one who is knowledgeable, healthy, motivated and engaged" (CDC, 2019). The model both requires and provides a mechanism for collaboration among the ten components. In doing so, it has the potential to reduce silos creating a shared model and serves to inform the development of other policies.

Recognizing there are both "possibilities and pitfalls" (O'Sullivan, 2004) for PE as a subject area within a public health agenda (and, if we are not careful, whole school approaches can be reduced to such), we argue for PE to embrace these approaches for multiple reasons. First, these public policy efforts combine educational and health agencies in support of a shared vision of a healthy child. Second, while each of the four previous proposals might be viewed as increasingly more comprehensive systems of collaboration and engagement by teachers in support of their students, the whole school models provide a mechanism for both collaboration and up-scaling the first four proposals within and across educational jurisdictions. Third, initial results from these programmes in which PE and health are components are compelling.

A recent review of the Health and Wellbeing aspect of the Scottish initiative (OECD, 2015), reported high academic achievement in science and reading equally spread across students accompanied by high levels of resiliency, inclusive environments supporting positive attitudes, and connections with peers and school. Furthermore, in reviews conducted to determine the association between academic behaviours and health, "physical activity has the most consistent findings" (Michael *et al.*, 2015, p. 740). As such, PE represents a key component of efforts to implement whole school models and thus has political leverage (see Chapter 14) as a subject matter contributing to the model.

Policy and practice lesson drawing

The five proposals presented have some common elements. First, they represent national level interventions, yet they are practices that can be operationalized locally. Second, they represent proposals where teachers can be held equally accountable for the processes used as much as the outcomes produced in students. These characteristics are also present in the World Health Organization's (WHO) health promoting school movement (WHO, 2019). A health promoting school is one that constantly strengthens its capacity as a healthy setting for living, learning and working (WHO, 2019). Health promoting schools are multicomponent interventions focused on children's health using educational, curricular, environmental practices, and policies designed to positively impact the school and community where the child lives.

An important dimension of health promoting schools is that, while the essential components remain a focus of all implementation (Mannix-McNamara and Simovska, 2015), it is operationalized differently within and across countries. In conceptualizing how the five proposals might be used, the health promoting school's movement presents some important lessons. Three of these lessons implicate longevity, the need to focus on the best approach, and the often underestimated, spillover effect.

The recognition of the fleeting and repetitive nature of educational changes suggests that while change is constant it also acknowledges as fact that many teachers recognize that "this too will pass" (see Chapter 14). Longevity is essential if a culture is to develop and be sustained. It requires that new educational reforms be embedded into existing practices rather than supplanting previous reforms. Longevity also requires that new reforms designed to replace existing practices are not merely ideologically based, but have strong evidence showing they are substantively better than what is currently being done.

Revolving door educational reforms often suggest, at the very least, either a lack of due diligence in the selection of the reform or a lack of confidence in the reform. Using effective educational reforms over time strengthens and stabilizes both the understanding and the use of a shared technical culture and language (Lortie, 1975). In this sense, the health promoting school movement provides a time-tested model that continues to grow (Mannix-McNamara and Simovska, 2015). It fits the exigencies of different settings and, as such, it provides a useful framework to implement fundamental change.

Longevity also requires attention to identifying the best processes and outcomes in education. The current multiplicity of options means that choosing what is most effective is challenging. A growing body of research points to the critical role of multi-dimensional interventions embedded in more than one dimension of school life (Maxwell *et al.*, 2017). Such reforms typically provide the best value for schools and communities. These interventions provide an infrastructure that is both supportive and large, and, as a result, better able to weather inherent challenges.

Importantly, these interventions also strengthen students' psychological positive identification with the school culture (Maxwell *et al.*, 2017). The five proposals, similar to the health promoting school, represent evidenced-based processes impacting a student's health, equity and learning.

Spillover effects speak to the effects that teachers have of influencing outcomes beyond the impact they have on their own students (Opper, 2019). Spillover effects can be positive or negative. Here we talk about the positive outcomes. One reason a teacher may have broader impact is that by increasing the ability of their own students, effective teachers increase the number of students who model desired behaviours to other groups of students. These other students are affected by their peers' behaviours. Importantly, spillover effects occur most strongly within groups of students who are of the same race and gender (Opper, 2019).

Recommendations for a shared research and development agenda that would encourage the international PE and PETE community to work together collectively to enhance the standing and survival of school PE and PETE

A guiding vision for these proposals is they extend beyond subject-specific PE content because they offer the potential for a deeper connection across the school and community, allowing the realization of a strong integrated educational system, providing "children the right to achieve their full potential" (NCCA, 2017, p. 10). They recommend a shared research and development agenda with three priorities.

First, examining how these proposals are utilized by teachers, schools, and communities would allow insight into the realities of implementation. Questions might explore, "What process was used to determine the changes in settings?", "What barriers were overcome?", and "How were the barriers overcome?".

Second, the effects of these proposals in meeting their stated objectives should be examined This examination should occur not just in terms of processes, but also in terms of student outcomes. The assessment of effects should be meaningfully comprehensive, reflecting the multidimensional characteristics of the endeavour.

Third, the professional learning of future and in-service teachers should be examined. Future teachers should graduate with, and in-service teachers be supported in developing, the skills and knowledge to use these proposals. Examining and assessing how teachers are prepared and how they use these skills in practice across the teacher education continuum (see Chapter 11) should form the basis of such investigations.

In concluding this chapter we acknowledge that these proposals, as are all endeavours of this kind, works in progress subject to the conditions of the times. Although the conditions change, we argue for a concerted effort to make the best of educational reform efforts. In particular, give teachers an opportunity to produce the kind of outcomes that are founded on their raison d'être.

References

Antonovsky, A. (1996). The salutogenic model as a theory to guide health promotion. *Health Promotion International*, 11(1) 11–18.

Bartlett, J. (2019). Social-emotional learning, health education best practices, and skills-based health. *Journal of Physical Education, Recreation and Dance*, 90(2), 58–60.

Centers for Disease Control (2019). Whole School, Whole Community and Whole Child Available at: www.cdc.gov/healthyschools/wscc/index.htm (accessed 31 March 2019).

Collaborative for Academic, Social, and Emotional Learning (n.d.). *What is SEL?* Available at: https://casel.org/what-is-sel/ (accessed 29 April 2019).

Fullan, M. and Quinn, J. (2016). *Coherence: The Right Drivers in Action for Schools, Districts, and Systems*. Thousand Oaks, CA: Corwin.

Gagnon, A. (2016). Creating a positive social-emotional climate in your elementary physical education program. *Strategies*, 29(3), 21–27.

Gutiérrez-Gracía, C. and Martinez-Alvarez, L. (2019). Physical education teacher education in Spain. In: A. MacPhail, D. Tannehill, and Z. Avsar (eds), *European Physical Education Teacher Education Practices*. Aachen, Germany: Meyer and Meyer, pp. 360–379.

Hellison, D. (2003). *Teaching Responsibility through Physical Activity*, 2nd edn. Champaign, IL: Human Kinetics.

Klobe, L.J., Allensworth, D.D., Potts-Datema, W., and White, D.R. (2015). What have we learned from collaborative partnerships to concomitantly improve both education and health? *Journal of School Health*, 85, 766–774.

Lortie, D. (1975). *Schoolteacher: A Sociological Study*. Chicago: University of Chicago Press.

Macdonald, D. (2019). Health and physical education: curriculum reform: an Australian story. Presented at the 2019 World Congress on Teaching, Learning, and Curriculum in Physical Education. Shanghai, China.

Macdonald, D., Enright, E. and McCuaig, L. (2018). Re-visioning the Australian curriculum for health and physical education. In L. Lawson (ed.), *Redesigning Physical Education: An Equity Agenda in Which Every Child Matters*. London: Routledge.

Mannix-McNamara, P. and Simovska, V. (2015). Schools for health and sustainability: insights from the past, present and for the future. In: V. Simovska and P. Mannix-McNamara (eds), *Schools for Health and Sustainability*. Dordrecht: Springer.

Maxwell, S., Renolds, K., Lee, E., Subasic, E. and Bromhead, D. (2017). The impact of school climate and school identification on academic achievement: multilevel modeling with student and teacher data. *Frontiers in Psychology*, 8, 2069. doi:10.3389/fpsyg.2017.02069

Merriam-Webster Dictionary (2019). Definition of culture. Available at: www.merriam-webster.com/dictionary/culture (accessed 31 March 2019).

Michael, S.L., Merlo, C.L., Basch, C.E., Wentzel, K.R. and Wechsler, H. (2015). Critical connections: health and academics. *Journal of School Health*, 85, 740–758.

National Council for Curriculum and Assessment (2017). *Junior Cycle Wellbeing Guidelines*. Dublin: National Council for Curriculum and Assessment.

National Association of State Boards of Education (2013). *Social-emotional Learning the Focus of New NASBE Resource*. 3 October. Retrieved from www.nasbe.org/press-release/social-emotional-learning-the-focus-of-new-nasbe-resource

Noddings, N. (1992). *The Challenge to Care in Schools*. New York: Teachers College Press.

Opper, I.M. (2019). Does helping John help Sue? Evidence of spillovers in education. *American Economic Review*, 109, 1080–1115.

Organisation for Economic Co-operation and Development (OECD) (2015). *Improving Schools in Scotland: An OECD Perspective*. Paris, France: OECD.

O'Sullivan, M. (2004). Possibilities and pitfalls of a public health agenda for physical education. *Journal of Teaching in Physical Education*, 23(4), 392–404.

Parker, M. and Patton, K. (2017). What research tells us about effective continuing professional development for physical education teachers. In: C. Ennis (ed.), *Routledge Handbook of Physical Education Pedagogies*. London: Routledge.

Scottish Government (2009). *Curriculum for Excellence: Health and Wellbeing: Experiences and Outcomes*. Glasgow: Learning and Teaching Scotland.

SHAPE America (2014). *National Standards & Grade-level Outcomes for K-12 Physical Education*. Champaign, IL: Human Kinetics.

Ward, P. (2016). Policies, agendas and practices influencing doctoral education in PE teacher education. *Quest*, 68, 420–439.

World Health Organization (2019). What is a health promoting school? Available at: www.who.int/school_youth_health/gshi/hps/en/ (accessed 9 May 2019).

Chapter 6

The interdisciplinary challenge

Preparing teacher educators and teachers to span knowledge, organizational and international boundaries

Louise McCuaig, Timothy Carroll, Susanna Geidne and Yoshinori Okade

As stated in Chapter 1, the interdisciplinary (ID) challenge signals the limitation of isolated programmes and teachers of Physical Education (PE) seeking to deliver an array of education, health and social agendas. Striving to enact these broad agendas has increasingly enmeshed the profession in "wicked problems", which typically involve complex interacting issues of poverty, health inequities, climate change and community safety (O'Flynn, 2011). Wicked problems have also been shaped by increasing precarity, a term used by social scientists to capture the impact of work insecurity, and its associated dynamics of uncertainty and instability on the wellbeing of individuals and families (Kirk, 2020). Precarious times and wicked problems have underpinned an ever-expanding recruitment of professionals, including PE teachers, into the provision of innovative responses to achieve the care, health and wellbeing of children and young people (Lawson, 2016; McCuaig *et al.*, 2019).

As Power and Handley (2019, p. 554) argue, these responses call for new organizational partnerships and "a shattering of traditional disciplinary boundaries". While PE teachers have tended to work independently and in isolation, shattering disciplinary and professional boundaries to enact the grand challenge of ID calls on current and future PE professionals to serve as boundary spanners (Williams, 2002). In this chapter, we focus attention on these notions of wicked problems and boundary spanning in response to Kirk's (2020) prediction that precarious social conditions will have an escalating influence on the PE profession. We begin with a brief overview of the characteristic qualities, knowledge and skills underpinning the enactment of boundary spanning. Following this, we draw on the expertise and experiences of authors to explore three of the many policy and practice boundaries of the PE profession. In conclusion, we focus attention on the potential of institutional change, collaborative leadership and longitudinal research in PE as three strategic responses to the challenge of ID.

Interdisciplinarity and boundary spanners

According to Frodeman (2017), ID is not simply about the integration of diverse disciplinary knowledge to solve social problems, it is equally a matter of the "challenges surrounding effective communication to different audiences" (Frodeman, 2017, p. 3). For Bhaskar *et al.* (2017, p. 3), the need for genuine ID is nowhere "more evident than in research [and practice] related to health and wellbeing". Although some believe that the current scholarship on ID lacks sophistication, there appears to be an emerging consensus on the benefits of ID. For example, Power and Handley (2019) consider these benefits to include stimulating current knowledge and disciplinary areas, provision of sustainable solutions to wicked solutions and development of new methodological approaches. Nonetheless, a critical success factor underpinning these benefits is the extent to which stakeholders and professionals are willing to confront and span the inter-personal and institutional boundaries that sustain ownership over "territories of knowledge" (Power and Handley, 2019, p. 556).

Herein lies the potential and significance of boundary spanners. Boundary spanners appreciate and overcome the complexities of working collaboratively, recognize and value multiple knowledges and possess tacit understanding of issues (Williams, 2002). According to Strange (2011), boundary spanners are skilful at creating strategic alliances and partnerships, as they must operate across the boundaries of "ideologies, disciplines, cultures, markets, peoples and entrenched worldviews" (Strange, 2011, p. s165). In the three case studies that follow, we demonstrate the need for, and challenges of, ID and boundary spanning in health, sport and PE contexts.

Case 1: crossing research discipline boundaries

Popular and professional commentary would suggest that a fundamental objective of PE is teaching people how to move (Bailey *et al.*, 2009), as a means of developing individual and community levels of physical literacy (Lundvall, 2015). It would be reasonable to argue, therefore, that engaging with new knowledge concerning the achievement of movement outcomes by the brain (or, more precisely, the central nervous system) should be an essential practice of the PE field's researchers and practitioners. The scientific discipline of neuroscience encapsulates the study of brain function, and has grown exponentially over the last few decades (Pautasso, 2012). Accordingly, powerful tools to understand brain function, such as functional Magnetic Resonance Imaging (fMRI), non-invasive brain stimulation, optogenetics, and simulation methods that include neural network modelling and machine learning, have been developed or more widely exploited.

An explosion of new approaches and knowledge has subsequently occurred in the branch of neuroscience most obviously related to PE and PE teacher education (PETE), a sub-discipline best termed "sensorimotor control". Leading edge scientific understanding of fundamental movement control principles and the organization of neuromotor systems has moved well beyond the frameworks of information processing models and dynamical systems theory, traditionally the theoretical bedrock of PE and Higher Education (HE) teaching degrees. One such advance is the growing recognition that fast sensorimotor feedback loops, traditionally thought of as "reflexes", are fundamental to essentially all voluntary movement and humans can learn to tune these feedback loops to improve motor performance (e.g. Carroll *et al.*, 2019).

An appreciation of this emerging knowledge has critical implications for multiple aspects of PE practice. Motor "decisions" emerging from such "low-level" feedback loops are taken too quickly for conscious deliberation, posing questions of the extent to which a player's explicit awareness of decision making strategies is necessary in some game and sport situations. This troubles high-stakes PE assessment practices which are often reliant on students' conscious reportage of decision making in games and sports to determine levels of achievement according to cognitive taxonomies (e.g. Bloom, 1956).

Engaging with leading sensorimotor control research will undoubtedly lead to many such tensions and perhaps uncertainties for PE and PETE. Such engagement, however, ultimately enhances a fundamental goal of the field, that is, to facilitate learners' acquisition and refinement of motor skills. Two major challenges will make the incorporation of new sensorimotor control knowledge into PE and PETE problematic. The first concerns the inertia that pervades academic programmes and curricula. Ideas, models and texts that have a long history of application in a field can be slow to reform and advance. PE teacher educators trained in theories of motor learning and control are rooted in Experimental Psychology from the 1950s, leaving them theoretically ill-equipped to embrace novel ideas about neural control relying upon recent advances in neurophysiology, cognitive neuroscience, engineering and computer science.

These issues relate to a second challenge. Many of the current advanced movement control theories incorporate complex, multidisciplinary models that require a working knowledge (or at least an appreciation) of basic principles drawn from a breadth of physical, biological and cognitive sciences. This sophisticated bedrock of scientific knowledge poses a barrier to the adoption of new sensorimotor control knowledge in the (typically) crowded curriculum of contemporary PETE programmes. Full engagement with new principles ideally requires a grounding in mathematics, neurophysiology, neuroanatomy and computer science. Despite these barriers, strategic boundary spanning by the profession offers the potential for PE and PETE to capitalize on some of the most critical and pertinent theoretical advances in sensorimotor control.

Case 2: crossing community health, sport and education boundaries

Health, in its broadest sense, is a well-studied and much advocated dimension of PE (Quennerstedt, 2008) (see Chapters 4 and 5). As personal and population health is determined by organizations other than those of the health sector (Commission on Social Determinants of Health, 2008), and shapes human living beyond biophysical factors (e.g. educational attainment), health promotion and education should be enacted where "health is happening". According to Kickbusch (2003), this orientation to health promotion aligns with a shift in public health practice from an exclusive focus on the individual towards strategies that address entire populations in specified settings.

A recognition that health and learning form the primary rationales of education, health and sport organizations, offers a compelling rationale for boundary spanning by PE and PETE professionals. Health, sport and education professionals typically address the same cohort of people, meeting them in the diversity of interconnected settings in which people enact their lives (Bloch *et al.*, 2014). More specifically, a health settings approach is clearly articulated in the international trend for community sports as part of a health-promoting policy that focuses on securing "all" young people's healthy upbringing through sport (Geidne *et al.*, 2019). Yet, it is within this mutually reinforcing context of community sport that the barriers and challenges facing boundary spanners within the PE profession are revealed.

Barriers emerge in relation to differences in perspectives between sectors and organizations (Israel *et al.*, 1998), when sport and PE mobilize health as solely a matter of physical health. Tensions are further evident in the considerable difference between the philosophical orientations of sports for all, as opposed to sports for performance (Stenling and Fahlén, 2016). Collaboration between the sports sector and PE can invariably produce "more of the same", both in the type and organization of sports and games, with PE tending to replicate sport instead of informing educative sport innovations. In addition to this, the employment status and qualifications of volunteer sport coaches can lead to power relations that are not conducive to building trust (Jones and Barry, 2018). Importantly, many of the tensions that emerge within community sport contexts are the result of different professions talking *about* each other, but not talking *to* or *with* each other.

More recently, Bloch and colleagues (2014) outlined a "supersetting" approach as a more comprehensive means of solving public health issues, striving to attain synergistic effects across multiple settings and employ intervention strategies that include local stakeholders from different settings. But how do these local stakeholders from different settings realize they have a joint problem and could solve it together? Where do they meet and how do they determine which strategy offers a best solution to the problem at hand?

Such questions emphasize the need for the creation of spaces that offer richer and more democratic opportunities to motivate and sustain boundary spanning. Supersetting approaches might offer a "next level" of collaboration, but they might also be predicated on the creation of meeting spaces *between* settings. This is not a question of who a boundary spanner is, could or should be, but how organizations can create environments that facilitate the growth and operations of boundary spanners. Establishing meeting spaces between settings also offers the potential of a more sustainable strategy than offered by the single boundary spanner, especially in sports clubs where real enthusiasts can be both a strength and weakness (Geidne *et al.*, 2013). Community sport, health and PE/PETE organizations seeking to create inter-setting spaces can find initial guidance in the education and schooling scholarship. Research that has explored crossings between preschool and school (Karila and Rantavuori, 2014), schools and teacher education (Williams, 2013), and teacher education and initial practice (Beuchamp and Thomas, 2011), offer insight into effective times and conditions for interdisciplinary collaborations.

Case 3: crossing global boundaries for effective PE curriculum

Over the past 30 years, Okade has worked on curriculum development, instructional research and teacher education for and with the Japanese PE profession (Okade *et al.*, 2012). This work has paved the way for PE curriculum development and implementation projects in three countries, including Cambodia, Myanmar and Bosnia Herzegovina. This experience in crossing the global boundaries of PE curriculum design and delivery has accentuated the importance of value orientations and reflective practice.

The rationales for, and expected outcomes of, a PE curriculum across nation states are not the same, as the design and delivery of a PE curriculum invariably reflects the value orientations of stakeholders and local PE teachers (Ennis and Chen, 1993). While the value of motor domain outcomes such as fitness, skill acquisition or game performance in PE are universally emphasized, social outcomes embedded in the affective domain were highly prized outcomes for the PE professions of Cambodia, Myanmar and Bosnia Herzegovina. In particular, developing cooperation, acceptance of others, communication skills and believing in others through PE experiences, were all greatly valued in these countries.

Establishing an understanding of the historical, social and political dynamics shaping stakeholders' value orientations, was to be a necessary prerequisite to securing these preferred objectives through collaborative PE curriculum reform. In Cambodia, for example, project members were reluctant to express their opinion in front of others, as civil war experiences had led them to believe that expressing their own opinion in public was a dangerous act. Through time and project discussions, Cambodian educators affirmed the importance of social domain objectives for their country's PE curriculum. Sensitive collaborative design was also critical to the clear articulation of social domain objectives in Bosnia Herzegovina, with objectives such as training for team work, quality interpersonal relations and tolerance emphasized in later iterations of the PE curriculum.

Additionally, Japanese curriculum experts were to discover that spanning global PE boundaries demands all stakeholders' willingness for change and reflection on taken-for-granted practices. For example, Bosnia Herzegovina committee members who visited Japanese junior high schools to observe PE lessons witnessed the Japanese PE teachers' allocation of push-ups to students who had failed to effectively perform learning activities. The demonstrating teachers were asked to share their opinion of this practice with the visiting teachers, generating a rich discussion on the impact of punishment on students' positive engagement with physical activity. Such conversations were informed by a recognition of students' negative experiences in Bosnia Herzegovina and a need for change in future PE programmes. These situations reveal the potential for change that can result from discussion, critique and reflection on the values underpinning personal and national practices in PE.

Communicating with education colleagues across the boundaries of country and subject discipline thus facilitated deep reflection on taken-for-granted practice, understandings of contemporary research evidence and strengthened personal motivation to engage in the improvement of Japanese PE programmes. In this sense, international collaboration on PE generates comparative dissonances that "make visible" customary home-country PE practices. Enacting this multi-directional process of sharing and reflection can alert PE professionals to the limited knowledge they possess about their own country's practice and highlights a need for ongoing engagement and learning.

Devising and enacting strategies for interdisciplinarity

Collectively, this chapter's three case studies reveal the potential of boundary spanning for knowledge diffusion, collaboration and innovation across local, intersectoral and global PE networks. Each case study highlights the role that new knowledge plays in driving innovative responses to the complex challenge of devising effective policy, curriculum and practice for PE (see Chapter 14). Ironically, a number of dynamics currently shaping PE and PETE affirm the grand nature of the ID challenge for the profession. While space does not permit a broad canvassing of the field's paradoxical dynamics, two dominant themes are pertinent.

As McCuaig and Enright (2017, p. 438) argue, in PE and PETE the "quest for rigorous accountability and an enthusiasm for assessment has come at considerable cost" which, Tinning (2006, p. 381) claimed, results in programmes becoming "less eclectic, more conservative and less adventurous". Within the context of the incessant audit culture shaping educational and research settings more broadly (Ball, 2003; Frodeman, 2017), the capacity of, and motivation for, individual's investment in boundary spanning and ID appears compromised. At a time when the need for innovation, creativity and collaboration appears vital, intensely monitored, standardized programmes of accredited Health, Sport and Physical Education (HSPE) appear anachronistic to the grand challenge of interdisciplinary PE.

Second, in summarizing the complexity of knowledge transmission, Weber and Khademian (2008, p. 344) state that such tasks are, "grounded in social and political relationships involving heterogeneous actors with diverse interests and

goals". Creating effective interdisciplinary networks in PE thus calls for boundary spanners who can recognize, analyse and synthesize the complex amalgama-
tion of values, experiences and cultures circulating across the profession. Such
skills would, we suggest, be predicated on a rich engagement with socio-critical
knowledges. Yet, in many PETE programmes across the globe, socio-critical
understandings and skills occupy a marginalized, and at times tenuous, position
(Shelley and McCuaig, 2018). An ongoing emphasis on biophysical sciences at
the expense of social sciences in PETE curriculum and research agendas leaves
graduates ill-prepared for the complexity of their work in precarious times (Kirk,
2020). These complementary dynamics of performativity and eroding socio-
critical agendas provide insight into some of the impediments that PE and PETE
professionals face in crafting ID strategies and action. In the remaining commentary, we explore three strategies concerning institutional structures, collaborative
leadership and longitudinal research that can address the grand challenge of ID.

Three strategies to overcome the interdisciplinary challenge

The first and most tangible strategy involves the creation of interstitial spaces
where the intellectual, interprofessional education (IPE) and international collaboration underpinning ID can be cultivated. As Power and Handley (2019,
p. 559) advise, the "most prevailing facilitator of embedding ID within HE was
professional bodies – the policies of which are key to driving changes in HE strategy". PE's professional bodies, including global research communities (e.g. Association Internationale des Écoles Supérieures d'Éducation Physique/International
Association for Physical Education in Higher Education) and councils for sport
and physical education (e.g. International Council of Sport Science and Physical
Education), offer unique social interaction sites that stimulate trust, reciprocity,
knowledge sharing and adoption of innovations (Marchiori and Franco, 2019).
For example, a key response to challenges posed in case study one would involve
the creation and nurturance of collaborations between PE/PETE practitioners
with a diverse collective of researchers in sensorimotor control. Invitations to
contribute to the literature and conferences of professional organizations, with an
emphasis on devising synthesis publications that distil and highlight important
findings and applications, would be a crucial first step.

Modifications of the physical and human resources of schools offer additional
potential for the creation of spaces where ID and boundary spanners can flourish.
Industrial age schooling, created to tame the children of industrial age workers
(Lawson, 2016) with delineated use of spaces, time and personnel, fails to meet
the far-reaching work teachers perform in precarious times. As the second of
our case studies explained, health, sport and PE have mutually supportive objectives and target populations. As such, advocacy for comprehensive investment
in school-based health care "hubs" poses a vital response to the ID challenge
(McCuaig *et al.*, 2019). Staff of health and welfare organizations located in school

supersettings can effect timely and substantial responses to support school communities' endeavours to promote the wellbeing of children. Creating health–welfare–education hubs can also drive mutual mentorship and interprofessional collaboration for isolated PE teachers. Health-settings advocates have identified some useful practices for the formal and informal interdisciplinary work that can be conducted in these spaces, including thematic lectures and the promotion of mutual trust through talking, listening, arguing, discussing, socializing and being visible to each other (Eriksson *et al.*, 2011).

Our case studies also point to the need for institutional change in HE contexts where PE professionals of the future are prepared for the rigors of work in precarious times. For some time, the education of health professionals in tertiary settings has promoted strategies of IPE that can expand students' "exposure to other professionals, both to develop a better understanding of multiple roles and to learn how to collaborate to improve service delivery" (McCroskey and Roberston, 1999, p. 70). PETE programmes have been slower to embrace IPE strategies, perhaps due to their common location in faculties of education and the earlier identified control and resistance from professional accreditation agencies (McCuaig *et al.*, 2019). Beyond professional-oriented degrees, a broader agenda of ID has been advocated by Power and Handley (2019) who nominate a number of enablers to guide tertiary educators. Programmes seeking to build students' interdisciplinary understanding and skills are most successful when they are placed outside formal curriculum to promote shared ownership and a removal of knowledge "territories". Other critical success factors include physical and mental thinking spaces, rewards and formal target measures, mutual respect and a clear articulation of benefits, values, impact, barriers and facilitators that drive localized strategies of ID.

A second strategy, authentic leadership, is a widely advocated enabler of ID (Power and Handley, 2019). For Head and Alford (2015), responding to wicked problems demands new models of leadership that eschew traditional top-down orthodoxies. Simply put, responding to these challenges is "beyond the cognitive capacities for any individual to identify what is wrong and determine ways of addressing it" (Head and Alford, 2015, p. 729). Instead, Head and Alford argue that adaptive and collaborative perspectives offer a "means of eliciting collaborative contribution without having formal authority" (Head and Alford, 2015, p. 731). Collaborative leadership, or "leading in a shared-power world", can drive other's engagement in the network through the tasks of determining who gets invited, how issues are framed, recognition of expertise, seeking and fostering innovations, achieving win–win negotiations and sustaining diplomacy across the network (Head and Alford, 2015).

Fostering collaborative leadership skills, and the leadership dynamics highlighted in our three PE case studies, emphasizes the unique potential and vital role that tertiary researchers and educators can play in responses to the ID challenge. For example, PETE faculty located in sport science and kinesiology departments are uniquely positioned to invite their neuroscientist and health promotion colleagues to engage in the collaborative knowledge sharing practices identified above. By virtue of their need to translate new knowledge into the content and pedagogical knowledges of PETE, these educators can promote the initial reception and integration of new knowledge and innovation into the practices of future teachers of PE. As our third case demonstrated, PE researchers are increasingly engaged in the process of national curriculum design and implementation, further enhancing their capacity to build research–practice bridges and facilitate the transmission of knowledge within, and beyond, national boundaries.

Finally, the ongoing commitment of PE scholars to the global collaboration, dissemination and critique of research is a crucial component of the field's capacity to create networks across which knowledge and innovation can diffuse and flourish. Collaborative research agendas that encourage academics within PE to engage with their neuroscience colleagues appear necessary, if the ultimate aim of embedding new sensorimotor control concepts within practical PE teaching and training is to be realized. However, it is also worth noting McCuaig and Enright's (2017) recognition of the need for long-term programmes of scholarship in PETE that question, amongst other things, the relationships between what PETE students learn and what they do following graduation. Simply put, we know so little of how our PETE graduates are managing the demands of precarity and wicked problems. Devising PETE content and pedagogies that promotes authentic IPE and effective responses to the ID challenge, necessarily demands systematic investment in longitudinal research that explores the barriers and enablers of effective boundary spanning within and beyond school PE programmes.

Conclusion

The case studies presented in this chapter have afforded an identification of the institutional, leadership and research strategies that drive robust responses to the grand ID challenge. We have also drawn attention to the critical role that PE researchers and faculty can play when they create inter-setting spaces that promote knowledge diffusion, innovation and collaborative learning across a diverse network of stakeholders. Notwithstanding this potential, the limited availability of PE-specific research on the barriers, critical success factors and impact of ID may impede the field's advocacy for, and capacity to enact, this chapter's proposed responses. Furthermore, there is an acknowledgement of the tensions associated with PETE faculty's investment in the arduous, time-consuming work of boundary spanning and the performativity of the contemporary university (Frodeman, 2017). We suggest this state of affairs may underpin Frodeman's (2017) warning that faculty claiming to conduct ID work tend to forsake their role as "thinkers of the 'in-between'" (Frodeman, 2017, p. 3) to maintain their status as experts and the inward-looking perspective akin to that discussed in Chapter 1. In countering this trajectory, we do not simply call on members of the PE profession to turn up and be counted at the education "party" (Kirk, 2020). Instead, we encourage PE practitioners and faculty to create their own wicked problem parties, reaching out across disciplinary, professional and national boundaries to invite as many stakeholders as possible to the task of devising innovative initiatives that can secure the care, health and wellbeing of young people in precarious times.

References

Bailey, R., Armour, K., Kirk, D., Jess, M., Pickup, I., Sandford, R. and Education, B.P. (2009), The educational benefits claimed for physical education and school sport: an academic review. *Research Papers in Education*, 24(1), 1–27.

Ball, S.J. (2003). The teacher's soul and the terrors of performativity. *Journal of Education Policy*, 18(2), 215–228.

Beauchamp, C. and Thomas, L. (2011). New teachers' identity shifts at the boundary of teacher education and initial practice. *International Journal of Educational Research*, 50(1), 6–13.

Bhaskar, R., Danermark, B. and Price, L. (2017). *Interdisciplinarity and Wellbeing: A Critical Realist General Theory of Interdisciplinarity*, New York: Routledge.

Bloch, P., Toft, U., Reinbach, H.C., Clausen, L.T., Mikkelsen, B.E., Poulsen, K. and Jensen, B.B. (2014). Revitalizing the setting approach – supersettings for sustainable impact in community health promotion. *International Journal of Behavioral Nutrition and Physical Activity*, 1(1). doi.org/10.1186/s12966-014-0118-8.

Bloom, B.S. (1956). *Taxonomy of Educational Objectives, Handbook I: The Cognitive Domain*. New York: David McKay Co Inc.

Carroll, T.J., McNamee, D., Ingram, J.N. and Wolpert, D.M. (2019). Rapid visuomotor responses reflect value-based decisions. *Journal of Neuroscience*, 39(20), 3906–3920.

Commission on Social Determinants of Health (2008). *Closing the Gap in a Generation: Health Equity Through Action on the Social Determinants of Health: Final Report of the Commission on Social Determinants of Health*. Geneva: World Health Organization.

Ennis, C.D. and Chen, A. (1993). Domain specifications and content representativeness of the revised value orientation inventory, *Research Quarterly for Exercise and Sport*, 64(4), pp. 436–446.

Eriksson, C., Geidne, S., Larsson, M. and Pettersson, C. (2011). A research strategy case study of alcohol and drug prevention by non-governmental organizations in Sweden 2003–2009. *Substance Abuse Treatment, Prevention, and Policy*, 6(1), 8.

Frodeman, R. (2017). The future of interdisciplinarity. *The Oxford Handbook of Interdisciplinarity* (Google books). Accessed 26 July 2019. doi:10.1093/oxfor dhb/9780198733522.013.1.

Geidne, S., Quennerstedt, M. and Eriksson, C. (2013). The youth sports club as a health-promoting setting: An integrative review of research. *Scandinavian Journal of Public Health*, 41(3), 269–283.

Geidne, S., Kokko, S., Lane, A., Ooms, L., Vuillemin, A., Seghers, J., … and Van Hoye, A. (2019). Health promotion interventions in sports clubs: can we talk about a setting-based approach? A systematic mapping review. *Health Education & Behavior*, 46(4), 592–601.

Head, B.W. and Alford, J. (2015). Wicked problems: implications for public policy and management, *Administration & Society*, 47(6), 711–739.

Israel, B.A., Schulz, A.J., Parker, E.A. and Becker, A.B. (1998). Review of community-based research: assessing partnership approaches to improve public health, *Annual Review of Public Health*, 19(1), 173–202.

Jones, J. and Barry, M. (2018). Factors influencing trust and mistrust in health promotion partnerships, *Global Health Promotion*, 25(2), 16–24.

Karila, K. and Rantavuori, L. (2014). Discourses at the boundary spaces: developing a fluent transition from preschool to school. *Early Years*, 34(4), 377–391.

Kickbusch, I. (2003). The contribution of the World Health Organization to a new public health and health promotion. *American Journal of Public Health*, 93, 383–388.

Kirk, D. (2020). *Precarity, Critical Pedagogy and Physical Education*. London: Routledge.

Lawson, H.A. (2016). Categories, boundaries, and bridges: the social geography of schools and the need for new institutional designs, *Education Sciences*, 6, 32. doi:10.3390/educsci6030032.

Lundvall, S. (2015). Physical literacy in the field of physical education – a challenge and a possibility. *Journal of Sport and Health Science*, 4(2), 113–118.

Marchiori, D. and Franco, M. (2019). Knowledge transfer in the context of inter-organizational networks: foundations and intellectual structures. *Journal of Innovation & Knowledge*, accessed 4 August 2019. doi.org/10.1016/j.jik.2019.02.001.

McCroskey, J. and Robertson, P.J. (1999). Challenges and benefits of interprofessional education: evaluation of the inter-professional initiative at the University of Southern California. *Teacher Education Quarterly*, 26(4), 69–87.

McCuaig, L. and Enright, E. (2017). Effective health and physical education teacher education: a consideration of principled positions. In: C.D. Ennis (ed.), *Routledge Handbook of Physical Education Pedagogies*. London: Routledge, pp. 428–446.

McCuaig, L., Rossi, T., Enright, E. and Shelley, K. (2019). Schools, student health and family welfare: exploring teachers' work as boundary spanners. *British Educational Research Journal*, accessed 31 July 2019. doi.org/10.1002/berj.3548.

O'Flynn, J. (2011). Some practical thoughts on working across boundaries. *State Services Authority and Australia and New Zealand School of Government Occasional Paper No. 14*.

Okade, Y., Hasegawa, E., Miki, H. and Miyazaki, A. (2012). The tasks and trials in PETE at the university level in Japan. *Journal of Physical Education & Health*, 2(3), 5–12.

Pautasso, M. (2012). Publication growth in biological sub-fields: patterns, predictability and sustainability, *Sustainability*, 4(12), 3234–3247.

Power, E.J. and Handley, J. (2019). A best-practice model for integrating interdisciplinarity into the higher education student experience. *Studies in Higher Education*, 44(3), 554–570.

Quennerstedt, M. (2008). Exploring the relation between physical activity and health – a salutogenic approach to physical education. *Sport, Education and Society*, 13(3), 267–283.

Shelley, K. and McCuaig, L. (2018). Close encounters with critical pedagogy in socio-critically informed health education teacher education. *Physical Education and Sport Pedagogy*, 23(5), 510–523.

Stenling, C. and Fahlén, J. (2016). Same same, but different? Exploring the organizational identities of Swedish voluntary sports: possible implications of sports clubs' self-identification for their role as implementers of policy objectives. *International Review for the Sociology of Sport*, 51(7), 867–883.

Strange, K. (2011). Refocusing knowledge generation, application, and education: raising our gaze to promote health across boundaries. *American Journal of Preventative Medicine*, 41(4), s164–s169.

Tinning, R. (2006). Theoretical orientations in physical education teacher education. In D. Kirk, D. Macdonald and M. O'Sullivan (eds.), *The Handbook of Physical Education*. London: Sage, pp. 369–385.

Weber, E.P. and Khademian, A.M. (2008). Wicked problems, knowledge challenges, and collaborative capacity builders in network settings. *Public Administration Review*, 68(2), 334–349.

Williams, J. (2013). Boundary crossing and working in the third space: implications for a teacher educator's identity and practice. *Studying Teacher Education*, 9(2), 118–129.

Williams, P. (2002). The competent boundary spanner. *Public Administration*, 80(1), 103–124.

World Health Organization (1986). *Ottawa Charter for Health Promotion*. www.who.int.

Chapter 7

The professional socialization challenge

Teacher education for a preferable future for physical education

K. Andrew R. Richards, Cassandra Iannucci, Eileen McEvoy and Angela Simonton

Occupational socialization theory (Templin and Schempp, 1989) has helped to facilitate inquiry into the recruitment, education and careers of physical education (PE) teachers (Richards et al., 2014). When occupational socialization theory is applied to physical education teacher education (PETE), the need for collaborative practice is apparent. Pre-service and in-service teachers, teacher educators, and professional development providers can and should work together to address a multifaceted professional socialization challenge. This challenge begins with teacher recruitment and extends to PETE and initial and long-term socialization in schools, all of which frame teachers' identity development (Richards et al., 2014). The challenge centres on how PE can break the cycle of reproduced programmes, policies and personnel, given evidence indicating that these result in sub-optimal programmes and outcomes.

Teacher socialization is a mechanism for programme reproduction, and reproduced programmes promise to maintain inherited patterns of socialization. This patterned relationship necessitates a dual strategy: revisit the purposes of PE and revise teacher socialization mechanisms to fit better programme designs. Questions of purpose invite debate. Acknowledging the dynamic nature of PE over time and across cultures and contexts, in many parts of the world, the preparation of youth for a lifetime of engagement with physical activity can be taken as the current overarching purpose (McEvoy et al., 2015).

We begin with the assumption that this overarching purpose of PE paves the way for analyses of the facilitators and challenges associated with teacher socialization processes. Mindful of international and intra-national differences and the risks and dangers accompanying "one-size-fits-all" proposals, our writing team is committed to a context-sensitive, collaborative model for teacher socialization, a model in which teachers, teacher educators, and professional developers work, learn and improve together.

Further, two related limitations should be acknowledged when reading this chapter. First, while we focus narrowly on the recruitment and professional socialization of PETE recruits, socialization processes span beyond initial teacher education and include teachers' experiences in the social milieu of the schools in which they work, which are framed by larger social and political forces (see Chapters 4 and 8). Second, teacher socialization and professional learning do not end with initial teacher education and need to be attended to through continuous professional development for both physical educators and PETE faculty members (see Chapter 13).

Framing the professional socialization challenge

Three interrelated sub-challenges invite attention because all are instrumental in the reproduction of sub-optimal programmes and teacher socialization: (a) passive teacher recruitment; (b) persistence of recruits' subjective theories through teacher education programming (Grotjahn, 1991); and (c) pressures to meet institutional standards and accreditation requirements for teacher education. These sub-challenges are related, as indicated in Angela's reactions in Table 7.1.

Table 7.1 A practitioner's perspective on the sub-challenges related to professional socialization

Sub-Challenges	Angela's Response from a Practitioner Perspective
Passivity and Reproduction in Teacher Recruitment	During my senior year before completing my bachelor's degree I was asked by a PETE faculty member to be a tour guide for prospective students. I would represent the view of a PETE student and be accompanied by another senior in the Kinesiology and Health programme. At the last minute, the faculty member said I was not needed because there was no interest in PETE, just Kinesiology and Health. I feel this was a mistake because most freshmen may not know exactly what they want to do when they get to college. This was an opportunity to recruit future PETE students, and we failed to capitalize on it. Reflecting back on that experience has led me to appreciate the importance of taking a more active approach to recruitment.
Persistence of Recruits' Subjective Theories	The alternative routes to certification are problematic in our field. From those that I have spoken with that took the alternative route, many had the mindset that teaching PE is "easy". At times, I think this comes from a belief that if you are good at sports, you will be a good physical educator. Additionally, many who think they are good coaches perceive themselves to be a good teacher of PE, which is not always the case. When speaking with PETE faculty members, they have indicated that it is also very hard to find quality cooperating teachers for field experiences. This represents a challenge because if a pre-service teacher is placed with a cooperating teacher that does not support the content and methods taught in the PETE programme, teacher education could be "washed out". For instance, if a pre-service teacher is placed with someone who rolls out the ball, they may start asking "why do I need to adopt these other teaching behaviours if this is okay in the real world?"

continued

Table 7.1 Continued

Sub-Challenges	Angela's Response from a Practitioner Perspective
Pressures to Meet Institutional Standards and Accreditation Requirements	I remember taking an exercise science class during my last semester of PETE and thinking, "much of this information does not apply to me or my field". The content was so specific it no longer became applicable to PE. Additionally, there were times during the PETE programme when I wish we had more time and space to invest in deeper conversations about content and the lives and careers of physical educators. For example, we spent two or three class periods discussing case studies of teachers in the field. I would have preferred this to be an entire class because I learned so much in the short time period.

Note
PE = physical education, PETE = physical education teacher education.

Passive teacher recruitment reproduces programmes

Professional socialization challenges and opportunities begin with new member recruitment. The profession appears in some nations to lack a structured approach to recruiting new members, particularly in ways that challenge the status quo (Richards and Templin, 2019). When recruitment is *passive*, recruits choose to enter PETE based on their respective experiences, which give rise to ideas of what PE is or should be (Curtner-Smith, 2017). Teachers and coaches recruit individuals who mirror their preferences, share their experiences, and promise to replicate teaching styles. While acknowledging important contributions made to promoting innovative practices (Lorente and Kirk, 2013), in many countries there continues to be an emphasis on team sport using multiactivity and teacher-driven pedagogies (MacPhail *et al.*, 2019). Accordingly, many prospective recruits associate PE with sport.

The continuous recruitment of these individuals contributes programme reproduction, inadvertently undermining programmes' grand purpose. Sport content continues to dominate in the programmes, despite evidence these activities do not promise to result in physical activity participation during adulthood (Fairclough *et al.*, 2002). Passive recruitment persists despite a growing literature that emphasizes the importance of *active*, research-informed initiatives (see Ayers and Richards, 2019). There is a need to attract, recruit and select a diverse teacher candidate pool (Richards and Templin, 2019). Recruitment of a more diverse PE workforce includes factors such as race, ethnicity, gender and socio-economic status, as well as physical activity preferences (Flintoff and Webb, 2012).

Active recruitment facilitates better teacher candidate selection. Selection is structured by entry requirements developed through institutional policies and accreditation requirements. These requirements vary across contexts, with example criteria including academic profiles, scores on examinations, admissions exams, and motor skill and fitness performance tests (MacPhail *et al.*, 2019). Motor ability, sport-specific skills tests, and fitness tests sometimes act as gatekeepers to PETE programme entrance, as is the case in a number of European countries (MacPhail *et al.*, 2019). Ward (2019) lamented that stringent entry requirements related to high cognitive abilities, including academic achievement and standardized test scores, may preclude some otherwise promising students from entering PETE.

Persistence of recruits' subjective theories

Although non-traditional, teacher certification programmes are increasing (Ward, 2019) and school-based teacher education has become more common in some European countries (MacPhail *et al.*, 2019), PETE programmes in higher education settings remain the dominant teacher education mechanism. An important dynamic occurs inside this PETE experience: teaching recruits with subjective theories focused on sport content and teacher-centred pedagogies are likely to be met by teacher educators who emphasize content beyond sport (MacPhail *et al.*, 2019). These differences signal an implicit power struggle over the purposes of school programmes, and they justify socialization frameworks called "dialectical". Freely translated, PE teaching recruits can and do exercise their sense of agency and resist the forces of those seeking to socialize them (Schempp and Graber, 1992), while PETE faculty members serve in powerful roles as gatekeepers to programme completion. Mindful of an imbalance of power in this dialectical relationship, pre-service teachers may opt for strategic compliance and impression management or engage in covert acts of resistance (Lacey, 1977).

Significantly, recruits may not be cognizant of how their prior socialization experiences influence how they perceive PE content and how they react to PETE programmes (Gillespie, 2011). Without intentional disruption, the socialization process can be somewhat automatic and with predictable results. A cycle of passive recruitment leads to reproduction of current practices and beliefs, followed by a resistance to PETE learning experiences that challenge such beliefs and the preservation of traditional practices and attitudes. The second professional socialization sub-challenge thus relates to developing and implementing innovative PETE curricula. These curricula are designed to pose challenges that enable pre-service teachers to reconsider their subjective theories.

Pressures to meet institutional standards and accreditation requirements

In many countries, accreditation bodies provide a framework of requirements for teacher education programmes (Johnson *et al.*, 2005). While accreditation bodies provide guidance, there is typically space for flexibility in programme structure and content. As such, opinions and approaches about the specific knowledge and skills needed to teach PE vary, even within a single PETE programme (Ayers and Housner, 2008). Some teacher educators and practising teachers, for example, have emphasized the importance of integrating social justice into teacher education (Walton-Fisette and Sutherland, 2018), whereas others have stressed the importance of preparing physical educators for the socio-political aspects of teaching (Richards *et al.*, 2013). Such a variety may not be inherently problematic. However, it does frame a consequential choice for PETE design (Metzler, 2009). PETE programme leaders are forced to decide: depth or breath.

The structural location of PETE in higher education also can create challenging conditions. For example, the development of sports science curricula in departments around the world has resulted in an increase in performance analysis courses (e.g. biomechanics, exercise physiology), oftentimes necessitating accommodations in PETE (Lawson and Kretchmar, 2017). As PETE curricula are adapted in response to these institutional expectations and professional accreditation requirements, space for content knowledge, pedagogical knowledge, and field experiences is limited, and opportunities to gain qualifications for teaching more than one subject are constrained, and so are opportunities for PETE faculty to interact with teaching recruits.

Further, these realities potentially inhibit PETE faculty members' ability to prepare students for the technical and socio-political aspects of teaching, perhaps provoking them to consider their subjective theories (Richards *et al.*, 2013).

Addressing the professional socialization challenge

The three sub-challenges indicate needs for a coordinated approach that involves (a) active recruitment, (b) constructivist-oriented PETE curricula, and (c) advocacy for better alignment in institutional and accreditation requirements. Each is summarized next. Angela's reactions from the perspective of an in-service physical educator are included in Table 7.2.

Table 7.2 A practitioner's perspective on the proposed solutions to the professional preparation challenge

Solutions	Angela's Response from a Practitioner Perspective
Active Recruitment into PE Teacher Education	I wanted to be a teacher when entering college because of my father who was a music teacher. I was not initially sure, however, what I wanted to teach. I decided to enter PE because I was active and wanted to help others become active. This route aligns with the recruitment of teachers of PE rather than the recruitment of PE teachers. I also believe that one of our most influential recruitment tools are in-service teachers. I try to provide

Solutions	Angela's Response from a Practitioner Perspective
	my students with a well-rounded curriculum that targets a diverse set of learners. I have become critical of more sport-centric curricula because they can create an environment that disadvantages lower skilled students. I also believe that it is important for teacher educators to develop relationships with in-service teachers that can help with recruitment and may also lead in-service teachers to question their practices.
Constructivist-oriented PE Teacher Education Curricula	During PETE, I was introduced to a variety of physical activity experiences that broadened my subjective theory of PE. These experiences included non-traditional team-sport experiences such as swimming, skiing, hiking and fishing. My professors also encouraged reflection on and comparison with my own PE experiences. Additionally, I believe that my teaching experience in the schools during PETE helped me to better understand and support the purpose and goals of PE. We used systematic observation tools to code teaching behaviour and would debrief based on the results of these evaluations. The constant reflection allowed me to formulate my own ideas and develop an identity that aligned with programme goals. One of my professors used cased-based learning to discuss socio-politics and marginalization. We would read case studies and discuss how we would handle a case, which was a great learning experience.
Advocacy for Better Alignment in Institutional and Accreditation Requirements	There were multiple classes I took during PETE that I thought to be irrelevant. The content was so specific to exercise science that I could not see the connections to PE. To make these courses relevant, I think there needs to be collaboration with the PETE faculty members, or courses should be adapted for PETE students. I also see value in relocating PETE into colleges of education. This could help reduce the number of recruits who enter the field because they simply want to coach and help foster a teaching-focused rather than sport-oriented outlook. Having the ability to work with other educators in different subject areas would also help address marginalization issues encountered in schools. There have been so many instances as a practitioner where I am trying to persuade other teachers that I am something other than a babysitter. They are unaware that PE has standards, goals, and a purpose. Developing stronger connections with other educators may help to reduce this occurrence.

Note
PE = physical education, PETE = physical education teacher education.

Active recruitment into physical education teacher education

An active approach to recruitment "reconceptualises recruitment as an intentional activity through which inservice physical educators and PETE faculty members attempt to identify, communicate with, and recruit highly qualified students" (Richards and Templin, 2019, p. 16). By taking an active, intentional approach, the PE profession can work to promote diversity within the field. This diversity refers to characteristics such as ethnicity and linguistics, as well as gender. It involves an alternative to an international mould: the athlete-turned-physical-educator. Teacher educators can become involved in recruitment, for example, by talking with students during campus visits and at secondary schools and by marketing their programmes through social and print media (Ayers and Woods, 2019). Many universities have recruitment offices that can provide resources that integrate with PETE faculty member efforts to ensure accurate messages about the nature of careers in PE are communicated (Bulger *et al.*, 2015).

Another approach is to recruit teachers of PE rather than PE teachers. This conceptual shift promotes a *teacher-first* identity rather than the emphasis on PE content. Such an approach may involve addressing populations interested in teaching as a career and offering PE as the medium. This contrasts with the current paradigm in which individuals tend to be recruited based on their affiliation with sport and see PE as a continuation of their sport identity (Curtner-Smith, 2017). It is also crucial that recruitment efforts involve in-service PE teachers as partners and advocates. In-service teachers can act as key agents of change in the socialization of future physical educators. Providing high-quality instruction that models effective practices to help potential recruits to develop subjective theories aligned with the goals of the field may help to challenge the intergenerational socialization cycle. Intentional strategies can include (a) having conversations with students who have diverse physical activity backgrounds about careers in PE, including those who want to teach and could use PE as a medium; (b) setting up campus visits for students who are interested in teaching; and (c) sharing PE resources (e.g. journal articles) with students (Ayers and Woods, 2019).

Importantly, active activities require that recruitment agents have subjective theories that align with effective practices. Recruitment partners should, therefore, be selected intentionally, and professional development can be coordinated to aid in defining and articulating goals for the discipline and the type of students who should be recruited. Further, PETE faculty members have often not been prepared for the challenges accompanying the recruitment of pre-service teachers (Kern *et al.*, 2019). If they are to become involved, they would need adequate support, which could be provided first in the context of doctoral education. It should also, however, be scaffolded through professional development for in-service PETE faculty members (Chapter 13) and targeted supports on campus, such as a relationship with offices of admissions.

Constructivist-oriented physical education teacher education curricula

When initial socialization experiences lead recruits to associate PE with team sports, and this reproductive pattern needs to be interrupted, something new and compelling must be offered in PETE. Further, it is one thing to adopt innovative ideas, but another to have the requisite knowledge and skills for implementation within school contexts. All pre-service teachers need preparation in the technical and socio-political aspects of teaching (Richards *et al.*, 2013), so it is likely that elements of their subjective theories will need to be reformulated. When teacher education adopts a constructivist perspective (Richardson, 1997), PETE faculty members are positioned as partners in the process of learning to become a teacher. They can, therefore, help pre-service teachers question and reformulate their subjective theories rather than telling them what they should think or forcing the outward projection of dispositions that do not result in lasting change (Graber, 1991).

Field-based PETE programmes that provide pre-service teachers adequate time in schools are essential (Chapter 4). The best ones are framed by constructivist theories of learning (Hanson and Sinclair, 2008). Such approaches recognize pre-service teachers' biographies as relevant to their developing professional identities, and they also provide a platform to discuss the purposes and goals of the field. Furthermore, these constructivist approaches can help pre-service teachers to consider and prepare for the realities of teaching in schools (MacPhail *et al.*, 2019). They proceed with open and honest discussions of school socio-politics and the influence of policies, programmes, and people who marginalize the discipline and isolate its teachers (Laureano *et al.*, 2014). This PETE preparation can help promote early induction, whereby pre-service teachers begin to understand and view schools as a teacher rather than as a former student (Lawson, 1983).

Examples of teaching and learning strategies that align with the constructivist agenda include case-based learning, project-based learning, critical incident reflection, and small- and large-group discussions. Discussions should empower pre-service teachers to articulate and navigate their own ideas of what PE is and could be so as to help them take ownership over their professional identities (Gillespie, 2011).

Advocacy for better alignment in institutional and accreditation requirements

Ideally, institutional strategies and professional body requirements foster learning environments in which intentional recruitment is prioritized and time is dedicated to assisting students in confronting their subjective theories. Such a scenario, however, requires institutional supports and accreditation requirements which support the creation of such a learning environment. The decision-making committees within institutions and accreditation bodies usually involve significant representation from academia and the professions. Accordingly, it is therefore not "them" but "us" who can control key decisions. Both PETE faculty members and in-service teachers should ensure their voices are represented on such committees so that they can continue to advocate for space and time in the curriculum for the kinds of activities that will, in the long term, address the professional socialization challenge and advance the field toward a favourable future. Teachers and teacher educators can advocate for policies that provide flexibility within curricula so as to maximize the quality of contact time with pre-service teachers.

Professional organizations also have an important role to play in this new teacher socialization initiative because they are in a position to represent the voice of the profession. In some contexts, professional organizations are involved in the development of accreditation policies that guide the content of teacher education (Scanlon *et al.*, 2019). These organizations can serve as advocates for change to government policies that restrict who can enter teacher education programmes and what they need to become certified teachers. This is particularly critical in considering that challenges associated with becoming a teacher have become increasingly burdensome in some contexts (Darling-Hammond, 2017), giving rise to alternative pathways that circumvent teacher education (Ward, 2019).

In many countries, education policy changes at the national level are slow to take shape and play out in fluid, densely packed spaces that are difficult to navigate (Scanlon *et al.*, 2019). As a result, PETE programme faculty members may consider the ways in which they can effect short-term change locally through their institutions while simultaneously attempting to influence accreditation and institutional requirements in the longer term. For example, it is possible that a specific course could be developed to collapse science requirements from several courses into one that more directly meets the content and pedagogical needs of PETE students.

Finally, and related to programme structure, we suggest the need to revisit discussions about the positioning of PETE programmes on university campuses (Lawson and Kretchmar, 2017). We argue that there may be some value added to repositioning PETE in departments focused on education rather than those focused on sport science. We believe that positioning PE in education could further accentuate the educative nature of PE as opposed to the focus on sport. When PETE programmes reside in departments of sport science, this organizational location implicitly suggests that PE is more aligned with disciplines such as exercise physiology, sport management and health sciences, than with education. This perception can perpetuate the attraction of recruits with sport-oriented subjective theories.

A programme relocation could also promote multisubject specialization, where graduates are qualified to teach multiple school subjects (Iannucci *et al.*, 2018). Currently, when multisubject specialization does occur, it sometimes requires education across multiple units (e.g. sport science and the school of education; Iannucci and MacPhail, 2018). It is possible that such arrangements could promote a teacher-first identity and also help teachers of other subjects value PE, thereby reducing marginality (Laureano *et al.*, 2014).

Conclusions and future research directions

While the sub-challenges proposed in this chapter and the corresponding solutions are discussed individually, we believe the connections between them are key. Both PETE recruitment and curricula, for example, are influenced by institutional and accreditation requirements (Lawson and Kretchmar, 2017). The overarching socialization challenge requires a return to occupational socialization theory and a reconceptualization of the profession towards a teacher-first attitude. Teacher socialization tends towards reproduction, and is cyclical in nature. Left uninterrupted, teacher socialization reproduces PE, PETE, and policy (Richards and Templin, 2019). Teacher socialization theory and research has the potential to frame and recommend strategic action. In addressing the challenges, the intention is for those who study and work within this cycle to become more responsive to the ever-evolving purpose of PE, while also working toward a favourable future for the discipline.

An important priority for future research and practice relates to evaluation of recruitment initiatives that seek to draw in a more diverse cadre of pre-service teachers. Similarly, the design of PETE programmes should be considered more carefully in relation to constructivist approaches that engage pre-service teachers in purposeful critique of their initial subjective theories and the development of identities aligned with the purpose of PE. Acknowledging that the purpose of PE shifts over time, a learning orientation that will prompt physical educators to remain engaged in continuing professional development throughout their careers is equally important (Chapter 13). This work should be supported by policy and advocacy research in the field of PE, focused on promoting an international agenda related to the role of PE in children's overall education and schooling.

Chapter epilogue

The development of this chapter represented an interactive, non-linear process for our writing team. Despite logistical challenges associated with managing an international authorship team, we found time to communicate over video conference and drafted the first version of the chapter. Following editorial review, however, we realized that the first draft did not include an explicit focus on the practitioner perspective and was overly US-centric. We asked Angela to review the chapter content, to which she had contributed, and provide reflective text that we could integrate into the chapter. We explored multiple different approaches for highlighting this contribution, eventually settling on the development of two tables that highlight Angela's reactions to the challenges and proposed solutions. The US-centric nature of the chapter reflected Kevin's experience and was influenced by the fact that most socialization research has been done in the US. Cassandra and Eileen were able to revise sections of the narrative to provide a stronger international flavour and move the chapter toward conceptual rather than comparative analysis.

References

Ayers, S.F. and Housner, L.D. (2008). A descriptive analysis of undergraduate PETE programs. *Journal of Teaching in Physical Education*, 27, 51–67.

Ayers, S.F. and Richards, K.A.R. (eds) (2019). PETE recruitment and retention: state of affairs. *Journal of Teaching in Physical Education*, 38, 1–74.

Ayers, S.F. and Woods, A.M. (2019). Chapter 5: Recruitment in PETE: survey results and discussion. *Journal of Teaching in Physical Education*, 38 (1), 37–44.

Bulger, S., Jones, E.M., Taliaferro, A.R. and Wayda, V. (2015). If you build it, they will come (or not): going the distance in teacher candidate recruitment. *Quest*, 67, 73–92.

Curtner-Smith, M. (2017). Acculturation, recruitment, and the development of orientations. In K.A.R. Richards and K.L. Gaudreault (eds), *Teacher Socialization in Physical Education: New Perspectives*. New York: Routledge, 33–46.

Darling-Hammond, L. (2017). Teacher education around the world: what can we learn from international practice? *European Journal of Teacher Education*, 40(3), 291–309.

Fairclough, S., Stratton, G. and Baldwin, G. (2002). The contribution of secondary school physical education to lifetime physical activity. *European Physical Education Review*, 8, 69–84.

Flintoff, A. and Webb, L. (2012). "Just open your eyes a bit more": the methodological challenges of researching black and minority ethnic students' experiences of physical education teacher education. *Sport, Education and Society*, 17, 571–589.

Gillespie, L.B. (2011). Exploring the "how" and "why" of value orientations in physical education teacher education. *Australian Journal of Teacher Education*, 36(9), 58–74.

Graber, K.C. (1991). Studentship in preservice teacher education: a qualitative study of undergraduates in physical education. *Research Quarterly for Exercise and Sport*, 62, 41–51.

Grotjahn, R. (1991). The research programme subjective theories: a new approach in second language research. *Studies in Second Language Acquisition*, 13, 187–214.

Hanson, J.M. and Sinclair, K.E. (2008). Social constructivist teaching methods in Australian universities – reported uptake and perceived learning effects: a survey of lecturers. *Higher Education Research & Development*, 27, 169–183.

Iannucci, C. and MacPhail, A. (2018). One teacher's experience of teaching physical education and another school subject: an inter-role conflict? *Research Quarterly for Exercise & Sport*, 89, 235–245.

Iannucci, C., MacPhail, A. and Richards, K.A.R. (2018). Development and initial validation of the Teaching Multiple School Subjects Role Conflict Scale (TMSS-RCS). *European Physical Education Review*.

Johnson, D.D., Johnson, B., Farenga, S.J. and Ness, D. (2005). *Trivializing Teacher Education: The Accreditation Squeeze*. New York: Rowman & Littlefield.

Kern, B.D., Richards, K.A.R., Ayers, S.F. and Killian, C.M. (2019). Chapter 6: Recruitment in PETE: interview results and discussion. *Journal of Teaching in Physical Education*, 38(1), 45–52.

Lacey, C. (1977). *The Socialization of Teachers*. London: Methuen.

Laureano, J., Konukman, F., Gümüşdağ, H., Erdoğan, S., Yu, J. and Çekin, R. (2014). Effects of marginalization on school physical education programs: a literature review. *Physical Culture and Sport: Studies and Research*, 64, 29–40.

Lawson, H.A. (1983). Toward a model of teacher socialization in physical education: the subjective warrant, recruitment, and teacher education (part 1). *Journal of Teaching in Physical Education*, 2(3), 3–16.

Lawson, H.A. and Kretchmar, R.S. (2017). A generative synthesis for kinesiology: lessons from history and visions for the future. *Kinesiology Review*, 6, 195–210.

Lorente, E. and Kirk, D. (2013). Alternative democratic assessment in PETE: an action-research study exploring risks, challenges and solutions. *Sport, Education and Society*, 18, 77–96.

MacPhail, A., Tannehill, D. and Avsar, Z. (eds) (2019). *European Physical Education Teacher Education Practices: Initial, Induction, and Professional Development*. Munich, Germany: Meyer & Meyer Sport.

McEvoy, E., Heikinaro-Johansson, P. and MacPhail, A. (2015). Physical education teacher educators' views regarding the purpose(s) of school physical education. *Sport, Education and Society*, 22(7), 812–824.

Metzler, M.W. (2009). The great debate over teacher education reform escalates: more rhetoric or a new reality? *Journal of Teaching in Physical Education*, 28, 293–309.

Richards, K.A.R. and Templin, T.J. (2019). Chapter 3: Recruitment and retention in PETE: foundations in occupational socialization theory. *Journal of Teaching in Physical Education*, 38, 14–21.

Richards, K.A.R., Templin, T.J. and Gaudreault, K.L. (2013). Understanding the realities of school life: Recommendations for the preparation of physical education teachers. *Quest*, 65, 442–457.

Richards, K.A.R., Templin, T.J. and Graber, K.C. (2014). The socialization of teachers in physical education: Review and recommendations for future works. *Kinesiology Review*, 3, 113–134.

Richardson, V. (ed.) (1997). *Constructivist Teacher Education: Building a World of New Understandings*. Washington, DC: Falmer.

Scanlon, D., MacPhail, A. and Calderón, A. (2019). Original intentions and unintended consequences: the "contentious" role of assessment in the development of Leaving Certificate Physical Education in Ireland. *Curriculum Studies in Health and Physical Education*, 10, 71–90.

Schempp, P.G. and Graber, K.C. (1992). Teacher socialization from a dialectical perspective: pretraining through induction. *Journal of Teaching in Physical Education*, 11, 329–348.

Templin, T.J. and Schempp, P.G. (eds) (1989). *Socialization into Physical Education: Learning to Teach*. Indianapolis, IN: Benchmark Press.

Walton-Fisette, J.L. and Sutherland, S. (2018). Moving forward with social justice education in physical education teacher education. *Physical Education and Sport Pedagogy*, 23, 461–468.

Ward, P. (2019). Chapter 2: The teacher pipeline in PETE: contexts, pressure points, and responses. *Journal of Teaching in Physical Education*, 38, 4–13.

Chapter 8

The cultural competence challenge

Readying schools and university programmes for student, teacher and faculty diversity

Kim Oliver, Carla N. Luguetti, Jackie Beth Shilcutt, Raquel Aranda, Savannah Castillo, Oscar Nuñez Enriquez and Traci Prieto

In this chapter, we feature an Activist Approach to teaching (Oliver and Kirk, 2015) as one way of responding to the "Cultural Competence Challenge". Our aim is to strive to make progress in meeting the physical activity, sport and health-related needs of children and youths worldwide. This Activist Approach is grounded in feminist theories (Anzaldua, 2007; Fine, 2007; hooks, 2000) and critical pedagogies (Freire, 1987, 1998) and was developed through work with marginalized populations (e.g. girls, people of colour, people in poverty). An Activist Approach challenges and changes power relations in education (Fine, 2007), revealing how complicated power dynamics are in the reality of classrooms, and affirming Cook-Sather's recommendation to "take small steps toward changing oppressive practices even if complete change seems or is unattainable" (Cook-Sather, 2002, p. 6).

We outline the four critical elements of an Activist Approach and how we have used these critical elements in PE and PETE programmes. Then we describe how we used an Activist Approach to create a model for working with youth from socially vulnerable backgrounds. Next we discuss how people around the world have taken up an Activist Approach to meet the diverse needs of the young people they work with in a variety of educational and community settings. We conclude with a discussion of how an Activist Approach – while only one way and not void of its own challenges – allows us to cater our pedagogy specifically to the contexts within which we work. We consider the Activist Approach as a way to name, critique and negotiate inequities people face in their own setting. It allows us to disrupt the status quo, engage in questioning and uncertainty, and challenge power relations in our specific contexts.

An activist approach to PE and PETE

As outlined in Chapter 1, there is no one way to approach the grand challenges of our time. For each given solution, we can always find a counter example. Rather than fixate ourselves on all the possible ways of meeting the diverse needs within our programmes, we have chosen to highlight one way and show examples that cut across contexts and cultures. If we hope to accommodate various forms of diversity, then as educators we must create and seek opportunities for multiple perspectives (Oliver and Oesterreich et al., 2015). We have come to believe in the power of activism because it allows us to attend and respond to diverse cultures, contexts, and communities. Despite enduring challenges, activism allows us to listen to what others need and to work in collaboration, and in action, to meet those needs as best as possible (Luguetti et al., 2017; Oliver and Oesterreich, 2013; O'Sullivan, 2018).

There are four critical elements to an Activist Approach: (i) student-centred pedagogy; (ii) attentiveness to issues of embodiment; (iii) inquiry-based education centred in action; and (iv) listening and responding over time (Oliver and Kirk, 2015). We have used *Student Centred Inquiry as Curriculum* (SCIC) (Oliver and Oesterreich, 2013) to describe a *process* for activist teaching. Certainly, teachers and teacher educators have taken the four critical elements from our Activist Approach and used them in very different ways (Lamb et al., 2018; Walseth et al., 2018) than the SCIC process that we currently use in our work (e.g. Luguetti et al., 2015, 2018).

Student-centred pedagogy

The first critical element of an Activist Approach is student-centred pedagogy. We agree with Cook-Sather (2002), who claims that students have unique perspectives about what goes on in their worlds. So, as long as teachers exclude students' perspectives from conversations about how to best engage them in PE, teachers will continue to make decisions based on an incomplete picture. We have strong, consistent evidence that suggests that when teachers are student-centred, it better facilitates active engagement in PE (e.g. Enright and O'Sullivan, 2010, 2012; Fisette, 2011). These findings echo repeated recommendations from scholars, all of whom report students' increased interest and engagement when the student voice is central in teachers' pedagogical decisions. Thus, we claim that if we hope to meet the grand challenge of readying schools and universities for diversity, student-centredness must play a part of what we do (for a more elaborate discussion of student-centred pedagogy, see Oliver and Kirk, 2015).

Attentiveness to issues of embodiment

The second critical element in an Activist Approach is the pedagogical attentiveness to students' embodiment (Oliver and Kirk, 2015). That is, what we have learned is that how people think and feel about their bodies matters and, as such, is critical to any educational reform that seeks to enact a social justice agenda (Anzaldua, 2007; Collins, 1990). Over the past three decades, PE scholars have also shown how students' embodiment is crucial to our understandings of teaching

PE, particularly to girls (e.g. Fisette, 2011; Oliver and Lalik, 2000; Vertinsky, 1992). Like student-centred pedagogy, attending to how students think and feel about their bodies has been critical to every research project we have done (e.g. Oliver and Lalik, 2004). While we attended to students' perceptions of their bodies differently when working in all-girl settings versus co-educational settings, it is important to students' interest and willingness to engage in PE and physical activity.

The more we learned from the girls with whom we worked, the more we began to realize that if PE was going to meet the needs of girls, it needed to be about more than just physical activity. Creating opportunities within PE for girls to explore their embodiment and how it related to their physical activity participation was central to making PE relevant for these girls. Many other activist scholars in PE have echoed this sentiment in their research (Enright and O'Sullivan, 2010, 2012; Fisette, 2011; Hills, 2007). As Kim's research has moved from all-girl settings to co-educational settings, we have found different ways of bringing issues of embodiment into the conversations about how to co-create a class environment with youth in physical activity (Oliver and Oesterreich *et al.*, 2015).

Inquiry-based education centred in action

Inquiry-based education centred *in* action is a third critical element in working from an Activist Approach (Oliver and Kirk, 2015). Activist research in PE demonstrates that when teachers use inquiry-based learning centred *in* action, they can and do facilitate students' active and willing engagement in PE (Fisette and Walton, 2014). Inquiry-based PE involves teachers engaging students in inquiry in order to help them (a) better understand what facilitates and hinders their engagement in school PE or physical activity outside of school, and (b) work with students toward challenging and transforming the barriers they identify in order to assist them in finding ways to increase their physical activity participation in ways meaningful to them. Inquiry-based learning within an Activist Approach (Oliver and Kirk, 2015) offers a response to the calls from feminist activist scholars (Cochran-Smith and Lytle, 2009; Fine, 2007) for the need to move beyond studying "that which is", and begin systematically studying, "that which might be", as well as the calls from educators for teachers to use inquiry-based learning as a means of social transformation towards equity and justice (e.g. Freire, 1987; Shor, 1992).

However, inquiry is not only what teachers have students do, but it also means that teachers will use inquiry as a way of guiding their pedagogical decisions (Lamb *et al.*, 2018; Oliver *et al.*, 2017). Within their curriculum design, teachers embed ways of continually inquiring into what facilitates and hinders students' engagement, enjoyment and learning in physical activity, and they utilize this information in their planning and teaching (Oliver and Oesterreich, 2013). This approach is one way to address diverse students' needs.

Listening and responding to students over time

The fourth critical element is listening and responding to students over time (Oliver and Kirk, 2015). Here, we describe a systematic approach, *Student-Centred Inquiry as Curriculum* (SCIC) (Oliver and Oesterreich, 2013), as a means of listening and responding. It is our HOW TO DO of an Activist Approach. We developed this process working collaboratively with Traci's high school PE classes in conjunction with Kim and Raquel's university teacher education classes (Oliver and Oesterreich, 2013; Oliver and Oesterreich *et al.*, 2015). Since then, we have extended this work to community sports programmes for socially vulnerable youth (Carla), after-school sports and dance clubs (Jackie Beth and Oscar), dance classes in high school (Savannah), content courses for pre-service teachers (PSTs) (Jackie Beth and Raquel), and PETE methods courses (Carla and Kim). As an overview of our process, the SCIC approach starts with *Building the Foundation*.

Building the foundation

The foundation of SCIC is to co-create an environment that allows for mutual understanding, respect, and learning amongst all participants involved in the educational setting. We need to create valued spaces where students can speak (Cook-Sather, 2002) and where we as teachers re-tune our ears so that we can hear what they are saying and redirect our actions in response to what we hear. The foundation was designed to help Kim and Raquel's PSTs understand the needs and interests of Traci's high school students with respect to physical activity, PE, and the importance of a safe learning environment. This process helps the high school students feel valued for their knowledge and perceptions of their worlds and helps the teacher educator to better understand the PSTs' beliefs about youth and physical activity.

Building the foundation is ultimately about co-creating a class environment that facilitates students' interest, motivation, and learning. Once we have built the foundation, we move into the cyclical portion of *Student-Centred Inquiry as Curriculum*. This phase involves planning, responding to students, listening to respond, and analysing data.

Planning

Planning requires simultaneously matching young people's interests, motivation, and learning *with* teachers' knowledge of their content. Every time the PSTs developed lesson plans, they were required to identify how their lessons related to student voice. The content of the lessons needed to be connected to state/provincial/national standards in some capacity but not reflect pre-designed traditional curriculum. From planning, we move to responding to students.

Responding to students

Responding to students allowed the PSTs to learn about teaching from the perspective of a teacher and an outside observer. In this process, the PSTs either taught or observed and collected data. As the teacher they taught the class, reflected on their teaching, received observational data from their peers to analyse, and reflected on their data analysis.

In this observer role, the PSTs collected data on different aspects of the class such as high school students' peer interactions, teacher behaviours (feedback, interactions), and body language of students. Their observations centred on factors that influence young people's interests, motivation, and learning of the content.

Listening to respond

In this third phase, we debriefed with the high school students about their experiences. The purpose of this is two-fold. First, it creates a space for high school students to reflect on their experiences so that they can better understand what influences their personal and collective interests, motivation, and learning. Second, it continues to centre student voice to allow teachers to better understand how their students interpret their curriculum and pedagogy.

Analysing the responses

In this fourth phase, the PSTs analysed the data gathered during the *Listening to Respond* phase as well as from their observation data and reflections from the *Responding to Students* phase. In this way, PSTs utilized feedback from their experience as teachers and their students' experiences in the class. This analysis allowed them to articulate changes they would make in their future planning and teaching and gave them direction as to the types of readings or materials they needed in order to better facilitate their students' interests, motivation and learning. Following this phase, PSTs return to *Planning* and begin the process again. The four-phase cyclical process of *Planning*, *Responding to Students*, *Listening to Respond* and *Analysing Responses* thus becomes student-centred inquiry *as* curriculum so that the basis of all content and pedagogical decisions arises from the reiteration of the four phases.

A worked example of student-centred inquiry as curriculum in sport

In this example, we share how, over the past seven years, we have used an Activist Approach to develop an activist sport pedagogical model with and for youth from socially vulnerable backgrounds (Luguetti *et al.*, 2016, 2017). Our first study was Participatory Action Research (PAR) in Brazil with 17 young people, four coaches, a pedagogic coordinator, and a social worker, and the results of the study demonstrated that young people have the agency and capacity to analyse their social context (Luguetti *et al.*, 2015, 2016, 2017). In 2017 and 2018, we implemented this activist pedagogical model again in another context in Brazil in order to test the strength of the approach with a wider sample of youth (100) and explore how ten pre-service teachers learn to use this approach (Luguetti and Oliver, 2019).

The pedagogical model was designed as a means of listening and responding to youth in order to use sport as a vehicle for assisting them in becoming critical analysts of their lives and their communities to develop strategies to manage the very particular challenges they face. We co-constructed a pedagogical model *with* the youth and coaches. To do this, we used a *student-centred inquiry as curriculum* (Oliver and Oesterreich, 2013) process to activist teaching as a way of working. Our intent was to co-construct a prototype pedagogical model that would create empowering possibilities to assist youth in learning to name, critique and negotiate barriers to their engagement in their sport context.

The model combines key critical elements of student-centred pedagogy, inquiry-based learning centred in action, an ethic of care, attentiveness to the community, and a community of sport (Luguetti *et al.*, 2016). The key theme of this pedagogical model is to *co-construct empowering learning possibilities through sport with youth from socially vulnerable backgrounds*. In that sense, youth become agents in the process of transformative learning, seeking opportunities to reframe and re-imagine their sport experiences.

The first part of the process for co-constructing the pedagogical model involved the youth and teachers/coaches identifying barriers to learning opportunities through sport in their community. In the second part of the process, the youth, teachers/coaches, and researchers imagined alternative possibilities to the barriers identified. The five non-negotiable critical elements (student-centred pedagogy, inquiry-based education centred in action, ethic of care, attentiveness to the community, and a community of sport) formed a patchwork of practice as the basis of the model (Luguetti *et al.*, 2015). While these critical elements must be present in order to faithfully implement the model, it is important to highlight that, depending on the context, the critical elements will take different substantive forms in different settings. For example, the problems youth from socially vulnerable backgrounds face in Brazil might be different in other countries (e.g. safety, sanitation, opportunity to play), but teachers/coaches must consider the critical element "attentiveness to the community" to implement this model. What they have to attend to specifically, however, will depend on the specific features of their own local context. Through the *Building the Foundation* phase, researchers/teachers will seek to understand the form each of the critical elements takes in their specific context.

In the final part of the process we worked collaboratively to create realistic opportunities for the youth to begin to negotiate some of the barriers they identified in the *Building the Foundation* phase. Through the Activist Approach, the learning *aspirations* for the prototype pedagogical model emerged (Luguetti *et al.*,

2016, 2017). What we have learned is that these learning aspirations will always be context-specific.

An activist approach around the world

While an Activist Approach to working with youth is still in its infancy, we are starting to see people around the world implement this approach in a variety of settings in order to better meet the diverse needs of youth (Lamb *et al.*, 2018; Walseth *et al.*, 2018). For example, Lamb and colleagues have worked with PE teachers in Scotland who were interested in better meeting the needs of their female students. These teachers, working in single-sex contexts, wove the critical elements of an Activist Approach into their core standards in order to better facilitate girls' engagement and enjoyment in PE (Lamb *et al.*, 2018; Kirk *et al.*, 2018). These teachers discovered that the Activist Approach enabled them to listen to the stellar or the problematic students who are often most vocal as well as those in the middle, the ones often left out. These teachers' insights reveal the importance of contextualizing, negotiating, collaborating, and adapting as both teachers and students navigate comfort and discomfort as they co-create their experiences.

Kristen Walseth and colleagues have also used an Activist Approach to better meet the needs of girls in PE. Their intent was to use the critical elements to help girls begin to name, challenge, and negotiate messages they receive about their bodies and create a PE curriculum that was more relevant to their everyday lives (Walseth *et al.*, 2018).

Karen Lambert and colleagues are currently exploring how to weave an Activist Approach into a pre-existing fire-fighting camp curriculum for girls in Australia. Given the set curriculum, rather than co-create the content with the girls as others have done, they have sought ways of being student-centred, listening and responding, and bringing to the surface issues of embodiment in the context of the fire-fighting curriculum (Lambert, 2018). Part of what they are learning is that an Activist Approach can be implemented with other models or curricula. An Activist Approach does not have to stand alone.

Discussion

In our conversations about how to address the cultural competence challenge of readying schools and university programmes for student, teacher, and faculty diversity, what we have learned from each other is the value of working as a community to honour the forms of knowledge each person brings to table. An Activist Approach to teaching is a process of working in collaboration and in action with others. It is a process designed to create opportunities for listening and responding to those we teach. It is a process that demands attentiveness to inequity and how inequities threaten to shape who and what we can become. And it is a process that has opened our eyes to the value diversity brings to any educational setting (see Chapter 9).

An Activist Approach, however, is not a process void of challenge. The main challenges we continue to negotiate in our work together revolve around issues that arise when personal identities feel threatened through the process of pushing against inequities embedded within the status quo. For the authors, these issues emerged in the perceived incommensurability between our teacher identities and what an Activist Approach to teaching required. Some came from cultures that valued teacher-centred pedagogy. Thus, shifting to a student-centred focus created discomfort and difficulty. Others came from backgrounds where traditional sport and competition privileged PE content. Thus, learning to respond to students who disliked sport and/or competition challenged our perceptions of what PE looked like. Others yet were trained to believe that PE or dance should be taught as individual units of instruction (e.g. aerobics, soccer, basketball, ballet). When messages from youth continued to echo that variety of activity is what is motivating and interesting for them, we were placed in a position that demanded we move beyond the status quo of PE and dance curriculum design. Any time the status quo is challenged, there will be resistance from those privileged by that status quo. This will always be a challenge within an Activist Approach.

Among the authors, despite all the differences in who we are, we collectively believe the benefits of an Activist Approach outweigh its challenges. These benefits emerge when our conceptual understandings collide with the concrete realities voiced and silenced in our educational settings. It is the collision that allows us to re-evaluate what we believe about teaching, learning, and youth and in turn facilitates our growth as humans committed to social justice. As we think about the diversity challenge with respect to future research and practice, we hope that more people, working in collaboration across context, culture, and positionalities, will take up an Activist Approach and apply it in a multitude of physical activity and teacher education programmes. As this body of knowledge continues to grow and our understandings about how to embrace diversity expand, ideas about innovation and bold redesign of PE and PETE might become actualized. For us this actualization happens when we merge the voices of youth, PSTs, teachers and professors in one learning environment. Our collective work has morphed into this outcome as a result of using an Activist Approach to teaching and as such we have learned the value of multiple perspectives.

As authors, one of the things we have discussed is that we are at once all in positions of privilege and positions of marginality. We believe that our various positions of marginality have created spaces for us to want to use our positions of privilege to give back to our communities. It is the experiences of living on the margins when people knew our names, honoured our requests, supported our courses of action, and walked alongside us in the journey, that we saw the glimmer of hope for what might be possible. When we saw people's eyes light up, shouldered loads together, and joined the inquiries of those around us, the glimmer got a litter brighter. These experiences helped us realize we all have different opportunities that allow us to contribute to creating more socially just schools and communities, and it is our duty to use these places of privilege for the good.

References

Anzaldua, G. (2007). *Borderland/La Frontera: The New Mestiza*, 3rd edn. San Francisco: Aunt Lute Books.

Casey, A. (2014). Models-based practice: great white hope or white elephant? *Physical Education and Sport Pedagogy*, 19(1), 18–34.

Cochran-Smith, M. and Lytle, S.L. (2009). *Inquiry as Stance: Practitioner Research for the Next Generation*. London: Teachers College Press.

Cook-Sather, A. (2002). Authorizing students' perspectives: towards trust, dialogue, and change in education. *Educational Researcher*, 3(4), 3–14.

Collins, P.H. (1990). *Black Feminist Thought: Knowledge, Consciousness, and the Politics of Empowerment, Perspectives on Gender*. Boston: Unwin Hyman.

Enright, E. and O'Sullivan, M. (2010). "Can I do it in my pyjamas?" Negotiating a physical education curriculum with teenage girls. *European Physical Education Review*, 16, 203–222.

Enright, E. and O'Sullivan, M. (2012). Physical education "In all sort of corners": student activist transgressing formal physical education curricular boundaries. *Research Quarterly for Exercise and Sport*, 83, 255–267.

Fine, M. (2007). "Feminist designs for difference." In S. Hesse-Biber Nagy (ed.), *Handbook of Feminist Research: Theory and Praxis*. Thousand Oaks, CA: Sage, 613–620.

Fisette, J.L. (2011). Exploring how girls navigate their embodied identities in physical education. *Physical Education and Sports Pedagogy*, 16, 179–196.

Fisette, J.L. and Walton, T.A. (2014). "If you really knew me" … I am empowered through action. *Sports, Education and Society*, 19(2), 131–152.

Freire, P. (1987). *Pedagogia do Oprimido [Pedagogy of the oppressed]*, 17th edn. Rio de Janeiro: Paz e Terra.

Freire, P. (1998). *Teachers as Cultural Workers: Letters to Those who Dare Teach*. Boulder: Westview Press.

Hills, L. (2007). Friendship, physicality, and physical education: an exploration of the social and embodied dynamics of girls' physical education experiences. *Sport, Education and Society*, 12, 317–336.

hooks, b. (2000). *Feminism is for Everybody: Passionate Politics*. Cambridge, MA: South End Press.

Kirk, D., Lamb, C.A., and Oliver, K.L. with Ewing-Day, R., Fleming, C., Loch, A. and Smedley, V. (2018). Balancing prescription and teacher agency in curriculum-making: co-constructing a pedagogical model for working with adolescent girls in physical education. *The Curriculum Journal*. Epub ahead of print 21 March 2018. doi:10.1080/0958 5176.2018.1449424

Lamb, C.A., Oliver, K.L. and Kirk, D. (2018). "Go for it girl!": adolescent girls' responses to the implementation of an Activist Approach in a core physical education programme. *Sport, Education and Society*, 23(8), 799–811.

Lambert, K. (2018). Lessons from the field: the transformative potential of occupational movements to shape physical education. Paper presented at the International Association for Physical Education in Higher Education (AIESEP), Edinburgh, Scotland.

Luguetti, C. and Oliver, K.L. (2019). "I became a teacher that respects the kids' voices": challenges and facilitators pre-service teachers faced in learning an activist approach. *Sport, Education and Society*. Epub ahead of print 3 April 2019. doi:10.1080/13573322. 2019.1601620

Luguetti, C., Oliver, K.L., Kirk, D. and Dantas, L. (2015). Exploring an activist approach to working with boys from socially vulnerable backgrounds in a sport context. *Sport, Education and Society*, 22(4), 493–510.

Luguetti, C., Oliver, K.L., Dantas, L.E.P.B.T. and Kirk, D. (2016). "The life of crime does not pay; stop and think!": the process of co-constructing a prototype pedagogical model of sport for working with youth from socially vulnerable backgrounds. *Physical Education and Sport Pedagogy*. Epub ahead of print 5 June 2016. doi:10.1080/17408989.2016. 1203887

Luguetti, C., Oliver, K.L., Dantas, L.E.P.B.T. and Kirk, D. (2017). An Activist Approach to sport meets youth from socially vulnerable backgrounds: possible learning aspirations. *Research Quarterly for Exercise and Sport*. Epub ahead of print 11 January 2017. doi: 10.1080/02701367.2016.1263719

Luguetti, C., Aranda, R., Nuñez Enriquez, O. and Oliver, K.L. (2018). Developing teacher pedagogical identities through a community of practice: learning to sustain the use of a Student-Cantered Inquiry as Curriculum Approach. *Sport, Education and Society*. Epub ahead of print 15 May 2018. doi:10.1080/13573322.2018.1476336

Oliver, K.L. and Kirk, D. (2015). *Girls, Physical Education and Gender: An Activist Perspective*. London: Routledge.

Oliver, K.L. and Lalik, R. (2000). *Bodily Knowledge: Learning about Equity and Justice with Adolescent Girls*. New York: Peter Lang Publishing.

Oliver, K.L. and Lalik, R. (2004). Critical inquiry of the body in girls' physical education classes: a critical poststructural analysis. *Journal of Teaching in Physical Education*, 23, 162–195.

Oliver, K.L. and Oesterreich, H.A. (2013). Student-centred inquiry as curriculum as a model for field-based teacher education. *Journal of Curriculum Studies*, 45(3), 394–417.

Oliver, K.L. and Oesterreich, H.A., with Aranda, R., Archuleta, J., Blazer, C., De La Cruz, K., Martinez, D., McConnell, J., Osta, M., Parks, L., and Robinson, R. (2015). "The sweetness of struggle": innovation in PETE through student-centred inquiry as curriculum in a physical education methods course. *Journal of Physical Education and Sport Pedagogy*, 20(1), 97–115.

Oliver, K.L., Luguetti, C., Aranda, R., Nuñez Enriquez, O. and Rodriguez, A.A. (2017). "Where do I go from here?": learning to become activist teachers through a community of practice. *Physical Education and Sport Pedagogy*, Epub ahead of print 13 July 2017. doi: 10.1080/17408989.2017.1350263

O'Sullivan, M. (2018). PETE Academics as public intellectuals and activists in a global teacher education context. *Physical Education and Sport Pedagogy*, 23(5), 536–543.

Shor, I. (1992). *Empowering Education: Critical Teaching for Social Change*. Chicago: University of Chicago Press.

Vertinsky, P.A. (1992). Reclaiming space, revisioning the body: the quest for gender-sensitive physical education. *Quest*, 44, 373–396.

Walseth, K., Engebretsen, B. and Elvebakk, L. (2018). Meaningful experiences in PE for all students: an activist research approach. *Physical Education and Sport Pedagogy*, 23(3), 235–249. doi:10.1080/17408989.2018.1429590

The digital age challenge

Preparing physical and health educators to understand and support "online" youth

Kathleen M. Armour, Victoria A. Goodyear and Rachel Sandford

Introduction

In their introduction to this book (see Chapter 1), the editors highlight the need to identify and address the grand societal challenges that are likely to impact upon physical education (PE) and Physical Education Teacher Education (PETE). As the editors argue, some of these challenges will necessitate incremental changes while others will require a radical rethink if PE is to remain relevant and fit for purpose (see, also, Lawson, 2018). The task for the chapter author teams was to consider a specific challenge and to identify new ways forward for PE and PETE, taking into account local, national and international contexts.

The challenge addressed in this chapter is interesting because, by its very nature, it transcends local, national and international boundaries. The *Digital Age Challenge* refers to the exponential growth of young people who are, in one way or another, using digital technologies and devices, engaging online with vast amounts of content, and connecting with extensive and proliferating networks of people. This will, inevitably, impact on their learning needs and identities in contemporary PE. Moreover, there is a considerable amount of content available online that is physical activity – and health-related. Some of this content could be regarded as positive and helpful, while other aspects are negative, destructive and harmful. Either way, there are growing numbers of devices and apps that can inform, regulate and record young people's physical activity and health-related behaviours, with numerous opportunities to share data, comments and interests. The questions for this chapter are: What are young people's learning needs in PE in a digital age? Are some young people influenced by their digital engagement more than others? And how can PE teachers be – and be supported by PETE to become – optimally effective in the distributed and largely unregulated digital context?

Scoping the "digital age" challenge for PE teachers and PETE

Contemporary youth in physical and health education classes are growing up in a very different world in comparison to that experienced by their teachers

(Buckingham, 2016; Turkle, 2017). Many adults who are invested in young people's health and wellbeing (including teachers/teacher educators, parents/ guardians, health professionals/practitioners, policymakers and researchers) are aware that young people are prolific users of digital technologies, but these adults find it challenging to engage with and support young people's digital participation (Askari et al., 2018; Livingstone et al., 2017). There is considerable evidence to suggest that adults struggle to fully understand technological advancement and the digital/online spaces inhabited by young people (Askari et al., 2018; Turkle, 2017; Livingstone et al., 2017).

A wide range of international evidence identifies the gap between adults and contemporary youth in digital contexts (Askari et al., 2018; Gaplin and Taylor, 2017; Third et al., 2017). Given that adults can feel out of their depth in the digital age, there are new challenges for policymakers, schools, health and education professionals/practitioners and parents in finding the best ways to support young people (Clark, 2013). For example, it is unsurprising to find that the understanding of many of today's adults is grounded in their childhood experiences of passive media (e.g. magazines or TV) (Clark, 2013). This seems to suggest that, as a minimum, adults need access to appropriate levels of professional support and evidence-based guidance (Goodyear et al., 2019a, 2019b; Goodyear and Armour, 2019). We will return to this point later in the chapter.

Once we accept that digital technologies have come to represent a significant social space in the lives of young people in contemporary society, it becomes essential that we consider how this experience impacts upon them as learners in PE.

Extra-school influences merit special attention. A number of authors have identified the need to consider the impact of digital technologies on young people's social practice and, more specifically, on their constructions of identity (e.g. Sandford and Quarmby, 2019). Contemporary notions of identity have increasingly begun to take notice of the spaces and places that comprise young people's complex social landscapes (see Chapter 8). The rapid pace of technological change adds to the complexity of social life, changing individuals' experiences of how they live, learn, work and communicate with one another (Shulman, 2016). Content relevant to that offered in PE lessons is widely available and young people have considerable agency in how and what they access. There can be little doubt that this should impact upon what is taught in PE, although there is limited evidence to suggest that it does.

Digital spaces are central in young people's lives, such that their online and offline worlds are "mutually constituted" (Collin et al., 2010; Handyside and Ringrose, 2017; Maclsaac et al., 2018). The dissolution of an offline/online binary creates new challenges for adults who wish to support young people's engagement in digital spaces. Adults tend to believe that support involves disconnecting youth from their digital worlds (Askari et al., 2018; Blum-Ross and Livingstone, 2018), but this is often unrealistic given the pervasiveness of digital technologies, and is simply unthinkable for contemporary youth (Goodyear and Armour, 2019). It is certainly apparent that young people use digital spaces in very complex and dynamic ways, where digital mediums have become a central resource in the development of identity, relationships, emotional regulation and learning.

One clear intersection point between PE classes and young people's online worlds is physical activity and health-related content and devices. It has been reported in numerous international contexts that young people make extensive use of a range of digital technologies to gain relevant and personalized information. Examples of these technologies include smartphones, tablets, gaming consoles, virtual reality, wearable devices (fitness trackers or motion cameras), voice activation/services (e.g. Alexa), and social media (OECD, 2018; Ofcom, 2018; Pew Research Centre, 2018). Indeed, over the last decade, the time young people spend on digital devices has almost doubled (OECD, 2018; Ofcom, 2018; Pew Research Centre, 2018). This research indicates that it is inevitable that this digital engagement impacts upon the ways in which contemporary youth engage with PE.

Beyond PE, intensive and extensive engagement with digital technologies impacts child and youth development. The consensus across disciplines ranging from neuroscience to psychology and biology is that adolescence is characterized by a period of dynamic brain development, and that interaction with the social environment plays a part in shaping the behaviours adolescents take forward into adult life (Patton *et al.*, 2016).

The research provides a dual scenario. On the one hand, there are compelling arguments to suggest that engagement with digital technologies can have an enduring and positive influence on young people's health and wellbeing (Orben and Przybylski, 2019). On the other hand, there is strong evidence to suggest that growth in technology use by young people has coincided with reported increases in poor mental health outcomes (Booker *et al.*, 2018; Kelly *et al.*, 2019) as well as an increase in sedentary behaviours (OECD, 2018).

It is important to note that the majority of evidence on young people, social media and health has been drawn from survey data (Orben and Przybylski, 2019). Yet, while caution is required in making claims about impact from associative data in large-scale social datasets (e.g. Booker *et al.*, 2018; OECD, 2018), there is enough evidence to suggest that digital technologies are making a difference to the health and wellbeing of young people in both positive *and* negative directions (Goodyear and Armour, 2019).

There are also particular concerns about how vulnerable youth – such as those in care, with mental health challenges, and/or body image concerns – engage with and use digital technologies (Holmberg *et al.*, 2018; OECD, 2018). This is a complex space and it presents challenges for adults, including teachers, who are trying to support young people. It also presents significant challenges for PETE professionals who have the responsibility to develop the next generation of PE teachers.

A grand challenge for physical educators, therefore, is to find ways to empower young people to maximize the opportunities of the digital age, while minimizing risks. This, in turn, presents a challenge for PETE professionals who will need to find new ways to help PETE students to understand the needs of future generations of young people "online", even though they may have quite limited digital experience themselves.

Intractable challenges

This challenge goes far beyond the PE context. Recently, there has been significant global policy attention focused on developing guidance for adults on how to support young people's engagement with digital technologies in the context of health and wellbeing (e.g. OECD, 2018). In the UK, for example, a number of 2018 and 2019 Government policy hearings involved working collaboratively with a range of researchers, national organizations and charities, and young people to develop new guidance.[1-3] Yet, as this work proceeded it became apparent that the strength of the evidence-base is, at best, moderate (Royal Society for Public Health, 2017). In a systematic review of reviews in the *British Medical Journal*, Stiglic and Viner (2019) identified the challenges presented by the apparent lack of consensus about the impacts of digital technologies on young people's health and wellbeing, and how to advise on boundaries and appropriate engagement. The Chief Medical Office for England has also voiced her concerns about the complexity of this issue, stating that the evidence-base and guidance on support is both sparse and contradictory.[4]

There have also been recent shifts in the guidance that is provided to schools, parents and paediatricians. In contrast to the authors' intentions, it could be argued these have added to the confusion and uncertainty that is experienced by many adults. For example, until recently the 2×2 rule (no screen time for those under two years, no more than two hours/day screen time thereafter) from the American Academy of Paediatrics had been used as a benchmark across the world for minimizing risk-related impacts of technology use (Blum-Ross and Livingstone, 2018). Yet, in the digital age, this advice is considered to be impossible and impractical to follow (Blum-Ross and Livingstone, 2018), particularly where it is argued that the research-informed effect sizes of screen time are too small to warrant policy change (Orben and Przybylski, 2019; Stiglic and Viner, 2019).

Most recently, the advice to adults has shifted to a more nuanced focus on the content, context and connections that inform young people's uses of digital technologies (Blum-Ross and Livingstone, 2018), as recently emphasized by the Royal College of Child Paediatrics and Child Health (2019). Yet, and as we have found in our own research, there are very clear gaps between the ways in which adults and young people perceive and interpret risks and opportunities in relation to content, context and connections (Goodyear and Armour, 2019). The ultimate fear for young people is that sharing too much of their digital lives with adults could result in a phone or online access ban (Goodyear and Armour, 2019), and this is where adults face very clear challenges in knowing how best to support and guide young people (Livingstone *et al.*, 2017; Third *et al.*, 2017).

The implications for PE and PETE are therefore quite clear, and apply to other professionals in clinical, educative and community settings. PE teachers will need to be better prepared to understand how young people engage with digital technologies and how this engagement impacts a wide range of curriculum designs and learning experiences in PE classes (Goodyear and Armour, 2019). Perhaps most importantly, teachers and other relevant adults will need to know enough about the individual young people in their care to recognize when they enter a period of vulnerability, and when the sheer scale, intensity and pervasiveness of digital technologies could act to intensify those vulnerabilities.

Interestingly, in much of our research, we have found that PE teachers rarely feature in young people's health-related thinking (Goodyear *et al.*, 2019a, 2019b). This may not be particularly surprising. In our recent work with PE teachers on digital technologies and learning on physical education, we found that teachers placed considerable emphasis on using technologies to support practice as usual, rather than seeking to understand them in the wider context of young people's online lives and to drive radical change (Casey *et al.*, 2016). This persistent gap between teachers and the young people they instruct and serve needs to be prioritized and bridged. In digital contexts, teachers and their students are likely to know and understand different things. It could be argued, therefore, that the only way forward is for both parties to share what they know, and to co-construct solutions that optimize the benefits of the digital age, while minimizing the risks.

What can we learn from collaborative research with young people and teachers?

Research example one

One of the chapter authors (Sandford) has been conducting research with a group of young people often identified as being more "at risk" or vulnerable compared with their peers. This research offers interesting insights for addressing our challenge. The "Right to Be Active" (R2BA) study was undertaken by Loughborough and Leeds Beckett Universities in the UK, and it sought to understand care-experienced young people's[5] (CEYP) engagements with sport and physical activity (Sandford *et al.*, 2018). Perhaps unsurprisingly, a frequently noted aspect of social practice for these care-experienced young people was their use of digital technologies and, in particular, social media.

As with other aspects of social practice in contemporary times, there has been something of a "moral panic" in the societal discourse around young people's engagements with digital technologies, with an emphasis on perceived risks (Ballantyne *et al.*, 2010; Sen, 2016). For young people such as care-experienced youth who are already categorized as "at risk" due to challenging personal circumstances, there are fears that the level of danger is higher than for their peers (Sen, 2016).

It has been argued, for example, that for many young people in care, the use of social media may be associated with risky contacts, which means it must be restricted/closely monitored as a result of legal orders or carers' rules (Wilson, 2016). For some of the young people within the R2BA study, access to social media (often via smart phones) was indeed controlled by carers, with the withdrawal of such access often used as a "punishment" or a threat for poor behaviour. Thus, although it could be argued that digital technologies offered care-experienced young people possibilities with regard to staying in contact, it also had disadvantages. As one young person in the study noted, "…our foster carers want to know where we are, what we're doing and who we're with every five minutes!" (Sandford et al., 2018, np).

What is evident from this research is that care-experienced youth perceive, engage with and experience digital technologies in similar ways to their non-care peers (Sandford et al., 2018). What this tells us is that wider research with young people and digital technologies will also apply to many care-experienced youth, and as long as PE teachers are aware of the specific constraints facing these young people, they can still apply many of the lessons that are apparent in the wider literature. Therein, however, lies another structural challenge. The R2BA work also revealed that teachers are often unaware of students who are in/have experienced care in their class and, moreover, what the care context means for young people and their engagement with learning.

Research example two

At the University of Birmingham in the UK, two of the chapter authors (Goodyear, Armour) have developed a programme of collaborative research focused on developing pedagogically informed understandings of how digital technologies shape and influence young people's health-related knowledge and behaviours.[6] We have co-constructed new knowledge with diverse groups of young people in participatory research designs (n = 1691; age 13–19) (Goodyear and Armour, 2019). In particular, we have investigated young people's agency and expertise in social media environments (e.g. Instagram, SnapChat, YouTube), health mobile applications ("apps" – e.g. MyFitnessPal, 7-minute workout) and wearable healthy lifestyle technologies (e.g. trackers such as Fitbits). We have also examined the impacts young people have reported on their physical activity, diet/nutrition, and body image behaviours, and related areas of wellbeing (see Goodyear et al., 2019a, 2019b, 2019c).

This participatory and collaborative approach to research (see Chapter 8) aligns with many contemporary global movements concerned with young people's online/offline rights (Livingstone and Third, 2017). It seeks to help key stakeholders – including young people – make informed decisions about how to use digital technologies in relation to health (Goodyear and Armour, 2019).

Social media

The young people reported that social media engagement did have an impact on their physical activity, diet/nutrition and body image behaviours. For example, 48 per cent of young people in the sample reported that they had changed their health-related behaviours because of something seen on social media. In contrast to existing evidence, however, most of the young people in the sample were critically-aware users and generators of health-related social media, and they reported a range of positive benefits.

To better understand the diverse ways in which young people experience social media, we constructed five composite narrative case studies to explain the different forms of content that appeared to be important in influencing young people's health and wellbeing behaviours. Examples of forms of content were: peer content (e.g. selfies), reputable content (e.g. celebrities, government), suggested content (e.g. YouTube), commercial content, and "likes". These all influenced young people to engage with health-related material on social media in different ways. This seems to be essential information for PE teachers, and it is apparent that analysing and understanding social media content and engagement should form a key component of training in PETE and continuing professional development. The fast pace of change in digital environments is a particular challenge for teachers, so ongoing professional learning is essential (see Chapter 7).

Addressing the grand challenge for PE teachers and PETE

The findings from the two projects reported above were reinforced in our collaborative research with a network of 35 international stakeholders in youth health and wellbeing. The group included teachers, practitioners/professionals from national health and wellbeing organizations and trusts, policymakers and researchers (Goodyear *et al.*, 2018). The focus of the research was to better understand the role of PE teachers in empowering young people in the digital age, while minimizing the much-reported risks. Three key findings are as follows.

1   *Digital literacy of PE teachers.* A key challenge for physical educators, as well as many other adults who wish to offer support, is to know when young people are in control of the digital mediums in which they are engaging, and when they shift to being out of control. Digital literacy support for teachers should aim to help teachers to critically evaluate the relevance of health-related information for their own and young people's lives, as well as developing the digital skills to navigate digital technologies so they can understand and offer appropriate support.

2   *Physical educators should harness the educative potential of digital health technologies and social media sites.* Access to digital technologies should be viewed as a right for young people, and as a powerful educative resource. Given that many young people can already recognize harmful, fake and/or untrue information, physical educators should focus on extending young people's existing digital, critical, safe and ethical skills and developing new understandings with young people about what critical, safe and ethical behaviours entail. To achieve that, the different forms of content noted

previously can be used to support young people's health-related understandings, and to inform the pedagogical design of lessons to address the contemporary learning needs of young people.

3   *Educative approaches should be co-constructed with young people.* Young people have undeniable agency in digital spaces, and this is at the core of the challenges facing teachers. It has been argued, therefore, that activist approaches (Luguetti *et al.*, 2017; Oliver and Kirk, 2015) or other comparable youth participatory approaches (Enright and Gard, 2019) are likely to be most effective. Activist approaches are grounded in the involvement and ownership of young people in creating and producing knowledge, with such knowledge then used to guide pedagogical decision- making and the co-design of learning experiences (Oliver and Kirk, 2015) (see Chapter 8). Through the adoption of activist approaches, young people could help adults to better understand about how their – the young people's – health-related understandings and behaviours are being shaped by technology, and, in turn, the types of educational support that will be relevant and of benefit to their needs (Oliver and Kirk, 2015). An activist approach also appears to be a fruitful way to harness young people's very specific levels of expertise in digital contexts in order to help adults better understand the complex and dynamic ways in which young people navigate digital technologies.

Conclusion

We have long argued that working across traditional disciplinary and professional boundaries is at the heart of addressing new challenges in PE and PETE. As Armour (2014) noted, the key challenge is to find new ways to close the multiple research/theory–practice gaps that restrict the growth of knowledge in our field. Indeed, Armour's work on Pedagogical Cases was in response to calls for new translational and collaborative mechanisms that bring research and theory together around the needs of young learners and in ways that practitioners can use and inform. With regard to the digital challenge addressed in this chapter, it is interesting to note that young people are already crossing boundaries, and are challenging our core pedagogical concepts of teacher, expert and content.

There can be little doubt that teachers have a role in addressing the digital challenges presented in this chapter, and that PE teachers are among those who should be supporting young people in the broad health and physical activity online/offline space. Yet, if they are to be effective, this requires much more than a token focus in PETE. Indeed, new trainees entering PETE today will already have a more intuitive understanding of digital technologies than most teachers in the profession and many PETE professionals. The digital challenge, therefore, appears to be primarily one of challenging researchers and educators to undertake more research that focuses on the digital challenge, but to do it in collaborative ways that engage young people, PETE professionals and teachers in co-constructing shared understandings. It is also essential to present the findings in accessible narrative formats and a range of novel digital mediums (see http://opencpd.net/ Socialmedia.html#msg-box10–39 for examples) so they can be shared and discussed online by all stakeholders.

We argue that digital technologies have the potential to make PE very relevant to contemporary youth, but only if we are willing to alter our content and pedagogies to meet young people where they are, rather than where they used to be. Adult stakeholders need to move beyond the pervasive technologies risk narrative, and focus instead on how young people's engagement with digital technologies should radically alter PE for the better. This requires new, brave, multidisciplinary and collaborative research, and new ways of sharing and communicating findings. The next stage, therefore, is to define a research agenda that focuses on new ways of learning collaboratively *with* young people and *across* PE/ PETE professional boundaries. Such an agenda would require funding at a level that could support large scale, transformative research. Doing nothing does not appear to be an option in the digital age challenge.

Notes

1 www.parliament.uk/business/committees/committees-a-z/commons-select/science-and-technology-committee/inquiries/parliament-2017/impact-of-social-media-young-people-17-19/
2 www.rsph.org.uk/our-work/campaigns/status-of-mind/appg.html
3 www.gov.uk/government/news/matt-hancock-warns-of-dangers-of-social-media-on-childrens-mental-health
4 www.gov.uk/government/publications/uk-cmo-commentary-on-screen-time-and-social-media-map-of-reviews
5 The term care-experienced young people refers to anyone who is currently, or has been at any stage of their life, under the care of local government. This includes, but is not limited to, those who have been removed from their biological families and placed in foster care, kinship care or local-authority run residential care (see Quarmby *et al.*, 2018).
6 http://opencpd.net/Guidelines.html

References

Armour, K.M. (ed.) (2014). *Pedagogical Cases in Physical Education and Youth Sport*. London: Routledge.
Askari, E., Brandon, D., Galvin, S. and Greenhow, C. (2018). Youth, learning and social media in K-12 Education: The state of the field. *International Society of Learning Sciences 2018 Proceedings*.
Ballantyne, N., Duncalf, Z. and Daly, E. (2010). Corporate parenting in the network society. *Journal of Technology in Human Services*, 28(1–2), 95–107.
Blum-Ross, A. and Livingstone, S. (2018). The trouble with "screen time" rules. Available at: https://nordicom.gu.se/sv/system/tdf/kapitel-pdf/16_blum-ross_livingstone.pdf?file=1&type=node&id=39905&force= (accessed 25 March 2019).
Booker, C.L., Kelly, Y.J. and Sacker, A. (2018). Gender differences in the associations between age trends of social media interaction and wellbeing among 10–15 year olds in the UK. *BMC Public Health*, 18, 231.

Buckingham, D. (2016). Is there a digital generation? In D. Buckingham and R. Willett (eds), *Digital Generations: Children, Young People and the New Media*. London: Routledge, 1–18.

Casey, A., Goodyear, V.A. and Armour, K.M. (2016). *Digital Technologies and Learning in Physical Education: Pedagogical Cases*. London: Routledge.

Clark, L.S. (2013). *The Parent App: Understanding Families in the Digital Age*. Oxford: Oxford University Press.

Collin, P., Rahilly, K., Third, A. and Richardson, I. (2010). *Literature Review: Benefits of Social Networking Services*. Sydney, Australia: CRC for Young People, Technology and Wellbeing.

Enright, E. and Gard, M. (2019). Young people, social media and digital democracy. In V. Goodyear and K. Armour (eds), *Young People, Social Media and Health*. London: Routledge.

Gaplin, A. and Taylor, G. (2017). Changing behaviour: children, adolescents and screen use. Available at: www.bps.org.uk/sites/beta.bps.org.uk/files/Policy%20-%20 Files/Changing%20behaviour%20-%20children%2C%20adolescents%2C%20and%20 screen%20use.pdf

Goodyear, V.A. and Armour K.M. (2019). *Young People, Social Media and Health*. London: Routledge.

Goodyear, V.A., Armour, K.M. and Wood, H. (2018). *The Impact of Social Media on Young People's Health and Wellbeing: Evidence, Guidelines and Actions*. Birmingham: University of Birmingham. Available at: http://epapers.bham.ac.uk/3070/ (accessed 25 March 2019).

Goodyear, V.A., Armour, K.M. and Wood, H. (2019a). Young people's engagement with health-related social media: new perspectives. *Sport, Education and Society*, 24(7), 673–688.

Goodyear, V.A., Armour, K.M. and Wood, H. (2019b). Young people learning about health: the role of apps and wearable devices. *Learning, Media and Technology*, 44(2), 193–210.

Goodyear, V.A., Kerner, C. and Quennerstedt, M. (2019c). Young people's uses of wearable healthy lifestyle technologies: surveillance, self-surveillance and resistance. *Sport, Education and Society*, 24(3), 212–225.

Handyside, S. and Ringrose, J. (2017). Snapchat memory and youth digital sexual cultures: mediated temporality, duration and affect. *Journal of Gender Studies*, 26(3), 347–360.

Holmberg, C., Berg, C., Hillman, T., Lissner, L. and Chaplin, J.E. (2018). Self-presentation in digital media among adolescent patients with obesity: striving for integrity, risk-reduction and social recognition. *Digital Health*, 4, 1–15.

Kelly, Y., Zilanawala, A., Booker, C. and Sacker, A. (2019). Social media use and adolescent mental health: findings from the UK millennium cohort study. *Lancet*, 6, 59–58.

Lawson, H. (2018). *Redesigning Physical Education. An Equity Agenda in Which Every Child Matters*. Oxon: Routledge.

Livingstone, S., Mascheroni, G. and Staksrud, R. (2017). European research on children's internet use: assessing the past and anticipating the future. *New Media & Society*, iFirst.

Livingston, S. and Third, A. (2017). Children and young people's rights in the digital age: an emerging agenda. *New Media & Society*, 19(5), 657–670.

Luguetti, C., Oliver, K.L., Dantas, L.E.P.B.T. and Kirk, D. (2017). An activist approach to sport meets youth from socially vulnerable backgrounds: possible learning aspirations. *Research Quarterly for Exercise and Sport*, 88(1), 60–71.

MacIsaac, S., Kelly, J. and Gray, S. (2018). "She has like 4000 followers!": The celebrification of self within school social networks. *Journal of Youth Studies*, 21(6), 816–835.

OECD (2018). *Children and Young People's Mental Health in the Digital Age: Shaping the Future.* Available at: www.oecd.org/els/health-systems/Children-and-Young-People-Mental-Health-in-the-Digital-Age.pdf (accessed 25 March 2019).

Ofcom (2018). *Children and Parents: Media Use and Attitudes Report 2018.* Available at: www.ofcom.org.uk/__data/assets/pdf_file/0024/134907/Children-and-Parents-Media-Use-and-Attitudes-2018.pdf (accessed 25 March 2019).

Oliver, K.M. and Kirk, D. (2015). *Girls, Gender and Physical Education: An Activist Approach.* London: Routledge.

Orben, A. and Przybylski, A.K. (2019). The association between adolescent wellbeing and digital technology use. *Nature*, 14, 1.

Patton, G.C., Sawyer, S.M., Santelli, J.S., Ross, D.A., Afifi, R., Allen, N.B. and Arora, M., ... (2016). Our future: a Lancet commission on adolescent health and wellbeing. *Lancet*, 387, 2423–2478.

Pew Research Centre (2018). *Teens, Social Media and Technology.* Available at: www.pewinternet.org/2018/05/31/teens-social-media-technology-2018/ (accessed 25 March 2019).

Quarmby, T., Sandford, R. and Elliot, E. (2018). "I actually used to like PE, but not now": understanding care-experienced young people's (dis)engagement with physical education. *Sport, Education and Society.* doi:10.1080/13573322.2018.1456418

Royal College of Paediatrics and Child Health (2019). *The Health Impacts of Screen Time: A Guide for Clinicians and Parents.* Accessed from: www.rcpch.ac.uk/sites/default/files/2018-12/rcpch_screen_time_guide_-_final.pdf

Royal Society of Public Health (2017). *#Status on Mind: Social Media and Young People's Mental Health and Wellbeing.* London: Royal Society for Public Health.

Sandford, R. and Quarmby, T. (2019). Space, place and identity: new pressures in the lives of young people. In V. Goodyear and K. Armour (eds), *Young People, Social Media and Health.* London: Routledge.

Sandford, R., Quarmby, T., Hooper, O. and Duncombe, R. (2018). Right to be active: dissemination of findings. Dissemination event held at Leicester City Football Club, September, 2018.

Sen, R. (2016). Not all that is solid melts into air? Care-experienced young people, friendships and relationships in the "digital age". *British Journal of Social Work*, 46, 1059–1075.

Shulman, D. (2016). *The Presentation of Self in Contemporary Social Life.* London: Sage Publications.

Stiglic, N. and Viner, R.M. (2019). Effects of screentime on the health and wellbeing of children and adolescents: a systematic review of reviews. *BMJ Open*, 9.

Third, A., Bellerose, D., Oliveira, J.D.D., Lala, G. and Theakstone, G. (2017). *Young and Online: Children's Perspectives on Life in the Digital Age.* Sydney: Western Sydney University.

Turkle, S. (2017). *Alone Together: Why We Expect More from Technology and Less from Each Other*, 3rd edn. New York: Basic Books.

Wilson, S. (2016). Digital technologies, children and young people's relationships and self-care. *Children's Geographies*, 14(3), 282–294.

Chapter 10

The PE school curriculum challenge

The shared construction, implementation and enactment of school physical education curriculum

Rachael Whittle and Ann MacPhail

Introduction

The physical education (PE) curriculum refers to a range of educational experiences, planned and unplanned, associated with student learning. Typically structured in relation to educational policy standards, it encompasses "all knowledge, skills, and learning experiences that are provided to students within the school program" (Lund and Tannehill, 2015, 6) with the grand aim of preparing "the physically educated student". In contrast to what might be considered a "PE programme" in some parts of the world, fully-developed PE curricula include a rationale; aims, goals and objectives; practical activities; and mechanisms for assessing student learning.

Curriculum is linked to assessment and pedagogy (Penney *et al.*, 2009). Optimal student learning depends on the alignment and coherence of these three components. Ideally, each informs and enriches the other, benefiting students. Mirroring other school subjects, particular kinds of PE curricula with their respective pedagogies and assessment systems have life histories. All are influenced and determined by designated missions for school systems as well as policy leaders' determinations regarding what students need to know and be able to do to thrive in host societies. In brief, societal change is a catalyst for curriculum innovation, altering the life histories of particular PE curricula and raising questions about how new curricula are constructed and who does this important work.

These questions regarding leadership for curriculum construction and quality assurance are addressed in this chapter. It features a collaborative approach to curriculum construction, implementation, enactment, and continuous improvement. Realizing the promise of this collaborative approach, particularly among teacher educators, teachers, and students, is a grand challenge with universal importance. It necessitates new curriculum discourses (i.e. language systems), and it positions teachers as expert co-designers of curricula (Petrie, 2017).

This collaborative approach is designed to disrupt an industrial-age linear discourse which conveys curriculum, implementation and enactment as a top-down, prescriptive system. In this view, "teachers are educational technicians enacting the design, and students are commodities whose subjectivity and individuality are mercilessly overlooked and deprived" (Ovens and Butler, 2017, 101). A collaborative approach presents curriculum as an, "organic and living process that is connected to place, community, and local knowledge" (Ovens and Butler, 2017, 101). Local leaders influence and make curriculum, responding to and building on school-community assets, while responding to and informing state/provincial/national curriculum standards.

Our intention is to articulate an operational framework for each disruption of PE curriculum development through which colleagues around the world can consider the professional responsibilities and practical dimensions related to their localized context.

Physical education curriculum construction – back to the future or future proof?

The "scientization" and "academicization" of school PE, particularly at the senior-secondary level, is manifested in the theoretical content and prevalence of written assessment tasks (Whittle et al., 2017). As PE has become more like other "academic" subjects, it risks losing its uniqueness (Green, 2008).

Competing priorities are part of the new curricular landscape, and in an era where accountability and assessment pressures may distract from the value and joy of movement that should be intrinsic in any quality PE programme, the increased pressure for PE to contribute to student wellbeing, while also meeting physical activity recommendations, creates tensions for teachers. For example, McKenzie and Lounsbery (2009) suggest that contemporary PE curricula are expected to improve a student's social, emotional, mental and physical health (see Chapter 5), while also combating childhood obesity and physical inactivity.

Physical Education has much to offer in terms of student wellbeing, the development of skills and behaviours that transfer to lifelong physical activity, but is this at the expense of more traditional objectives of PE curricula? Globally, designers of PE curricula often "borrow" from other jurisdictions. Sometimes they are pressured to inherit from others' curricula. Meanwhile, there is a call for PE curricula to be innovative, tailor-made designs that meet the needs of current and future generations of students, requiring a new generation of leaders (Lawson, 2018).

This growing complexity rules out a standardized, generalizable PE curriculum that is fit for purpose in every nation and its local contexts. Priorities for local curriculum design are inescapable. Toward this end, we consider the involvement of multiple players in the construction, implementation and enactment process.

Shared curriculum construction: whose voices and choices?

Providing the opportunity for a diverse range of stakeholders to come together and share their views, ideas and concerns in a way that allows all involved to be heard and valued is a process referred to as "structured democratic voice" (Smith and Benavot, 2019). While those involved always tend to bring preconceived ideas and advocate for curriculum inclusions specific to their perspective and priorities (Scanlon et al., 2018), the design process must be fluid, evolving through the interactions of the group.

Conflict is endemic. What is valued by some can be ridiculed or feared by others, in what Ennis (1997) called the "dreaded curriculum". The power differential within the group can result in some parties having greater influence than others (Scanlon et al., 2018) and may even control the behaviour of less powerful group members (Lau, 2001).

Student voices and student agency

It is noteworthy that students, as key stakeholders, are rarely involved in policy-making decisions and student agency has been missing from the curriculum construction process (Fitzpatrick et al., 2018; Lundy and Cook-Sather, 2015). Toward this end, MacPhail and Halbert (2005) called for student contribution to be the first step in the development of curriculum. However, student voices have been "mostly silent" in curriculum construction.

Student agency can improve teaching and learning outcomes for students (Bourke and Loveridge, 2016; Yonezawa and Jones, 2007; Baroutsis et al., 2016; Griebler et al., 2017), and student agency in curriculum construction may provide useful contributions from an alternate perspective to governments, authorities and other stakeholders (see Chapter 8).

One challenge thus is to ensure that students are positioned to be heard and valued if they are to make meaningful contributions to the curriculum construction process. This will likely require a shift in the distribution of power to ensure that the student voice informs curriculum construction decisions and student involvement is real and substantive, rather than a tokenistic addition to the process.

Teacher voices and teacher involvement

Consultation as an essential aspect of curriculum construction ensures input and feedback from other key stakeholders. For example, the development of the national, senior-secondary PE curricula in Australia and Ireland had representatives from curriculum authorities, departments of education, tertiary institutes (including teacher educators) and teachers on the advisory panels.

Curriculum development in the USA provides a contrast. MacLean et al. (2015) identified the lack of collaboration between policymakers and teachers as a key factor in the "implementation failure" of physical education policy (Dyson et al., 2011).

Teacher involvement in curriculum construction is essential to successful enactment and implementation (MacLean et al., 2015; MacPhail, 2007; Kirk and MacDonald, 2001; Evans and Penney, 2002). On the other hand, the value of teacher contributions to the construction of curriculum can be limited, especially when teachers' knowledge is limited to their local context (Kirk and MacDonald, 2001). However, teachers' local knowledge is an asset because teachers everywhere are being called on to articulate their expertise of their local context in the curriculum construction process.

An Asia-Pacific example: the construction phase

The review of the senior-secondary PE curriculum in the Asia-Pacific offers insights about the collaborative design process and the value of teachers' perspectives in the construction, implementation and enactment of the curriculum. Involved in the review panel responsible for the construction of the curriculum document were (i) seven teachers from government, catholic and independent educational sectors; (ii) four academics with subject specific expertise in exercise physiology, motor learning and skill acquisition and a socio-cultural perspective of PE; and (iii) an industry representative.

Teachers' input provided a check on the balance between theoretical intentions of the proposed curriculum and the practical interpretation and viability of the curriculum in the classroom. For example, the teachers reported a number of challenges: (i) understanding current knowledge in the field; (ii) dealing with change and time constraints imposed by the process itself in addition to the challenges involved in the actual curriculum; (iii) planning a curriculum that is relevant and interesting to the broader student cohort yet flexible enough to meet local context needs; and (iv) developing a course that was manageable at an operational level yet allowed for depth of learning and application of knowledge.

PE teacher educator voices and ongoing involvement

The role of academics, and specifically teacher educators, in the curriculum construction process is dualistic. Academics are often sought to provide "expert" advice on specific content inclusions and to provide insights to new and emerging research relevant to the curriculum. Yet, in their role as educators of the next generation of physical education teachers, it is imperative that teacher educators have a thorough knowledge of curriculum developments (MacPhail and Halbert, 2005). Familiarity with the relevant curriculum impacts on the teacher educators' ability to deliver a programme that adequately prepares pre-service teachers (PSTs) (Melnychuk et al., 2011). Teacher education is responsible for preparing graduates to understand, deliver and assess the aims and objectives of the designed curriculum and, as such, teacher educators have a pivotal role to play in the curriculum construction process. Those involved in PETE have a professional responsibility to actively engage in a collaborative approach to curriculum construction, implementation and enactment, providing a conduit to connect research, teacher education and schools.

Curriculum implementation: a multi-layer perspective

A new or revised curriculum, once approved by the appropriate governing body or authority, is "handed over to schools for implementation" (MacPhail and Halbert, 2005, 297). Olson (2000) suggests that teachers are at the "nexus of curriculum implementation" because they are the ones entrusted with the responsibility of bringing the curriculum to life within the classroom. Implementation in this context is the adoption of the curriculum as policy. At the national level, it can be argued that consistency in curriculum implementation is needed to ensure the learning objectives and overarching aims of the curriculum are met.

Local factors and actors remain important. Implementation decisions made at the school level, described as the "local context of implementation" (Kirk and MacDonald, 2001), are made in relation to school management, availability of facilities in schools and community organizations, and specific cohorts of students. Local adaptation during curriculum implementation is inevitable and essential.

Curriculum enactment: from policy to practice

PE curricula are structured by governmental standards, and these standards are policy instruments. Policy enactment is a complex process where teachers are expected to interpret curriculum and develop teaching and learning programmes (Hume and Coll, 2010) and "the intentions of the policy makers may or may not be realised through enactment" (Paveling et al., 2019).

The "how" and "what" teachers teach can be considered the enacted curriculum. As Penney (2013) states, it is here that "the rubber hits the road", both for teachers and teacher educators. The reminder here is that few curriculum policy documents are clear and self-explanatory (see Chapter 14). The onus is placed on teachers, teacher educators, and school officials to unpack, understand and interpret the curriculum policy document.

Enactment occurs in many places within a system where curriculum is "translated and transformed" (Remillard and Heck, 2014). In such instances, teachers take a curriculum document to deliberate and make decisions on how they interpret and operationalize the content in their specific context.

Enactment rarely is uniform across all school and community settings. Hume and Coll (2009) identified numerous "sites of influence" that impact on the interpretation and consequent enactment of the curriculum, and some were not aligned with the intent of the prescribed curriculum policy. Similarly, Doyle and Rosemartin (2012) reported that teachers do not enact curriculum solely according to design.

Differences between the intended curriculum and the enacted curriculum are thus normative because teachers are curriculum interpreters, not implementation puppets (MacLean et al., 2015). They adapt the curricula to meet the needs of the local context. They also filter curriculum specifications through the lens of their perceived competencies and teaching preferences (see Chapter 7). These inevitable local variations hold promise for "bottom-up" curricular policy innovation and continuous improvement – an important benefit associated with the collaborative approach recommended in this chapter.

Teachers and teacher educators: curriculum change agents?

Curriculum change is more likely when those involved in the implementation of the policy are actively involved in the construction phase of the process (Voogt et al., 2016). Goodwill is generated when teachers and teacher educators are viewed and treated as co-designers as they implement and enact a new curriculum, and policy provisions are based in part on their professionalism and their capacity to make solid decisions through the implementation and enactment phases.

Such a collaborative approach to curriculum and its close relations, pedagogy and assessment, depends in part on special provisions for timely communications among the key stakeholders – representative students, teachers, teacher educators, school leaders, and policy officials. The ideal is a potent combination of top-down and bottom-up organizational learning and improvement. Focused on fidelity, alignment, coherence, and the achievement of desirable outcomes (see Chapters 2 and 4), this collaborative approach makes curriculum a dynamic entity, potentially benefiting all participants. Practical examples illustrate this approach's import.

Returning to the Asia-Pacific example: the implementation and enactment phases

The implementation phase involved materials developed by the government curriculum and assessment authority and delivered in workshops by teachers, including those involved in the construction process and others who had not been involved. Involving additional teachers in this aspect of the process further contributed to teacher agency, while ensuring consistency in the message delivered. While the workshops allowed teachers scope and flexibility to provide advice on practical implications for classroom enactment of the curriculum, further teacher collaboration and development of learning resources and activities within a local context was necessary.

At the local level (school and classroom), it has been argued that teacher control over curriculum is needed to, "sustain professional engagement and to impact positively on pupils' learning" (Wyse et al., 2012, 82). The relationship between the official curriculum and the school PE programme is influenced by local factors including the perceived purpose and value of PE within the whole school programme and other considerations such as mandated times for PE and physical activity (see for example the mandate for physical education and sport in Victorian schools – State Government Victoria, 2019). The curriculum provides a framework for teachers to design teaching and learning programmes that, "can be responsive to individual school contexts and groups of students" (Brown and Penney, 2017, 128). There exists a tension between teacher autonomy and accountability and teachers have shown some wariness of the flexibility a non-prescriptive curriculum offers (MacLean et al., 2015; Simmons and MacLean, 2016). Without sufficient leadership and guidance from curriculum policymakers, teacher confidence to act as change agents may be diminished (Simmons and MacLean, 2016). Teacher confidence and competence to enact a new curriculum is increased with greater awareness, resources and guidance (Nanayakkara et al., 2017), which can impact on the ability of teachers to "use the curriculum as a tool to achieve success" (Wyse et al., 2012, 80). For success, a level of professional trust is needed and a shift in power to teachers working alongside a curriculum policy that encourages teachers to use their professional judgement to enact curriculum in their school context. This will allow teachers to take ownership of the process and enable change to occur.

Reflecting on teacher involvement in the Asia-Pacific

The involvement of teachers in the example provided previously across the three aspects of construction, implementation and enactment provides a unique perspective of the frustrations, successes and challenges faced by teachers through this process. On reflection, those involved in the process found the experience to be rewarding, as noted by one of the teachers:

> I think this has actually been one of the best parts of being involved in the process, recognising the challenges in developing a course. Appreciating the expertise of those on the panel and the rigorous process involved. I have felt a responsibility to support others in the implementation of the course and a desire to see the course deliver on our goals.

Ongoing and continued support beyond the implementation phase through a professional learning community may provide the additional mechanism needed that allows teachers to close the gap between the intended and enacted curriculum. The role of higher education institutes, professional associations and governing authorities to provide continuing professional development (see Chapter 13) to both in-service and PSTs to increase awareness and comfort with the new curriculum is necessary for successful enactment (MacPhail and Halbert, 2005). Teacher educators play an important role in ensuring graduating teachers understand content and pedagogical implications and the requirements of curriculum documents if the graduating teachers are to successfully enact curriculum documents once in schools (Culpan, 2017; MacPhail and Halbert, 2005). The role of relevant stakeholders in following through the construction, implementation and enactment of curriculum is imperative to the success of student learning outcomes.

An Irish example: the reality of including numerous stakeholders throughout the curriculum reform process

The usual starting point for any curriculum development (i.e. the construction) resides with a government statutory body agency responsible for advising the government on curriculum for school-aged children. Such an agency tends not to be responsible for implementing curriculum change but rather suggesting to the government changes in the curriculum that are necessary for young people to flourish in an educational context. The support for school educational change is therefore typically provided by the agency through developing a range of support materials and by working with those educators responsible for introducing new curriculum developments.

In this example, Ireland was considering the construction of a new curriculum. It was prudent for the specific government agency charged with oversight of curriculum development to reflect on research evidence, good practice and international experience that informs meaningful, relevant and worthwhile PE curriculum. This government agency approached a PE teacher educator with extensive experience in researching and delivering effective PE practices (specifically related to curriculum and instruction models). The agency sought this teacher educator's vision for school PE that places the student at the centre of the learning experience in their final two years of post-primary school (aged 16 to 18 years). All were aware of the extent to which research findings from numerous contexts would need to be reconsidered to apply to a specific educational environment. The vision presented by this teacher educator was innovative in that it moved away from the traditional approach of constructing a PE curriculum around discrete physical activities (e.g. games and athletics) to considering a PE curriculum based on six curriculum and instruction models as the framework through which a range of physical activities could be taught (MacPhail et al., 2018).

This initial consultation was the first step in a new process of curriculum development that involved educational discourse designed to ensure all those involved in, and throughout, the curriculum process had a shared involvement and voice in the construction, implementation and enactment of curriculum. This was the beginning of a formalized relationship between the agency responsible for curriculum construction, the teacher educator, and practising teachers in curriculum design. The intent was to disrupt the traditional linear discourse that conveys curriculum, implementation and enactment as top-down, prescriptive systems.

Discussions and deliberations took place among associated members of the national agency to consider the desirability and feasibility of the curriculum being proposed, conscious of the extent to which the national educational landscape would be able to promote and support such a curriculum and the associated consequences that would arise (i.e. enactment). The teacher educator was available to further qualify the premise of the proposed PE curriculum as well as consider, in partnership with the national agency, the reality of enacting such a curriculum in the specific country context. The committee structure "managing" the development of this specific PE development, and the process by which curriculum development was "managed" by the appointed committee, is reported elsewhere (MacPhail, 2015).

Once initial agreement was reached on the proposed PE curriculum framework, the associated document was made available online for consultation by anyone with an interest in contributing to the refinement of the curriculum, e.g. teachers, schools, teacher educators, teaching unions, parent organizations. Practising teachers were viewed as the key to this curriculum being viable in the country context for which it was intended. Therefore, teachers were invited and encouraged to take part in this consultation, acknowledging that they were seen as the drivers of curriculum development and, ultimately, its implementation and enactment.

The open consultation phase provided an opportunity for individuals and PE professional bodies to comment on the proposed PE curriculum. Focus groups with school students were facilitated by the national agency in a bid to capture young people's views on the proposed PE curriculum framework, their role in its design, and their engagement in the curriculum itself at the implementation stage. Those young people involved in these discussions gained insight into the various curriculum and instruction models, how they would/could be introduced, and how their voice would be sought at different stages of design and enactment in schools.

Once the curriculum was finalized (National Council for Curriculum and Assessment, 2015), the same PE teacher educator was commissioned to work with the national agency in upskilling a group of teachers to be confident in delivering the curriculum (i.e. implementation). Subsequently, there were national agency representatives, a teacher educator, teachers (and by association students) all working together towards the implementation of the curriculum.

Over a three-year period, teachers were invited to take part in a "teachers training teachers" professional development experience. Each semester, one of the curriculum models was the focus. Teachers learned about the model, experienced "living" the model, studied the learning outcomes intended for student learning of the model, and designed a unit of learning framed by the model. The teacher then taught the unit of learning, reflected on their teaching of it, talked to students on their learning within the specific unit, and came back for discussion and sharing with the other teachers engaged in the professional development. This process engaged teachers as a learning community, allowing them to draw support from one another and empower them as leaders in the curriculum change process.

In turn, the teachers involved in the professional development on curriculum and instruction model design were upskilled and prepared to teach other teachers. The continual involvement and participation of the teacher educator throughout the process has allowed teacher education programmes to consider the most effective ways to educate future PE teachers who are expected to effectively deliver the proposed curriculum. The collaborative process thus yielded multiple benefits to many stakeholders.

Conclusion

The "grand challenge" of engaging relevant stakeholders in the curriculum construction, implementation and enactment process involves students, teachers, teacher educators and curriculum and/or government authorities who have a collective professional responsibility to construct, implement and enact curriculum that meet the needs of the students for whom the curriculum serves. As illustrated in the examples in this chapter, this process is already gaining momentum in some jurisdictions.

The challenge to include the views, ideas and concerns of not only the established voices, but of those not ordinarily heard, is ongoing (see Chapter 8). Future research is needed to identify mechanisms that will allow for equal and effective contributions from students, teachers, teacher educators, as well as relevant authorities. Reflection on current practice that has identified power differentials between those at the table suggests that, while there may be involvement of students, teachers, teacher educators and the relevant authorities in this process, not all contributions are viewed or valued equally. It is imperative that key stakeholders accept, and share, the responsibility and have agency in the process.

Furthermore, research to identify strategies for pre-service and in-service teachers to support and build teacher capacity to enact official curriculum documents is warranted if we are to make progress in achieving the ambitious goals of school PE in the twenty-first century. The relationship between those involved in construction, implementation and enactment needs to be dynamic and constantly evolving to ensure an iterative process is achieved. Each must play a role in the evolution of the curriculum and in closing the gap between the intended curriculum and the reality as this will require different solutions at multiple levels of influence.

References

Baroutsis, A., McGregor, G. and Mills, M. (2016). Pedagogic voice: student voice in teaching and engagement pedagogies. *Pedagogy, Culture & Society*, 24, 123–140.

Bourke, R. and Loveridge, J. (2016). Beyond the official language of learning: teachers engaging with student voice research. *Teaching and Teacher Education*, 57, 59–66.

Brown, T.D. and Penney, D. (2017). Interpretation and enactment of senior secondary physical education: pedagogic realities and the expression of Arnoldian dimensions of movement. *Physical Education and Sport Pedagogy*, 22, 121–136.

Culpan, I. (2017). Criticality in physical education teacher education: do graduating standards constrain and or inhibit curriculum implementation? *Australian Journal of Teacher Education*, 42, 84–94.

Doyle, W. and Rosemartin, D. (2012). The ecology of curriculum enactment. *Interpersonal Relationships in Education*. Switzerland: Springer, 137–147.

Dyson, B., Wright, P.M., Amis, J., Ferry, H. and Vardaman, J. M. (2011). The production, communication, and contestation of physical education policy: the cases of Mississippi and Tennessee. *Policy Futures in Education*, 9, 367–380.

Ennis, C. (1997). Defining the dreaded curriculum: tensions between the modern and the postmodern. In J.-M. Fernandez-Balboa (ed.), *Critical Postmodernism in Human Movement, Physical Education, and Sport*. Albany: State University of New York Press, 207–220.

Evans, J. and Penney, D. (2002). *Politics, Policy and Practice in Physical Education*. London: Routledge.

Fitzpatrick, J., O'Grady, E. and O'Reilly, J. (2018). Promoting student agentic engagement through curriculum: exploring the Negotiated Integrated Curriculum initiative. *Irish Educational Studies*, 37: 453–473.

Griebler, U., Rojatz, D., Simovska, V. and Forster, R. (2017). Effects of student participation in school health promotion: a systematic review. *Health Promotion International*, 32, 195–206.

Green, K. (2008). *Understanding Physical Education*. London: Sage.

Hume, A. and Coll, R.K. (2009). Assessment of learning, for learning, and as learning: New Zealand case studies. *Assessment in Education: Principles, Policy & Practice*, 16, 269–290.

Hume, A. and Coll, R. (2010). Authentic student inquiry: the mismatch between the intended curriculum and the student-experienced curriculum. *Research in Science & Technological Education*, 28, 43–62.

Kirk, D. and MacDonald, D. (2001). Teacher voice and ownership of curriculum change. *Journal of Curriculum Studies*, 33, 551–567.

Lau, D.C.-M. (2001). Analysing the curriculum development process: three models. *Pedagogy, Culture and Society*, 9, 29–44.

Lawson, H. (2018). *Redesigning Physical Education: An Equity Agenda in Which Every Child Matters*. Oxon: Routledge.

Lund, J. and Tannehill, D. (2015). *Standards-based Physical Education Curriculum Development*. Boston, MA: Jones & Bartlett Publishers.

Lundy, L. and Cook-Sather, A. (2015). Children's rights and student voice: their intersections and the implications for curriculum and pedagogy. In D. Wyse, L. Hayward and J. Pandya (eds), *The SAGE Handbook of Curriculum, Pedagogy and Assessment*. London: Sage, 263–277.

MacLean, J., Mulholland, R., Gray, S. and Horrell, A. (2015). Enabling curriculum change in physical education: the interplay between policy constructors and practitioners. *Physical Education and Sport Pedagogy*, 20, 79–96.

MacPhail, A. (2007). Teachers' views on the construction, management and delivery of an externally prescribed physical education curriculum: higher grade physical education. *Physical Education and Sport Pedagogy*, 12, 43–60.

MacPhail, A. (2015). The story of representation (or not) in contributing to the development of a school subject curriculum. *Irish Educational Studies*, 34, 225–243.

MacPhail, A. and Halbert, J. (2005). The implementation of a revised physical education syllabus in Ireland: circumstances, rewards and costs. *European Physical Education Review*, 11, 287–308.

MacPhail, A., O'Sullivan, M., Tannehill, D. and Parker, M. (2018). Redesigning physical education in Ireland: significant redesign over modest reforms? In Lawson, H. (ed.), *Redesigning Physical Education. An Equity Agenda in Which Every Child Matters*. Routledge: London, 171–181.

McKenzie, T.L. and Lounsbery, M.A. (2009). School physical education: the pill not taken. *American Journal of Lifestyle Medicine*, 3, 219–225.

Melnychuk, N., Robinson, D., Lu, C., Chorney, D. and Randall, L. (2011). Physical Education Teacher Education (PETE) in Canada. *Canadian Journal of Education*, 34, 148–168.

Nanayakkara, J., Margerison, C. and Worsley, A. (2017). Importance of food literacy education for senior secondary school students: Food system professionals' opinions. *International Journal of Health Promotion and Education*, 55, 284–295.

National Council for Curriculum and Assessment (2015). *Physical Education Framework*. Dublin: NCCA.

Olson, M. (2000). Curriculum as a multistoried process. *Canadian Journal of Education/ Revue canadienne de l'education*, 169–187.

Ovens, A. and Butler, J. (2017). Complexity, curriculum, and the design of learning systems. In C. Ennis (ed.), *Routledge Handbook of Physical Education Pedagogies*. London: Routledge, 97–111.

Paveling, B., Vidovich, L. and Oakley, G. (2019). Global to local tensions in the production and enactment of Physical education curriculum policy reforms. *Curriculum Studies in Health and Physical Education*, 1–15.

Penney, D. (2013). *Making a Difference: Policies, People and Pedagogy in Physical Education and Sport*. Wilf Malcolm Institute of Educational Research, Faculty of Education, University of Waikato.

Penney, D., Brooker, R., Hay, P. and Gillespie, L. (2009). Curriculum, pedagogy and assessment: three message systems of schooling and dimensions of quality physical education. *Sport, Education and Society*, 14(4), 421–442.

Petrie, K. (2017). Curriculum reform where it counts. In C. Ennis (ed.), Routledge Handbook of Physical Education Pedagogies. London: Routledge, pp. 173–186.

Remillard, J.T. and Heck, D.J. (2014). Conceptualizing the curriculum enactment process in mathematics education. *Zdm*, 46, 705–718.

Scanlon, D., MacPhail, A. and Calderón, A. (2018). Original intentions and unintended consequences: the "contentious" role of assessment in the development of Leaving Certificate Physical Education in Ireland. *Curriculum Studies in Health and Physical Education*, 1–20.

Simmons, J. and MacLean, J. (2016). Physical education teachers' perceptions of factors that inhibit and facilitate the enactment of curriculum change in a high-stakes exam climate. *Sport, Education and Society*, 23(2), 186–202.

Smith, W.C. and Benavot, A. (2019). Improving accountability in education: the importance of structured democratic voice. *Asia Pacific Education Review*, 1–13.

State Government Victoria (2019). *Physical and Sport Education*. Available at: www.education. vic.gov.au/school/principals/spag/curriculum/Pages/sport.aspx.

Voogt, J.M., Pieters, J.M. and Handelzalts, A. (2016). Teacher collaboration in curriculum design teams: Effects, mechanisms, and conditions. *Educational Research and Evaluation*, 22, 121–140.

Whittle, R.J., Benson, A.C. and Telford, A. (2017). Enrolment, content and assessment: a review of examinable senior secondary (16–19 year olds) physical education courses: an international perspective. *The Curriculum Journal*, 28, 598–625.

Wyse, D., Baumfield, V.M., Egan, D., Hayward, L. and Gallagher, C. (2012). *Creating the Curriculum*. London: Routledge.

Yonezawa, S. and Jones, M. (2007). Using students' voices to inform and evaluate secondary school reform. In D. Thiessen and A. Cook-Sather (eds), *International Handbook of Student Experience in Elementary and Secondary School*. Dordrecht: Springer, 681–709.

Chapter 11

The research and development challenge

Better aligning teachers' and teacher educators' needs, priorities and demands

Tim Fletcher, Alex Beckey, Håkan Larsson and Ann MacPhail

Introduction

A physical education (PE) teacher's role is complex, partly because the lines are blurred between teacher of curricular PE (teaching PE for all students), teacher of academic PE (teaching PE for examination) and school sport coach. You are employed mainly as the former but often judged by outcomes from the latter two. Much of what you do day to day in lessons goes unnoticed and in my early career it was sporting success that defined me as a PE teacher and influenced my lessons.

After ten years of teaching I thought I had nailed my craft. My proof was that I had coached one of the best seasons in the school rugby team's history. Two years later I was full of doubt.

The doubt came from a chance meeting with a former student on a train. Sam had been instrumental in the successful school rugby team. I asked about his studies and life, curious to find out the directions he had taken. We spoke to each other like long-lost friends. However, talking about school rugby turned things cold. Sam explained that he had not played since his final game for the school. He had fallen out of love with it. Sam paused, unsure whether to speak his mind. He went on, saying it was my fault, telling me firmly, but kindly, what I had done: the constant repetition of isolated set piece moves, highlighting tactical and technical mistakes in practices and games, the inability to hide my disappointment when they failed in training or in matches, the singling out of individuals, the constant pressure to win. Sam offered an honest reflection of me and my coaching and his words led me to think about how this reflected my PE teaching too.

I still feel the guilt. How did I get things not just so wrong, but believe I was so right when doing them? The guilt led to doubt and the doubt led me to look for problems rather than to continue believing I had all the solutions. Two incidents reinforced these doubts. First, a photographer came to take publicity photos for a new school website. When going through the hundreds of photographs taken of our students in PE, not one child was smiling. Second, I tried to search for problems within our department's teaching but could not find them whilst I was teaching. This led me to ask an administrator for time to observe other teachers. I saw constant lines, laps and lectures. By having the time and space to step back from the action I was better able to find potential problems. A series of photographs and the space to step away from the act of teaching, all in a short period, made me realise that I had professional development needs, priorities and demands I had been unaware of. Six years later I'm still looking to clarify the problems of my teaching. Developing the craft of my teaching has been a difficult, often isolated, process.

In medieval times a craftsperson went through three stages of developing expertise, supported throughout by a guild. The first stage was an "apprentice", focusing mainly on imitating the practices of other, more experienced, craftspeople. The second stage was a "journeyman", which was defined as a period of experimentation and hybridization of existing practices. The final stage was achieving the status of the "master craftsperson", which was categorized by innovation and transformation of practices. The difficulty is that whilst my initial teacher education (ITE) and the PE departments I have worked in gave good grounding to become an apprentice, they have not been sufficient to move me to the latter two stages. From my experience, the guild (or an extended professional learning community) does not exist within PE. Without a sustained support network to become part of, PE teachers will be destined to stay in the apprentice phase, imitating and repeating the same flawed practices over and over. A guild may help us find the problems of our teaching and either transform our practice to solve them or innovate our practice so the rest of the PE community can benefit and share in the wisdom. If the medieval idea of the guild might be a potential answer to finding and solving the professional development needs, priorities and demands of PE teachers, what would its modern-day equivalent look like?

The introductory narrative was written by Alex, who is a secondary PE teacher and blogger. The thrust of his narrative represents our focus in this chapter. That is, identifying how PE teachers and teacher educators[1] can be better organized to occupy the same space as members of a professional learning community (or what Alex referred to as a "guild"). Put simply, how can the work of teachers and teacher educators become better aligned? While we highlight reasons why a distance remains between teachers and teacher educators and their work, most of the chapter represents an emboldened vision of a professional learning community for PE teachers and teacher educators.

Physical education teachers and teacher educators: together or apart?

Despite PE teachers and teacher educators having similar missions, objectives and tasks (see Chapter 13), and often sharing the same initial preparation and induction (i.e. many teacher educators were teachers), several processes and experiences serve to distinguish each role from the other. Insights into these processes can be offered by field theory (Bourdieu, 1984) and occupational socialization theory (Richards *et al.*, 2014) (see Chapter 7).

Bourdieu (1984) would suggest that teachers and teacher educators pursue their work on different fields, which may explain why they tend to value things differently. Being positioned in different fields contributes to various socializing experiences that may produce specific ideas about who teachers are (their identities) and what they should do, and likewise for teacher educators. These socializing experiences can be conservative in that traditional ideas about the work done in and to fields may be reproduced, or they can be progressive by offering new and alternative approaches. Socialization also carries implications for how teaching texts, such as curriculum documents, are interpreted in the different fields, which may in turn lead to different ideas about what teachers want to, or should, learn as part of their continuing professional development (CPD) (see Chapter 13).

Many teacher educators express good intentions in wanting to work *with* teachers rather than *on* teachers (see Chapter 4). However, institutional pressures, cultures, and expectations contribute to a distancing between the demands and expectations of teachers and work done by teacher educators *with* teachers. This point is emphasized when considering Alex's opening narrative and similar narratives from other teacher educators (e.g. Casey and Fletcher, 2017).

Some analysts would suggest that neoliberal governance, and therefore organizational socialization, in higher education and schools makes new and open types of collaboration especially difficult (Zeichner *et al.*, 2015). This political and economic imperative makes it difficult to conduct academic work that does not have measurable outcomes that can be identified along budgetary lines or contribute directly to a university's status, such as conducting "fundable" research programmes or working directly with fee-paying students. This does not mean that "self-serving" research agendas based on personal preferences and special appeal to large-scale funders are in place solely because of the structures and governance of higher education. It means that meeting teachers' needs requires changes to be made at the personal level (i.e. individual teacher educators) *and* the organizational level if they are to be realized properly, particularly in relation to how CPD is funded. For example, for sustained changes to be made, bridge-building and the injection of ongoing investments in approaches that support teachers teaching each other would be made, and teacher educators' work with teachers would be acknowledged by university administrators as contributing to the teaching profession, to the individual teacher educator's mission, and that of the university.

In order to create an integrated approach to teachers' and teacher educators' work, it is useful to consider the dominant conceptualizations of the processes of teaching. This is presented in Table 11.1, where three main and linear "phases" of teaching are offered. The first phase involves a teacher enrolling, participating in, and completing ITE according to the requirements of the particular teaching and political context. Interaction with teacher educators is represented by an "x".

The induction phase follows completion of formal ITE qualification, typically involving the first five years of a school teaching career. During induction, teachers often cease interacting with teacher educators (note unmarked cells in Table 11.1) and are socialized into the cultures of the school or school district (Richards *et al.*, 2014) (see Chapter 7).

Following induction most teachers are required to engage in some form of CPD (Parker *et al.*, 2017), which will vary depending on the organizational culture of the school. For example, teaching and teacher learning might be isolated (as mentioned by Alex in the opening narrative) or it may take place in a learning community. In collaborative forms of CPD, much of the learning will be informal and involve interactions with colleagues of varying levels of experience and ways of participating themselves.

Significantly, many participants in collaborative CPD may be construed as teacher educators given they are involved in their own lifelong learning as well as that of others. It is these types of teachers we suggest may be appropriately identified as the "master craftsperson" as they seek to transform their own practice and that of others. However, in its current form, "master teacher" status is often determined by career stage or years of teaching experience (Woods *et al.*, 2017) rather than through peer review of teaching practice or engagement in innovative and/or exemplary practices.

The structures and processes of teacher education are not as easily marked by the linear phases representing teaching. Although teacher educators have their own induction and are often involved in their own CPD and that of others, commitment to working with teachers is usually voluntary and piecemeal. There are typically no obligations nor recognitions for teacher educators to commit to teachers' professional learning. Consequently, many teacher educators may never work with teachers beyond ITE. As mentioned, the neoliberal climate in higher education is partially responsible for these conditions.

In the following sections, we provide alternatives to these traditional conceptualizations by proposing a continuum where the processes of teaching and

Table 11.1 A representation of the traditional linear process of teaching

Typical processes of teaching	ITE →	Induction →	CPD →
Typical involvement of teacher educators	x		

teacher education are integrated. We also provide an illustrative example from Håkan's experience working with teachers in Sweden, presenting lessons that may be helpful in considering a path forward.

A continuum for physical education teachers and teacher educators

In proposing a continuum whereby the fields of teaching and teacher education overlap, it should be acknowledged that ongoing teacher and teacher educator learning is contextually situated (Opfer and Pedder, 2011). That is, teacher educators cannot rely on working *on* teachers from a distance. They need to work *with* teachers, both in terms of CPD and research, in the specific contexts of teachers' work (see Chapter 12). Although this collaborative arrangement may seem straightforward, Kennedy (2016) suggests it has not been enacted authentically, suggesting "CPD providers, such as teacher educators expect their words to alter teachers' behaviors inside the classroom" (Kennedy, 2016, 947).

Casey and Larsson (2018) address this need in PE. They argue that research and "expertise" have tended to reside externally to the main functions of the profession. They also suggest that when "expertise" or knowledge generation is internal to the profession (e.g. practitioner research produced by teachers), there may be different impacts in, and for, teaching. One only has to look at engagement with informal practitioner research reported by teachers on Twitter to see the potential impact for the profession.

In proposing a continuum, we adopt a broad conceptualization of teaching and teacher education. Here, becoming and "doing the work of" a PE teacher and/or teacher educator are lifelong processes. This necessitates a revision to Table 11.1 in that teacher educators become involved in all phases of teaching, as represented by the marked cells in the second row of Table 11.2.

The clearly marked boundaries or cells indicate that the identities and practices of those involved in these processes are somewhat fixed in current conceptualizations of teaching and teacher education. For example, in collaborative forms of CPD, many participants can be construed as teacher educators because they are involved in their own lifelong learning and that of others. However, we doubt many will self-identify or be identified by others as teacher educators and, therefore, may not engage with other work in the "field" of teacher education that

Table 11.2 A continuum of the processes of teaching and the ongoing involvement of teacher educators

Typical processes of teaching	ITE (4 yrs) →	Induction (5 yrs) →	CPD →
Proposal for involvement of teacher educators	x	x	x

would be helpful to their practices. A continuum can help blur the boundaries around each field, making identities and practices more fluid and flexible. This shift would also address several calls for a more democratic structure and epistemology of teaching and teacher education (Casey and Larsson, 2018; Zeichner *et al.*, 2015). These calls request that teachers' knowledge is given greater value and privilege alongside that of teacher educators and that teacher educators' work *with* teachers is given greater value in the academy.

Ideas about better integrating PE teaching and teacher education are not especially new. For example, O'Sullivan *et al.* (1999) described a four-year collaborative effort between a university and urban school district in the United States. The outcomes and experiences were generally positive for teachers and their students. While we advocate for this type of approach, O'Sullivan *et al.* (1999) appeared to report a one-way relationship where teacher educators established relationships with and entered school contexts. It was not reported that teachers took on roles as teacher educators in their school district (e.g. as CPD facilitators) or in universities.

More recently, teacher educators at the University of Edinburgh in Scotland realized that the top-down approach to CPD was not working (Jess and McEvilly, 2015). They developed a collaborative initiative consisting of higher education and school-based teacher educators *and* teachers. Participants work together on practitioner research projects based on problems of practice identified by the teachers. Importantly, the school-based teacher educators are regularly involved in the ITE programme. This has led to the development of a large and integrated community of teachers and teacher educators, and resulted in aligned practice-based research agendas that have been collaboratively identified by the teachers and teacher educators involved (Jess *et al.*, 2018) (see Chapters 4 and 12).

In the following section, Håkan provides a narrative of his involvement in a sustainable collaborative relationship between teachers and teacher educators in Sweden.

An illustrative case of sustaining an integrated approach to teaching and teacher education

How we approach this grand challenge is primarily a question about understanding the different contextual, especially cultural (i.e. norms and values) conditions of teachers' and teacher educators' work. Therefore, this is about challenging the idea of teachers and teacher educators working on different fields and identifying new ways of thinking about how teachers and teacher educators can occupy the same space. Important questions to ask are "What are the ongoing needs and demands of teachers?" and "According to whom?" Moreover, there is a need to ask a corresponding question about teacher educators, "What are the needs and demands of teacher educators, if they are to be able to assist teachers in CPD?" While teacher educators often value asking these types of critical questions about teachers and teaching, there is a need to ask them *with teachers*.

From extensive involvement with CPD for teachers, Håkan has come across two kinds of questions teachers tend to ask. First and most common is "What can I do better (i.e. what can I improve) within my work?" The second less common question is precisely what Alex asked in the opening narrative of this chapter, "How can I improve by changing the framework I am working within?"

Since 2011, Håkan has acted as scientific leader of a doctoral programme for PE teachers and asked how teachers' interests intersect with what teacher educators' value. The doctoral programme is part of a government initiative to support school and teacher development. A third cohort is currently being recruited, consisting of PE teachers who will participate in a four-year doctoral programme while teaching in schools part-time. Arguably, such programmes are established on the assumption that science will provide "evidence" for good teaching. However, this particular programme adopted a more modest approach by providing a space where teachers and teacher educators have sustained opportunities to collaborate around mutual interests.

The teachers are expected to choose the focus for their research project in consultations with teacher educators. Meetings between teachers and teacher educators evoke two issues relevant to this chapter, particularly in relation to challenging, and coming to terms with, the institutional gap between the two fields.

The first issue is, "What views about science and research have to be negotiated between teachers and teacher educators?" Both groups share the same educational background in that they have all undergone similar ITE. The teachers have basic scientific training, including a very broad introduction to research in PETE. However, the diversity of scientific perspectives that they were exposed to in ITE is rarely problematized explicitly, which means that tensions between different research areas remain mostly implicit in teachers' thinking.

In contrast, the teacher educators have engaged with prolonged scientific training by focusing on one discipline, typically education, which does not have a dominant position in PETE nor within the academy at large (Larsson *et al.*, 2018). This means that throughout the programme, substantial time and energy is spent discussing what science and research can be. At the outset, ideas about what can be studied (and how) are quite heavily permeated by positivism, advocating a divide between researcher and the research object (teachers, teaching, learning, etc.). This is tantamount to the respective positions of expert (educational researcher or teacher educator) and recipient of expertise (teacher). It takes some deliberation merely to raise awareness among the teachers and teacher educators about these issues, let alone reach some form of agreement. For instance, it tends to be difficult for teacher educators to give up their interpretation preference.

The second issue is, "What norms and values related to teaching and researching (including supervision, seminars, etc.) have to be negotiated between teachers and teacher educators?" Early on, teachers did not respond to the culture of the research groups they were members of in the same way as other doctoral students. Doctoral students not in the teacher cohort often come directly from undergraduate studies, which means they are somewhat accustomed to frank ways of asking critical questions that characterize academia. The teachers have spent five to 40 years in schools, where a very different culture prevails. What the new "regular" doctoral students experience as an open discussion is often experienced by the teachers as criticism. It took quite a while to sort out misunderstandings and potential conflicts related to the different experiences of the research group discussions.

What lessons can be learned from our experiences working in this doctoral programme? And what are the implications for conceptualizing teaching and teacher education on a continuum within a shared occupational space? Besides the general necessity to respect and be interested in the perspectives of the other, it is worthwhile spending time discussing *explicitly* what the assumptions and expectations are about collaboration around graduate studies, research projects, CPD and the like. For Alex, this is an interesting discussion because he acknowledges the doubt he experiences. However, would it be as easy with a teacher who might be more or less convinced that they have "nailed their craft"?

This analysis takes us back to two questions: "What are the ongoing needs and demands of teachers?" And: "According to whom?" For example, is it the teacher educator's job to sow the seeds of doubt among teachers who are convinced they have achieved expert status? We might also ask what could be gained or lost when external observers introduce doubt.

Alternatively, we might ask if the teacher educator should settle instead for cooperating with teachers already in doubt. Teachers and teacher educators would therefore be required to establish relationships that foster a culture of collaboration to deeply probe the problems of practice that are present and arise in the milieu of day-to-day practice, and study those in depth from various theoretical or empirical angles to mutually benefit all participating stakeholders (see Chapter 12). This may also enable teachers' experiences of isolation in CPD to be reduced.

One thing is perhaps clearer. Teachers may be more likely to have their voices heard in this type of arena if, and when, the teacher educators are open to listening to those voices and taking them seriously.

A revisitation of Alex's opening narrative

If PE is to be reimagined for the better, we ought to begin thinking about the teaching community as a guild and the processes of teaching on a continuum. Having teacher educator, teacher, pre-service teacher, and school students working together must be a far better vision for improving practice than the model we appear to have at the moment. The current state of CPD within PE places each role in a silo [see Figure 11.1] with minimal interaction, due to organizational constraints that make teacher educators and teachers serve their own self-interests rather than to support each other's.

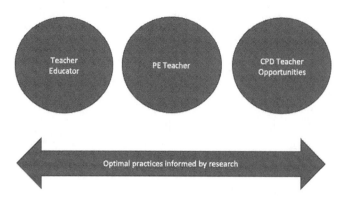

Figure 11.1 Physical education teachers and teacher educators in silos.

In my experience, teachers tend to like someone to blame for their misfortunes. When it comes to our CPD needs, priorities and demands not being met, we point to line managers, senior leaders, teacher educators and CPD providers. I have often heard the following or similar from colleagues: "My ITE did not prepare me for the demands of teaching PE" and "My CPD does not help me get better at teaching because it doesn't relate to my context". I've uttered versions of these myself. To break down the silos [Figure 11.1], PE teachers need to stop blaming others and start thinking how they can take responsibility for addressing and advocating for their CPD needs. For example, while we often say our CPD could be better, how often do we ask how we could contribute to making it better?

CPD providers also need to start offering support that is relevant to the needs and the demands of the teachers. Teacher educators need to think how they might position themselves so as not to appear as the problem solvers. Everyone in the guild must ask how they can support each other, otherwise the silos will remain.

Figure 11.2 presents one option for how we might do this by facilitating how teachers, CPD providers and teacher educators could work together. The arrows denote that the processes of teaching and teacher education are recurrent, integrated and ongoing, with members of the guild or learning community engaged in all processes collaboratively.

If we want to move PE forward, teachers must initially break the silos to create a guild for everyone in the profession, no matter where they are on the continuum. If we say our ITE did not prepare us well for teaching, then we need to work with teacher educators to help better prepare pre-service teachers and/or acknowledge that ITE cannot adequately prepare teachers for all their needs. Instead, ITE may better serve as an induction to the guild. Of course, this must also work the other way around, with teacher educators and CPD providers supporting teachers' needs and helping them identify

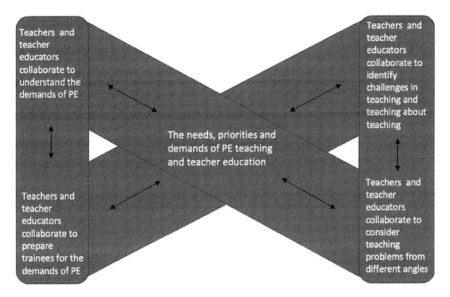

Figure 11.2 Representation of how members of the guild might work together.

problems they are facing, working collaboratively towards solutions that benefit the whole guild, not just certain groups within it. They must also be willing to welcome teachers into ITE, so they may contribute their own knowledge and expertise, and feel it is valued.

If we are reimagining PE, then we also need to reimagine the teacher's role. Teachers need to be at the centre of driving PE forward, but that will only come with the aforementioned shifts in mindset and a lot of time. Without these things it may well remain that PE teachers will continue to be myopic, looking only to their PE department as their guild, resulting in imitation and trying to fit in. In other words, we will not move far beyond the stage of apprenticeship.

If any "group" does not shift and take the time to think and act differently, we will continue to work in silos and the reimagining of PE will just be wishful thinking that will never come to pass. There is a saying in Africa, "If you want to go fast, go alone. If you want to go far, go together".

Conclusion

In this chapter, we have tried to both acknowledge and craft an agenda for pursuing work and experiences that are relevant and engaging for teachers and teacher educators in school PE. Examples from Scotland (Jess and McEvilly, 2015) and Sweden (Håkan's case) provide illustrations of the processes and potential outcomes of such an approach. With that said, we acknowledge that the link between stakeholders across the continuum has, to this point, been neglected to the extent that there is little in the way of a "chain of evidence" (Cochran-Smith, 2005) to support any impact that the integration of PE teaching and teacher education has on students' learning. In the current neoliberal era, providing such evidence will be crucial to convince administrators to support new, integrative agendas for teachers' and teacher educators' work. As such, specific projects that seek to identify connections between approaches to CPD and student learning are imperative.

We believe that our proposal may help to generate chains of evidence to enable more direct links be made between the experiences of students, the ongoing needs of teachers across the continuum, and the types of activities in which teacher educators are involved. Central to all of this is a shared appreciation of the importance of providing practice-based evidence on what works effectively in PE and PETE, and subsequently, what CPD challenges arise if we are to achieve desirable outcomes for PE teachers, PETE and the PE profession collectively.

Epilogue

In writing this chapter, each of us brought different perspectives and experiences based on our location on the teacher education continuum and what we believe to be important in our work and, ultimately, the experiences of students in PE. The writing process was both challenging and stimulating, and fostered discussion, debate, empathy, and respect for what we do individually and collectively for the PE profession.

Despite being positioned in different fields and in different countries, and without having worked together in such a capacity before, the collaborative process has facilitated some general points of agreement regardless of our own personal contexts and preferences, and led to growth in how we value each other's perspectives. This type of thinking and/or writing process involving collaboration from stakeholders on different locations on the continuum has short- and long-term value. For example, our particular collaboration may likely lead to other collaborative ventures not only across fields but in ways that allow fields to merge or, as we suggest in the chapter, for us to work along the continuum.

Note

1 We use the term "teacher educator" to refer to people who mostly work in PE in higher education.

References

Bourdieu, P. (1984). *Distinction: A Social Critique of the Judgment of Taste* (R. Nice, Trans.). Abingdon, UK: Routledge.

Casey, A. and Fletcher, T. (2017). Paying the piper: the costs and consequences of academic advancement. *Sport, Education and Society*, 22(1), 105–121.

Casey, A. and Larsson, H. (2018). "It's Groundhog Day": Foucault's governmentality and crisis discourses in physical education. *Quest*, 70(4), 438–455.

Cochran-Smith, M. (2005). Studying teacher education: what we know and need to know. *Journal of Teacher Education*, 56(4), 301–307.

Jess. M. and McEvilly, N. (2015). Traditional and contemporary approaches to career-long professional learning: a primary physical education journey in Scotland. *Education 3–13*, 43(3), 225–237.

Jess, M., Atencio, M. and Carse, N. (2018). Integrating complexity thinking with teacher education practices: a collective yet unpredictable endeavour in physical education? *Sport, Education and Society*, 23(5), 435–448.

Kennedy, M.M. (2016). How does professional development improve teaching? *Review of Educational Research*, 86(4), 945–980.

Larsson, L., Linnér, S. and Schenker, K. (2018). The doxa of physical education teacher education–set in stone? *European Physical Education Review*, 24(1), 114–130.

Opfer, V.D. and Pedder, D. (2011). Conceptualizing teacher professional learning. *Review of Educational Research*, 81(3), 376–407.

O'Sullivan, M., Tannehill, D., Knop, N., Pope, C. and Henninger, M. (1999). A school-university collaborative journey toward relevance and meaning in an urban high school physical education program. *Quest*, 51(3), 225–243.

Parker, M., Patton, K. and Tannehill, D. (2017). Professional development experiences and organizational socialization. In K.A.R. Richards and K.L. Gaudreault (eds), *Teacher Socialization in Physical Education: New Perspectives*. Abingdon, UK: Routledge, pp. 98–113.

Richards, K.A.R., Templin, T.J., and Graber, K. (2014). The socialization of teachers in physical education: Review and recommendations for future works. *Kinesiology Review*, 3(2), 113–134.

Woods, A.M., Gentry, C. and Graber, K.C. (2017). Research on physical education teachers' career stages and socialization. In K.A.R. Richards and K.L. Gaudreault (eds), *Teacher Socialization in Physical Education: New Perspectives*. Abingdon, UK: Routledge, pp. 81–97.

Zeichner, K., Payne, K.A. and Brayko, K. (2015). Democratizing teacher education. *Journal of Teacher Education*, 66(2), 122–135.

Chapter 12

The evidence-based decision-making challenge

Developing research-supported, data-informed, structures and strategies in schools and teacher education programmes

Peter Hastie and Andy Vasily

In his paper "Closing the gap ... between the university and schoolhouse", Jack Schneider (2014) notes that the parties involved in education have, across time, been endowed with a separate set of professional powers and responsibilities. Teachers, in the main part, have won command of the instructional core without ever gaining jurisdiction over scholarship or policy. Equally, policymakers have become well-positioned to interpret scholarship and issue general directives, but have failed to secure real control over classroom teaching. Finally, due to expectation of a continuous climbing of the status ladder, academics have increasingly detached themselves completely from K-12 classrooms. The result of all this is an environment highly inhospitable for moving scholarship into classrooms.

The purpose of this chapter is to outline ways in which teachers, teacher educators, and pre-service teachers (PSTs), can participate in experiences that might serve to defy this doomsday scenario. To that end, this chapter has two main parts. In the first part, we present our understanding of evidence-based decision-making and practice, and postulate why this process is rarely witnessed within physical education (PE) practice in schools and in teacher education programmes. In the second part, we describe experiences that need to be introduced during teacher preparation that will allow PSTs to develop the skills and dispositions needed to conduct research-supported, data-informed practice. In this second part, we focus on sport pedagogy researchers, university faculty and PE curriculum policymakers, and their important contributions in removing barriers and providing ideas that are perceived as significant, are philosophically compatible with teachers, and are realistic.

It is important to first provide a common language for the various concepts presented in the title of this chapter. According to the USA's Centers for Disease Control and Prevention, *evidence-based decision-making* "is a process for making decisions about a program, practice, or policy that is grounded in the best available research evidence and informed by experiential evidence from the field and relevant contextual evidence" (CDC, n.d., p. 1). The intent of this process is perhaps best presented by Jim Hmurovich, President and CEO of Prevent Child Abuse America, when he states,

> when somebody on staff asks what we should do to address a problem, the first questions I now ask are "What does the research say? What is the evidence base? What information can we gather to determine if it will fit in different contexts?" It's become a way of life.
>
> (CDC, n.d., p. 1)

The CDC framework recognizes that contributions from researchers *and* practitioners provide a more comprehensive view of evidence that is appropriate and necessary for decision-making. By consequence, in terms of *data informed*, we are suggesting that in addition to the research evidence being informed by data, we would expect that the practice of teachers as they work with students is informed by data from those particular students. The reason for this is that we understand that research in one particular context may not necessarily translate fully to a different setting.

Elements of the grand challenge

Figure 12.1 presents a model of how we conceptualize this "evidence-based decision-making" grand challenge as it relates to teaching PE. In examining the figure, it is important to note that while the teacher is central to the challenge process, the extent to which problems can be addressed are often constrained by certain structural determinants (particularly those relating to curriculum). In today's accountability-rich policy and practice environments, these curriculum structures are consequential. Nonetheless, although the language employed is variable and imprecise, policies in support of both programmes and implementation-oriented practices emphasize data, evidence and research.

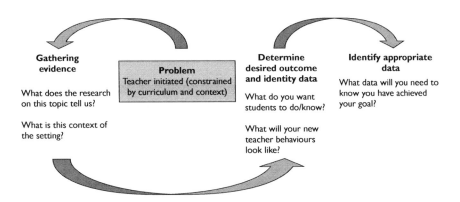

Figure 12.1 Conceptualizing the "evidence-based decision-making" grand challenge.

At the centre of the challenge lies the teacher, and the teacher is central in this model. The notion of teacher *dispositions* is critical here. Indeed, *if* a teacher does not see a need for, or see the value in, changing some aspect of their practice, then none of the other elements of the model apply. Teachers who do not have the temperament in which they consistently ask how they may improve their practice, or how more importantly they may have a positive impact on students' learning and achievement, are unlikely to spend the time necessary fulfilling the other elements in the model. Examples of these elements include reading research and creating assessments that provide the necessary data that inform adjustments to their teaching, or that serve to confirm that their interventions are being effective.

A number of authors (e.g. Evans, 2017; Kirk, 2010) suggest, unfortunately, that many in the PE profession have failed to adopt such a reflexive approach to their practice. One overall result is a PE community that is notoriously resistant to change (Kirk, 2010).

Assuming, however, that a teacher *has* identified an aspect of their professional work that they wish to either accommodate, change, or strengthen, the next step in the model is for them to gather evidence from the best available research, as well as to collect contextual information about factors important for the decision. Based on their interpretation of the evidence gained from this reading/study, the next step requires the teacher to identify a desired outcome that they believe is realistically achievable with their students. At this point, the teacher will ascertain what data would be necessary to make a decision as to whether the desired outcome has been achieved or not.

Where do teachers get their evidence?

In the perfect educational world, teachers and policymakers would make well-informed decisions by putting the best available evidence from research at the heart of policy development and implementation. Indeed, if this were the case, this entire chapter would be rendered moot. More likely, however, is that teachers rely on opinion-based evidence, which is heavily dependent on the untested views of individuals or groups, often inspired by ideological standpoints, prejudices, or speculative conjecture. Nonetheless, it should be pointed out that the research on this assertion is essentially invisible, and as equally anecdotal as the claim that teachers do not read educational research.

Fleer (2001) found that the preferred resources of early childhood teachers included in-service programmes, professional conferences, and curriculum materials. Journals and books were a fourth resource area, but the preference was for "curricula and practical teaching books." Research was nominated by only a small number of respondents. As Harrison *et al.* (2006, p. 218) comment,

> these data confirm the concern of many early childhood teacher educators
> that PSTs eschew research in favor of practical materials when seeking means

to improve teaching practice or to solve particular challenges, and that students prefer more practical activities in their coursework – something they can use in the classroom – rather than more theory, analysis, or research.

Why do teachers not consider research evidence as an option?

Given this limited support for the lack of research as the first port of call for solving educational challenges, we suggest that there are a number of factors that contribute to this mindset. These can be collected into three main categories: institutional barriers, the difficulty of reading research, and lack of incentives to change.

Institutional barriers

At a macro level, it would seem that institutions who prepare teachers have a reluctance to allocate time in their programmes for their teacher candidates to learn about research, and to seriously address issues regarding research-based or evidence-based practice in teaching (Hunter, 2017; Munthe and Rogne, 2015).

At a more micro level, while the focus of her study was on reading instruction, Moats (2014) has noted that many scientifically grounded concepts are not taught in the majority of teacher preparation institutions. Indeed, Moats suggests that of the many reasons why coursework for teachers has remained impervious to scientific evidence, one is the gulf between science and the educational philosophies held by many faculty members. A clear example in physical education teacher education (PETE) would be the continued insistence on the promulgation of short units relying on direct instruction as the most appropriate way to conduct a PE programme. This practice continues despite the clear evidence that models-based practice in PE can achieve many of the aims and objectives of multiple national curricula (Casey and Goodyear, 2015; Harvey and Jarrett, 2014; Hastie *et al.*, 2011).

The difficulty of reading research

Across a number of studies that have attempted to engage teachers in the research process (and as such have involved teachers in reading research), one consistent finding is that "research papers are hard to read". Further, due to "impenetrable language" and "badly written papers" (Gorard *et al.*, 2014), many teachers who are originally described as excited and keen to use research are left misunderstanding and misinterpreting much of the evidence present in the papers. A second feature identified as frustrating for teachers is a lack of examples or resources that they could use in their instruction, "These could be as simple as clarification of technical terms with several examples, or as in-depth as videos of successful implementations of the intervention being used for training" (MacLellan, 2016).

Lack of incentives to change

Moats (2014) suggests that teachers are rarely provided any incentives to change their practice, and further, citing Brady *et al.* (2009), notes that most experienced teachers tend to be the most sceptical of professional development projects and are the most inclined to reject information if it challenges their prior beliefs. Within PE, Casey (2014) provides critical insight into how this barrier can be overcome. Casey noted that despite the difficult undertaking of adopting models-based practice, "the biggest factor in engendering change was the sustained support offered through collaborative partnerships between schools and universities. These supportive relationships allowed the teachers to continually reconsider their practice with the help of experienced colleagues" (Casey, 2014, p. 18).

Configuring PETE to be responsive and "fit for purpose" in developing evidence-based practitioners

In this section, we outline a number of strategies and activities that can be incorporated within teacher education programmes that are aimed at building the self-efficacy of PSTs towards conducting evidence-based inquiry in their teaching and, hopefully, strengthening their dispositions to engage in such practices post-graduation.

It should be noted that we are not starting from scratch here, which would be to suggest that there are no models currently in place, and that there is no evidence of research conducted in PETE programmes. In fact, the educational literature has many examples of the use of action research projects serving as a capstone experience for PSTs (Gibbs *et al.*, 2017). In essence, PSTs are asked to identify with their cooperating teacher some area of concern or challenge related to their teaching. From there, they source a number of papers that might inform a course of action which is then carried out and reflected upon. Finally, the students present their work to their peers and university faculty and, in some cases (see Kinchin, 2012), this results in published work.

Limitations of action research projects

We question if a "one shot" experience is sufficient in building research capacity, or becomes more a task that involves a series of hoops to jump through in order to achieve final certification. In fact, Volk (2010) found that the likelihood of graduates utilizing or applying action research once they become teachers was "less than convincing" (Volk, 2010, p. 315). Volk's rationale was that many teachers associate action research with the sophisticated project and formal paper (similar to what was required in their undergraduate programme). While this reasoning is certainly legitimate, we are suggesting that a lack of experience, mastery, and self-efficacy with the building blocks of evidence-based inquiry are perhaps better predictors of this abandonment.

The need for a scaffolded sequence of experiences

It is our belief that PSTs need *multiple* and *progressive* experiences in the various elements of evidence-based practice if they are truly going to embrace this facet of their future professional work. This section outlines a series of strategies that relate to our first model (Figure 12.1), and is strongly grounded in the notion of scaffolding. In this way, PSTs can experience repeated and increasingly sophisticated ways to learn how to eventually become independent evidence-based practitioners. Our opinion of the importance of scaffolded experiences is highlighted from our reading of the research on action-research based, capstone projects. Few, if any of these projects, contained information that informs us as to the background skills necessary for the students to be able to successfully complete these tasks, the struggles they experienced, and how they selected their issues and created their plans.

Van de Pol *et al.*'s (2010) description of scaffolding is particularly relevant here. First, students need a variety of instructional techniques to help them move progressively toward stronger understanding and, ultimately, greater independence in the learning process. Second, PETE faculty need to provide temporary levels of support that help students reach higher levels of comprehension and skill acquisition that they would not be able to achieve without assistance. Finally, these supportive strategies are incrementally removed when they are no longer needed, and the teacher gradually shifts more responsibility over the learning process to the student.

Strategy 1: helping students to ask research questions that require data and necessitate evidence-based decision-making

If we want our PSTs, and by association our future teachers, to conduct mini projects that are evidence based, we need to help them find an entry point, which is typically that point in which they identify the problem (see Figure 12.1). In this section of the chapter, however, we will change that starting point to one of "asking good questions" as, ultimately, such questions come as a result of an issue or a situation. Figure 12.2 provides a graphic of the three experiences we consider to be necessary for PSTs to adopt an inquisitive disposition.

Our recommendation is that at the very beginning of a PETE programme, this questioning comes in the form of observation led by PETE faculty. Unlike those of us who have experienced early-level PST research, they do not have a repertoire of experience at that point to essentially identify situations, particularly those that are problematic to their own teaching. Guided observation provides PSTs with examples of questions which we, in professional preparation, propose

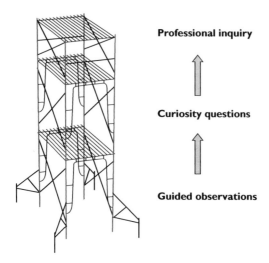

Figure 12.2 Scaffolding the process of "asking good questions".

are important to consider. Crafted well, such questions can help PSTs appreciate the value of asking questions. An example of one such observation appears below:

> Observe a student in a class taught by a teacher in your school (or by a classmate) who seems to be having little success. To what extent (if any) did the teacher address this student's needs (with either feedback or task modification)? How did the students respond after any teacher interaction?

In the second stage, we are ready for PSTs to begin creating their own questions. At this second stage however, rather than present the task to PSTs in terms of "identifying an issue", we reframe this more as a "curiosity". We believe that terms such as "issues" or "challenges" present a sense of "deficit". If we present PSTs with the question, "What are you most curious about at this point of your teaching training?" we have a greater potential to pique their curiosity about their teaching. We also believe it is this notion of curiosity that encourages them to consider a researcher lens, as the next step is to formulate that curiosity as a question. We have also found that allowing PSTs to examine aspects of their teaching/learning that they are curious about presents a less threatening frame of reference, and allows them to detach emotionally from it. This, in turn, only serves to help them to become more curious about it.

It is only after experiences with guided observation and developing curiosity-based questions that we can move PSTs into professional inquiry. It is important, however, that PETE faculty steer these PSTs towards inquiries that have something directly related to the school students who are in front of them each day. The rationale for this is that in the case of practising teachers, there are some who do not wish to be challenged about their teaching. These are teachers who want their professional inquiry to be more of an interest rather than an identified area in need of focus in regards to their teaching practice. As an example, Andy, the second author of this chapter, has experienced one teacher who wanted to have his professional inquiry focus on social and emotional learning and its value throughout his school. In Andy's words,

> He appeared as if he was trying to steer clear of his own pedagogical practice and look at the bigger picture of the school and the school culture. This is indeed a noble act in itself but it's not going to make him more effective for the students he dealt with each day.

It is important at this point, however, that in his role as pedagogical coach (or the PETE faculty or cooperating teacher), Andy was able to take this teacher's interest in social emotional learning and move that into the classroom and examine what he was doing on a daily basis. In fact, the evidence of that teacher's own use of language contrasted with respect to the things he valued. That is, there was disconnect between the goals and the way he spoke to students.

Strategy 2: helping students to source evidence

The second stage of the model presented in Figure 12.3 deals with pre-service and practising teachers assessing information from three sources (published research, data from experts and examination of context), to gather information about how they might best go about answering their research question. Similar to Strategy 1, we consider that three sets of experiences are important in developing a teacher's mindset that empirical evidence is indeed a resource that provides added value over the more easily accessible anecdotal suggestions. These are presented in Figure 12.3.

We believe that it is during a PST's earliest dealings with pedagogical subject matter that links between theory/research and practice are made explicit. This then allows those links to be placed in the foreground of discussions. Further, specific examples of how the research informs pedagogical practice should be presented to PSTs early in their teacher education experience.

The most obvious place for this introduction to pedagogy research is the text-books read by PSTs as they learn to become teachers. Capel and Whitehead (2015) provide wonderful examples of the interweaving of theory/research data with tasks that PSTs can conduct in schools. Indeed, the text contains over 150 such tasks that are designed to help novice teachers identify the key features of a particular research finding within the reality of the classes they teach. This model of deliberately foregrounding the academic work, in published work in sport pedagogy, to inform appropriate teacher practice is a strategy that more authors of texts might wish to consider.

The second stage in learning to become research literate is for university faculty to provide summaries of research that outline or list the key points of an article. As Andy has noted from his experience, a lot of teachers do not want to

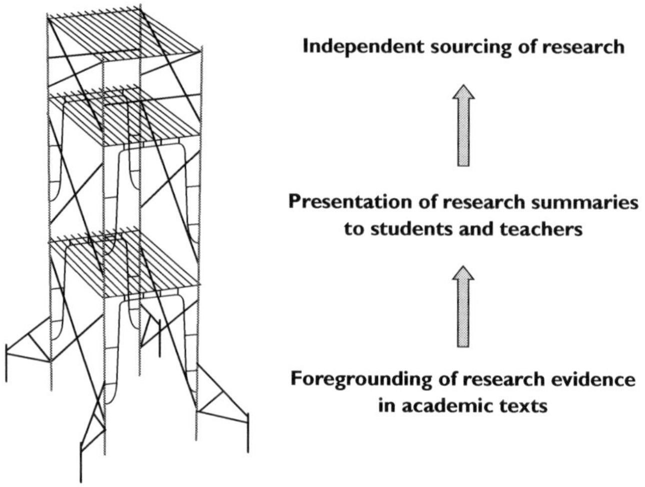

Independent sourcing of research

Presentation of research summaries
to students and teachers

Foregrounding of research evidence
in academic texts

Figure 12.3 Scaffolding the process of "valuing empirical evidence".

do the heavy cognitive lifting when it comes to reading research. Lessening that load has the potential to change the dispositions of early career teachers towards seeing research and theory as an asset.

Perhaps the best model for presenting these research summaries has been the UnLock Research website developed by Professor Lawrence F. Locke, a leader in US sport pedagogy. Locke's goal was to connect teachers with the various aspects of doing, reading, understanding, and interpreting research. Fortunately, Shape America has renewed the original website in the form of monthly translated research articles, each of which is organized around three headings: (i) research summary, (ii) conclusion, and (iii) key takeaway. (www.shapeamerica.org/MemberPortal/prodev/research/UnLocking_Research.aspx).

Once PSTs are in a position where the PETE programme has developed an ethos in which instructional strategies and curriculum issues are seen to be grounded in research evidence, they should be allowed the opportunity to read, interpret and summarize papers so they can indeed begin to do some of this heavy cognitive lifting. These readings should be specifically guided by the fundamental question of, "What message or findings from this research can I translate into my own teaching (in my own context, with my own students)?". It is only then, in the final stages of a culture of reading and enacting research, and being able to do preliminary interpretations of research, that we should be asking PSTs to source papers independently of the university faculty.

Indeed, the intention of the text *Research and Practice in Physical Education* (Tannehill *et al.*, 2013), is to share, report and discuss research in ways that clarify the implications and applications for practice. The text assists those interested in quality PE and physical activity programmes in reading and understanding research in order to apply it to their own practice and subsequently contribute to their continuing professional development. The format of the text provides the reader with short summaries of research papers clustered under themes. The editors' then share insights on research and their discussions on what each research paper conveyed to them, the implications they drew from each study for their own teaching practice and how the reader might read and interpret research to meet their own needs and those of their students. The editors provide the lens of reading research as a primary/ elementary teacher, post-primary PE teacher, a teacher educator and a researcher.

Stage 3: identifying data that reflect impact

If our central interest is on the impact of our teaching on *student learning*, then we need to put that at the centre of our evidence-based inquiries. In Figure 12.4 we suggest there are three sets of experiences that provide students with the skills and self-efficacy that will allow them to comfortably and confidently collect data on their own teaching and, more so, to examine those data to assess the impact of their planned intervention.

In the first instance, PSTs need practice at collecting prescribed data that inform teaching practice before we ask them to identify what data might be relevant. One example is provided from the Capel and Whitehead (2015) text.

> Arrange for a lesson you teach to be video- and audio-recorded. After the lesson watch the recording and identify if and how you use autonomy-supportive behavior (e.g. pupil choices) and controlling behavior (teacher commands and rewards). Discuss the data collected with another student teacher and consider how you might increase your use of autonomy-supportive behavior in your lessons.
>
> (Capel and Whitehead, 2015, p. 111)

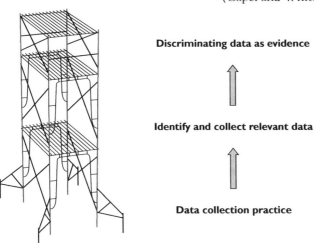

Figure 12.4 Scaffolding the data collection process.

Experiences such as these give PSTs a vocabulary of the various forms of data they might choose to use when conducting an evidence-based inquiry. They also help PSTs develop a familiarity with the whole concept of "data as evidence". It is useful and important for these PSTs to begin to operationally define what they understand as data, evidence (as determined by teachers in contexts), and research-based evidence. It is only then that, as teachers, they can make sense of data, and thereby decide if data-as-information qualifies as evidence. It is important to go through this exercise as it is this evidence that allows us to get to the point where teachers can have conversations.

In fact, it is often considered that these conversations are the most important elements in professional inquiries. As a case in point, Peters (2004) found that while teachers do not find reflective *writing* as a particularly valuable activity during their professional inquiries (i.e. they did not want to "formalise" their reflection in writing), they were certainly keen to reflect through *collegial dialogue*.

Conclusion

On reading the suggested set of learning experiences for PSTs described in this chapter, one's initial reaction may well be that, given the time constraints present in PETE programmes, such an endeavour is unrealistic. However, we would encourage readers that, on closer inspection, the intent is to add experiences within already existing courses that serve to *foreground* evidence-based inquiry and to give PSTs opportunities to *practice* the skills necessary to develop a level of self-efficacy with respect to "doing research". If we are to be true to our knowledge of skill development and self-confidence (which are the best predictors of future behaviours), then we need to give PSTs ongoing and repeated experiences with respect to creating research questions and developing the tools to answer these questions. We are aware of the role of practice in the development of competence and, more importantly, we are well aware of the need to structure that practice so that it is presented at appropriate levels of challenge, to be motivating and engaging, and to be supported by quality feedback.

We finish this chapter with five takeaway points that we believe encapsulate the factors that, if enacted during PETE and supported with teachers as they attempt to conduct evidence-based teaching, will allow for the grand challenge to be achieved. In order, these are:

1   "Doing" is critical – we must allow PSTs and teachers in schools opportunities to "do" inquiries with appropriate levels of support.
2   Doing should be based upon curiosity – as the notion of curiosity removes the deficit mentality concerning change.
3   Exposure and practice should be precursors to critique – critical reflection should not be the starting point (or the focus of one-shot experiences).
4   PETE should also examine its own evidence base – in order to provide a more comprehensive account of evidence to PSTs as they learn to teach.

5 PETE faculty should also adopt the culture of evidence-based practice – in order to be quality role models for those who they teach.

References

Brady, S., Gillis, M., Smith, T., Lavalette, M., Liss-Bronstein, L., Lowe, E. and Wilder, T.D. (2009). First grade teachers' knowledge of phonological awareness and code concepts: examining gains from an intensive form of professional development and corresponding teacher attitudes. *Reading and Writing: An Interdisciplinary Journal*, 22(4), 425–455.

Capel, S. and Whitehead, M. (2015). *Learning to Teach Physical Education in the Secondary School: A Companion to School Experience*. London: Routledge.

Casey, A. (2014). Models-based practice: great white hope or white elephant? *Physical Education and Sport Pedagogy*, 19(1), 18–34.

Casey, A. and Goodyear, V.A. (2015). Can cooperative learning achieve the four learning outcomes of physical education? A review of literature. *Quest*, 67(1), 56–72.

CDC (n.d.). Understanding evidence: evidence based decision-making summary. Available at: https://vetoviolencecdcgov/apps/evidence/docs/EBDM_82412pdf

Evans, J. (2017). *Equality Education and Physical Education*. London: Routledge.

Fleer, M. (2001). *An Early Childhood Research Agenda: Voices From the Field*. Canberra ACT: Department of Education Training and Youth Affairs Commonwealth of Australia.

Gibbs, P., Cartney, P., Wilkinson, K., Parkinson, J., Cunningham, S., James-Reynolds, C. and MacDonald, A. (2017). Literature review on the use of action research in higher education. *Educational Action Research*, 25(1), 3–22.

Gorard, S., See, B.H. and Siddiqui, N. (2014). Anglican schools partnership: effective feedback education endowment foundation. Available at: https://fileseericedgov/fulltext/ED581096pdf

Harrison, L.J., Dunn, M. and Coombe, K. (2006). Making research relevant in preservice early childhood teacher education. *Journal of Early Childhood Teacher Education*, 27(3), 217–229.

Harvey, S. and Jarrett, K. (2014). A review of the game-centred approaches to teaching and coaching literature since 2006. *Physical Education and Sport Pedagogy*, 19(3), 278–300.

Hastie, P.A., Martinez de Ojeda, D. and Calderón, A. (2011). A review of research on Sport Education: 2004 to the present. *Physical Education and Sport Pedagogy*, 16(2), 103–132.

Hunter, W.J. (2017) Evidence-based teaching in the 21st century: the missing link. *Canadian Journal of Education*, 40(2), 1–7.

Kinchin, G. (2012). Learning sport education through reflective inquiry: four case studies. In P. Hastie (ed.), *Sport Education: International Perspectives*. London: Routledge, pp. 166–176.

Kirk, D. (2010). *Physical Education Futures*. Abingdon, Oxon: Routledge.

MacLellan, P. (2016). Why don't teachers use education research in teaching. Available at: https://eic.rsc.org/analysis/why-dont-teachers-use-education-research-in-teaching/2010170. article

Moats, L. (2014). What teachers don't know and why they aren't learning it: addressing the need for content and pedagogy in teacher education. *Australian Journal of Learning Difficulties*, 19(2), 75–91.

Munthe, E. and Rogne, M. (2015). Research based teacher education. *Teaching and Teacher Education*, 46(1), 17–24.

Peters, J. (2004). Teachers engaging in action research: challenging some assumptions. *Educational Action Research*, 12(4), 535–556.

Schneider, J. (2014). Closing the gap between the university and schoolhouse. *Phi Delta Kappan*, 96(1), 30–35.

Tannehill, D., MacPhail, A., Halbert, G. and Murphy, F. (2013). *Research and Practice in Physical Education*. London: Routledge.

Van de Pol, J., Volman, M. and Beishuizen, J. (2010). Scaffolding in teacher-student interaction: a decade of research. *Educational Psychology Review*, 22(3), 271–296.

Volk, K.S. (2010). Action research as a sustainable endeavor for teachers: does initial training lead to further action? *Action Research*, 8(3), 315–332.

Chapter 13

The professional development challenge

Achieving desirable outcomes for students, teachers and teacher educators

Hal A. Lawson, David Kirk and Ann MacPhail

The challenges and opportunities accompanying teaching and learning with children and youths have been the primary priority worldwide, and justifiably so. Unfortunately, three companion priorities have not received sufficient attention: (1) desirable outcomes at scale for physical education (PE) teachers; (2) outcomes for their teacher educators (PETE); and (3) outcomes for doctoral programme faculty members who prepare teacher educators and provide research leadership. These three groups are related. What school-age students experience in the name of PE is influenced by their teachers. What PE teachers prioritize and do is influenced by PETE faculty. And what PETE faculty prioritize can be traced in part to their respective doctoral programmes (including mentoring and networking with student peers) and concurrent experiences (e.g. conference attendance, publication activities).

These relationships implicate an influential, mostly-invisible system with several components (Lawson, 2019). Systems theory offers three principles: (1) every component in a system influences and is influenced by one or more of the others; (2) every systems improvement depends fundamentally on adult learning; and (3) oftentimes unintended consequences stem from purposive social actions (Merton, 1938).

The first principle recommends against piecemeal improvement plans. The second raises profound issues regarding the profession's readiness, capacity, resources, and mechanisms for continuous professional development (CPD). These issues merit special attention and dedicated resources in fast-changing educational policy contexts and political environments, especially as it becomes clear that inherited PE and PETE programmes and practices are not fit for purpose in a fast-changing world (Kirk, 2019; Lawson, 2018; MacPhail, 2017).

For example, new school designs with unique programmes are increasing. Some offer opportunities to develop new curricula for physical literacy (Whitehead, 2010) or its companion, critical movement literacy (Standal, 2015). Other priorities include health literacy (McCuaig *et al.*, 2014), mental health literacy (Tully *et al.*, 2019), and a newcomer called trauma literacy (Lawson *et al.*, 2019). These innovative concepts necessitate widespread CPD, and the same need accompanies implementation demands associated with specialized PE curricular models (Kirk, 2010).

How will PE teachers and teacher educators learn and improve, individually and together? What are the incentives and disincentives? What are the most important learning priorities? Who will provide solid CPD opportunities and experiences? What can be done with, and for, teachers and teacher educators who have excused themselves from responsibilities for CPD? What implications and imperatives apply to doctoral programmes? What roles and responsibilities belong to the professional associations, professional development providers, the school systems and higher education institutions that provide employment for PE teachers and teacher educators?

These questions are consequential for the future of the profession, extending to the school-related opportunities for children and youth. In the remainder of this chapter, we selectively address these questions' meaning and significance, concluding with innovative strategies to achieve the potential of PE programmes, PETE programmes, and their connections. We begin with the vested interests of PE teachers, teacher educators, and leaders of professional associations because their futures depend on coordinated strategies for meeting the professional development challenge (see Chapter 11).

Safeguarding a professional monopoly as challenges mount

School PE programmes and companion PETE programmes are fixtures in national, state, and provincial education systems. Teachers and teacher educators enjoy an occupational monopoly in some of these places, i.e. they enjoy exclusive rights to practice in school systems and higher education institutions. This exalted professional status had to be earned by the profession's leaders who successfully organized and mobilized for collective action. Significantly, teachers and teacher educators worked together as they pursued common purposes.

This self-promoting collective action was, and is, hard work, but it is worth the effort because the profession's special status among all competing occupations depends on it. However, there is nothing automatic about these employment monopolies. Competition for the right and privilege to provide PE, by whatever name and in various forms, is on the rise. In some nations, this special status is being eroded by the neoliberal practice of outsourcing (Williams and Macdonald, 2015). For example, in England, many primary school PE programmes now are taught by part-time sports coaches (Griggs, 2010).

Meanwhile, what Kirk (2019) calls the growing "precarity" of children and youths is a worldwide phenomenon. Freely translated, increasing numbers do not come to school ready and able to learn. Multiple causes and correlates are implicated. Teachers and teacher educators must learn about them and explore together the implications for PE and PETE programmes. For example, when members of the PE profession do not rely on CPD to adapt and learn, they open occupational doors for programme competitors, and this problem is exacerbated when teacher educators and teachers work at cross-purposes.

CPD and the normative model for a profession

The professions are a special category of work and occupation. In contrast to occupations that do not require higher education degrees, people-serving professions enjoy comparatively higher prestige, are granted more discretion and autonomy, and receive better monetary and symbolic rewards. Higher education is foundational for the special status of "profession" because it provides three core characteristics (Lawson, 1979).

One is the pledge to service. Nested in this altruistic promise are two ethical imperatives: do no harm and work relentlessly to help the people in your charge achieve the desirable outcomes for which you and your profession are accountable (Lawson, 2018). These ethical imperatives are as salient to PETE faculty as they are to PE teachers.

Second, professions claim that their specialized practice is guided by solid theory and research. This claim is reinforced by the location of teacher education programmes in higher education institutions which provide organizational homes for researchers such as PETE faculty. This dynamic view of practice helps to explain why some scholars claim that scripted routines are the enemy of professionalism. However, there is a difference between assessment-driven, data-informed, and research-based routines which have been demonstrated to be fit for purpose, versus routines chosen and implemented because of convenience, a teacher's personal preferences, and mitigating circumstances.

This difference is a proxy for two types of school PE programmes. One is a loosely-supervised, multi-activity programme, the aim for which can be described as keeping students "busy, happy, and on good behavior" (Placek, 1983).

Third, national professional associations, oftentimes with state/provincial sub-organizations, monitor and provide CPD. Ideally, they work in partnership with higher education providers and governmental providers.

Like a spider's web, national associations are connected to nearly every aspect of the profession. For example, national associations accredit professional education programmes (e.g. teacher education), and some are involved in state/provincial licensure. Leaders in these associations also establish practice standards and engage in policy advocacy. Prominent among these standards are licensure requirements for CPD. These requirements give expression to the profession's claim that its researchers provide theory, research, and optimal practice models that facilitate the achievement of desired educational outcomes. Inside this positive claim is a powerful sanction: the failure to CPD, which enables practitioners to remain abreast of these important developments, means losing the licence to practice.

Does the profession measure up?

Comparisons between the above-described, generic model for the professions and current PE/PETE configurations are timely. It all starts with the following principle: dynamic, high-quality PE programmes, PETE programmes, and PETE doctoral studies programmes fundamentally depend on effective CPD because it serves as a quality assurance mechanism.

Readers are invited to inspect the CPD norms, requirements, and programme provisions emphasized by professional associations in their host nations. Next, consider educational policy requirements for CPD (Knapp, 2003). Are there firm requirements? For what? What are the incentives? What are the rewards? What sanctions are levelled against practitioners who ignore CPD norms and requirements? These questions connect CPD needs, demands, and provisions with educational policy environments, highlighting the extent to which professionals' refusal to engage in CPD is policy-enabled and without employment consequences.

From voluntary professional responsibility to external accountability mechanisms

Teachers of all school subjects are increasingly required to perform in accordance with policy requirements, oftentimes called "educational/professional standards". They are often prescriptive and evaluative. "Accountability" is the watchword. It means "answerability" and raises important questions. To whom are PE professionals answerable? For what educational processes? And for what educational outcomes? These questions signal evaluative rigor, the likes of which marks the end of "rolling out the ball and watching students play", while keeping them "busy, happy, and good" (Placek, 1983).

In other school subjects, these accountability requirements are prescriptive – for example, collect student assessment data, use the data to determine which intervention fits the students' needs, evaluate intervention implementation effectiveness, and repeat the cycle to learn and improve. Direct supervision by a school principal, or a professional development specialist, is a routine event. In this way, teachers are believed to be held accountable for work processes and student results or learning.

It is likely that PE teachers and teacher educators will be held accountable in some of the same ways. If so, it is plausible to predict that some will need to stop and "unlearn" some professional orientations and behaviours, substituting more appropriate ones. For veteran teachers and teacher educators, professional development leave may be needed. Viewed in this way, CPD is a vital lifeline for teachers and teacher educators as imperatives for outcomes-based accountability mount and another threat looms.

Continuing professional development with a self-interested purpose: safeguarding and enhancing the profession's status and employment markets

Every profession runs the risk of maintaining a nearly-exclusive focus on "insider operations and developments" at the expense of external environments and especially rapid and dramatic social changes. Every profession also develops routine practices structured in conformity with inherited programmes.

However, self-promotion and social marketing are essential. Self-promotion and social marketing in service of PE and PETE's occupational monopoly depend on five fixtures (e.g. Lawson, 2018): (1) demonstrable, important student outcomes for which teachers and teacher educators are prepared to be held accountable; (2) a solid, dynamic evidentiary base in support of the profession's claims, primary aims, and both voluntary and externally-imposed accountabilities; (3) PE and PETE curriculum models which lend practical expression to the connections between this knowledge base and desirable outcomes; (4) technically-competent teachers and teacher educators; and (5) partnerships for the simultaneous renewal, improvement and redesign of PE and PETE. These five fixtures also are CPD priorities.

An international perspective

The European Commission's (2012) definition of teacher education captures the notion of a continuum across initial teacher education, induction and CPD. Subsequently, PE teachers and physical education teacher educators need to be working collaboratively towards the shared goal of enhancing the attractiveness and quality of the teaching profession and, in turn, heightening the learning experiences of students. Collaborative relationships between PE and PETE are long overdue (Lawson, 2018). PE and PETE should collectively be involved in informing curriculum change at the school and higher education level, educating each other and advocating collectively for what is determined to result in the most meaningful, relevant and worthwhile PE experience for school students. As such, this will determine the current professional development challenges for PE and PETE if they are to be successful in facilitating such experiences for school students.

In many school systems, physical education teacher educators visit schools to offer advice and feedback to their pre-service teachers during the school placement practicum. This ubiquitous activity offers one concrete point of contact to develop a reciprocal relationship. In Scotland, for example, all reports on pre-service teacher learning must be co-authored by supervising teachers and teacher educators. The act of co-authoring reports, although not without its challenges, requires teachers and teacher educators to develop a shared language for pre-service teacher learning. This required point of contact and shared responsibility offers just one starting point for reciprocal professional learning between pre-service teacher, teacher supervisor, and teacher educator.

Other opportunities present themselves. Short-term (two years) teacher secondment from school to university, with the guarantee that the teacher–teacher educator is returned for a minimum period of two years to the school system, has clear potential for knowledge exchange and reciprocal learning. There would be political and economic challenges to institute such a practice. Nevertheless, as university requirements for scholarly accountability pull physical education teacher educators further and further from practice, the ongoing refreshment of experience from the chalk face could benefit PETE programmes considerably. As seconded teachers return to school, new insights into the professional preparation of teachers are introduced and embedded there. Moreover, such an initiative has potential for professional growth among teachers and teacher educators. Short-term sabbaticals for teacher educators to return to work as PE teachers in schools could further enhance such a scheme.

Variability and context-specificity in PE teachers' professional development.

The variability and context-specificity in PE teachers' professional development is captured in *European Physical Education Teacher Education Practices* (MacPhail *et al.*, 2019). It reports the initial, induction and professional development opportunities for PE teachers across 24 European countries. In the majority of the 24 countries, there is no coherent or systematic structured induction programme for novice PE teachers. This gap raises questions about CPD priorities and delivery systems – for example, how teacher professional learning is a key strategy for improving the quality of teaching practices and the learning of students (Schleicher, 2018). Despite this attention and increased funding to support a change in the focus and delivery of CPD, concerns persist about the quality of provision both in general education and physical education (Patton *et al.*, 2015). Teachers' content knowledge and pedagogical content knowledge are special priorities, and research is available to frame this CPD agenda, including its joint applications to teacher education and school practice (Kim *et al.* 2018).

Alongside practising PE teachers, teacher educators also have manifest professional development needs (MacPhail, 2011; Mitchell and Lawson, 2019). As with teachers, issues remain regarding incentives, rewards, resources, and conducive working conditions (McEvoy *et al.*, 2018). MacPhail *et al.* (2019) report a range of CPD provision across 24 countries, ranging from centralized compulsory CPD courses to decentralized optional opportunities to improve teaching practice and student learning. Differences were apparent in the aims, content, duration, and format of CPD experiences across the different countries as well as the provision of support materials and resources that accompanied those experiences. A range of providers was evident and included independent schools, government agencies, professional organizations, charitable bodies and higher education institutions.

Appreciation for variability and context-specificity in PE teachers' professional development does not dispel a requirement for systematic CPD models. Needs begin with the induction of novice PE teachers and include CPD for experienced teachers. All such CPD must be customized to fit specific jurisdictions, and they must be tailor-made for specialized programme models. Such models can serve to provide exemplars of how to design educative, cost-effective induction and CPD opportunities replicating existing successful elements of CPD, cognizant of contextual adaptations.

Variability and context-specificity in PETE professional development initiatives

Professional learning communities (Hadar and Brody, 2017) are gaining popularity as spaces in which PETE professionals can seek support for their CPD needs (Parker et al., 2012). Professional learning communities comprise groups of teacher educators who meet regularly for the purpose of increasing their own learning and that of their students. This holistic approach is known in some parts of the world as embedded professional development because learning occurs as practice proceeds. It is timely to consider how professional learning communities can embed professional responsibility and commitment to CPD among teacher educators and pre-service teachers (MacPhail et al., 2014).

However, a pivotal question remains. If the multi-activity exposure curriculum reigns supreme, and the aim is busy, happy and good students (Placek, 1983), why would teachers and teacher educators worry about and engage in CPD?

One answer may be through legislation that attaches professional learning to licensure. In Scotland, for example, all teachers are required to complete a Professional Update (PU) every five years to maintain their registration (and licence to teach) with the General Teaching Council of Scotland (GTCS). This requirement also applies to teacher educators. They too must maintain their registration with the GTCS as teacher educators through the PU.

Collaborative professional development for PE and PETE

The collaborative, simultaneous professional development of CPD for teachers and teacher educators, typically facilitated by school–higher education partnerships, is crucial to the work that lies ahead (Lawson, 2018). This configuration requires shared places and spaces that provide pre-service teachers, teachers and teacher educators with opportunities to learn from, and share knowledge with, each other, and to use the knowledge and understanding gained to determine how best to share the responsibility of teaching in service of student learning, both in the school and teacher education.

Such an innovative organizational configuration promises to enhance the quality and relevance of the learning of pre-service teachers alongside teachers and teacher educators. It promises a shared learning community. The premise, supported by teacher socialization research (Richards *et al.*, 2014) is that more effective teacher educators result in producing more effective teachers who in turn deliver meaningful, relevant and worthwhile school PE learning experiences.

Novice teachers are a special priority. Their technical competence rests on content knowledge and pedagogical content knowledge, both of which are manifested in professional skills and teaching competencies (Kim *et al.*, 2018). The best PETE programmes lay a foundation, i.e. they provide beginning competence, but they also ensure that prospective teachers know that their needs for CPD are career-long.

Meanwhile, research focused on best practices in CPD provision is also a practical necessity. While the generic CPD research is informative, PE is a special subject in many respects, and PE teachers inevitably encounter competing demands in variable school contexts. Presently there are more questions than answers. What are the main CPD needs of PE teachers and PETE faculty? What CPD delivery mechanisms are most promising and effective? How might teachers and teacher educators plan and complete CPD collaboratively? And, how might groups of teachers and teacher educators in the same locale develop CPD networks? What roles can professional association play? What educational policy changes are needed? These questions and others they implicate signal a long-overdue, CPD-focused research and development agenda launched by teachers, teacher educators, and leaders of professional associations.

Looking ahead

We have argued that continuing education and professional learning of teachers and teacher educators, alone and together, is of paramount importance for PE to survive and thrive in school systems.

In addition to our profession's moral responsibilities, important issues of professional expertise and practice competence are at stake, particularly as external accountability mandates increase. In principle, a higher education provides teachers and teacher educators with requisite commitments and abilities for research-informed practice and CPD to support it.

This value-added impact continues once practice begins. Teachers and teacher educators are obliged to collect relevant assessment and outcome data and use them as they practice; review and learn from research; and benefit from professional-development-related interactions with their colleagues. These value-effects for professionals translate to added value to the lives of the young people teachers are charged with serving.

These imperatives for what can be called adaptive competence, founded on technical teachers' competencies for teaching and learning, are gaining significance. In a world that appears to be increasingly unstable, uncertain and insecure, the challenge of enhancing the health and wellbeing of all young people increases. Standing still is an undesirable course of action, and so is looking back in time to a different set of conditions, yearning for their return.

Mindful of contextual variability, one-size-fits-all solutions to the question of professional learning of pre-service teachers and the CPD of teachers and teacher educators are inappropriate. Five broad principles offer guidance.

The first principle derives from the specialized branch of economics focused on workforce characteristics and development during periods of rapid technological change. Education's import for "human capital development" (Becker, 1994) is the priority. Human capital economists who study and seek to develop human capital emphasize two temporal components of adaptive competence (Wagner, 2019), and both are relevant to PE and PETE. The short-term component emphasizes the ability to transfer knowledge and skill from one context to another. For example, to what extent is a novice teacher with little or no preparation for a curriculum model such as Teaching Games for Understanding able to learn its components and implement it with fidelity? The long-term component of adaptive competence is founded on the accelerating rate of knowledge production during an era of rapid, dramatic societal and global change. The relevant concept is knowledge obsolescence. How do teachers and teacher educators keep pace with research and practice breakthroughs? More fundamentally, are they prepared to do so and are they committed to this CPD priority?

The second principle is that professional learning for pre-service teachers, teachers and teacher educators must be joined up. It might be argued that pre-service teachers learn from teachers when they engage in practicum activity in schools. This is so, but the potential for this process to work both ways, for pre-service teachers *and* for teachers, is seldom explored. There are opportunities, too, for teachers and teacher educators to collaborate and learn from each other through the practicum. Whatever this principle looks like in practice, we think that the current process, where professional learning is undertaken in silos, is tantamount to standing still.

The third principle is to incentivize teachers and teacher educators to engage in regular professional learning. There are various ways this might be done, from financial incentives to promotional opportunities. The example from Scotland provided earlier is noteworthy because it is legislated.

The fourth principle is to take a more systematic approach to professional induction in the first two years of a novice teacher's career. It is during this period that teachers are most likely to leave as they experience the reality shock of teaching as work (Richards et al., 2014). With developments in digital technology, the university could continue to play a role in partnership with schools, with novice teachers receiving support, and possibly gaining academic credits, towards higher degrees.

The fifth principle draws on systems frameworks when it emphasizes doctoral programmes structured to prepare PETE faculty. Worldwide, these programmes are key drivers for teacher preparation and research on teaching, teacher socialization and PE programmes. Some of the same questions surrounding adaptive competence development for pre-service teachers, novice and experienced teachers, and teacher educators can and should be raised about the design, conduct and outcomes of such programmes (Mitchell and Lawson, 2019).

The time has arrived to join up these principles and put them into practice at a time when, in some jurisdictions, PETE has lost its institutional base. In some cases, this is a result of the field's scientization, academicization, specialization and eventual fragmentation (Kirk, 2010). In some locales, PETE is either marginalized among the kinesiological sciences, or else re-located to departments of teacher education and away from its disciplinary base.

In other cases, economic factors are in play. Here, PETE undergraduate degree programmes are reduced to one-year postgraduate teaching certificates. Graduates entering these programmes to gain teacher qualifications come from a wide range of undergraduate programmes that may or may not be fit-for-purpose. In both cases, physical education teacher educators may have lost control of their programmes and the resources that make them possible.

For PETE programmes that remain in universities, institutional survival is an important and ever-pressing concern. They have the added burden of providing leadership on the issues we have discussed here. They must look inwards and outwards at the same time. The development of teacher education communities of practice will be important spaces for this leadership to take effect.

Professional associations also have an important role to play in taking forward teacher professional learning (Mitchell and Lawson, 2019). Where jurisdictions have established standards for entry into teaching and for remaining licensed to teach, professional associations have the substantive expertise to provide support through professional learning opportunities. In many countries they already do this. Less often do they work with governments to help establish teaching standards, or lobby to develop and extend them through legislation.

The provision of PE in schools, where it is staffed by specialist teachers, supported by appropriate facilities, equipment and timetabled as a recurrent programme, has the potential to make a significant contribution to the health and wellbeing of all young people. The fact that physical educators often struggle to show evidence of the educational benefits of their teaching leaves the field in a vulnerable position. This vulnerability increases when all members of the profession take a blind eye toward unintended, undesirable outcomes and side-effects, both short and long-term. Lack of CPD is one cause, and strategic CPD is a cure.

A balanced research agenda which attends to programme achievements, shortfalls, and unintended outcomes (e.g. Ladwig *et al.*, 2018) can be a catalyst for professional development, adaptive competence, and continuous quality improvement. Continuing professional development configurations that join up teachers and teacher educators are consequential for the profession's future. Most of all, they hold promise for improving students' experiences and outcomes.

References

Becker, G.S. (1994). *Human Capital: A Theoretical and Empirical Analysis with Special Reference to Education*, 3rd edn. Chicago: University of Chicago Press.

European Commission (2012). *Supporting the Teaching Professions for Better Learning Outcomes*. Commission Staff Working Document SWD (2012) 374. Strasbourg: European Commission.

Griggs, G. (2010). For sale – primary physical education. £20 per hour or nearest offer. *Education 3–13*, 38(1), 39–46.

Hadar, L. and Brody, D. (2017). Professional learning and development of teacher educators. *The Sage Handbook of Research on Teacher Education*. London: Sage, 1049–1064.

Kim, I., Ward, P., Sinelnikov, O., Ko, B., Iserbyt, P., Li, W. and Curtner-Smith, M. (2018). The influence of content knowledge on pedagogical content knowledge: an evidence-based practice for physical education. *Journal of Teaching in Physical Education*, 37, 133–143.

Kirk, D. (2010). *Physical Education Futures*. London: Routledge.

Kirk, D. (2019). *Precarity, Critical Pedagogy and Physical Education*. London: Routledge.

Knapp, M.S. (2003). Professional development as a policy pathway. *Review of Research in Education*, 27, 109–157.

Ladwig, M.A., Vazou, S. and Ekkekakis, P. (2018). My best memory is when I was done with it: PE memories are associated with adult sedentary behavior. *Translational Journal of the American College of Sports Medicine*, 3(16), 119–129.

Lawson, H.A. (1979). Paths toward professionalization. *Quest*, 31(2), 231–243.

Lawson, H.A. (2018). *Redesigning Physical Education: An Equity Agenda in Which Every Child Matters*. London: Routledge.

Lawson, H.A. (2019). The physical education system as a consequential social determinant. *Quest*. https://doi.org/10.1080/00336297.2019.1632214

Lawson, H.A., Caringi, J.C., Gottfried, R., Bride, B. and Hydon, S. (2019). Secondary traumatic stress, student trauma, and the need for trauma literacy. *Harvard Educational Review*, vol. 89(3), 421–447.

MacPhail, A. (2011). Professional learning as a physical education teacher educator. *Physical Education & Sport Pedagogy*, 16(4), 435–451.

MacPhail, A. (2017). "Physical education and sport pedagogy" and the three "A"s: apprenticeship, academia and administration. *Sport, Education and Society*, 22(5), 669–683.

MacPhail, A., Patton, K., Parker, M. and Tannehill, D. (2014). Leading by example: teacher educators' professional learning through communities of practice. *Quest*, 66(1), 39–56.

MacPhail, A., Tannehill, D. and Avsar, Z. (eds) (2019). *European Physical Education Teacher Education Practices: Initial, Induction, and Professional Development*. Maidenhead, UK: Meyer & Meyer Sport (UK).

McCuaig, L., Carroll, K. and Macdonald, D. (2014). Enacting critical health literacy in the Australian secondary school curriculum: the possibilities posed by e-health. *Asia-Pacific Journal of Health, Sport and Physical Education*, 5(3), 217–231.

McEvoy, E., MacPhail, A. and Heikinaro-Johansson, P. (2018). Research lives of physical education teacher educators. *Curriculum Studies in Health and Physical Education*, 9(1), 90–103.

Merton, R.K. (1938). Social structure and anomie. *American Sociological Review*, 3(5), 672–682.

Mitchell, M.F. and Lawson, H.A. (2019). Professional standards for research and scholarship: the case of PETE professors. Paper presented to the National Association of Kinesiology in Higher Education, Charleston South Carolina, USA, January.

Parker, M., Patton, K. and Tannehill, D. (2012). Mapping the landscape of communities of practice as professional development in Irish physical education. *Irish Educational Studies*, 31(3), 311–327.

Patton, K., Parker, M. and Tannehill, D. (2015). Helping teachers help themselves: professional development that makes a difference. *NAssP Bulletin*, 99(1), 26–42.

Placek, J.H. (1983). Conceptions of success in teaching: busy, happy and good? In T.J. Templin and J.K. Olson (eds), *Teaching in Physical Education*. Champaign, IL: Human Kinetics, pp. 46–55.

Richards, K.A.R., Templin, T.J. and Graber, K. (2014). The socialization of teachers in physical education: review and recommendations for future works. *Kinesiology Review*, 3, 113–134.

Schleicher, A. (2018). *Valuing our Teachers and Raising their Status: How Communities can Help*. Paris: Organisation for Economic and Social Development.

Standal, O. (2016). *Phenomenology and Pedagogy in Physical Education*. London: Routledge.

Tully, L.A., Hawes, D.J., Doyle, F.L., Sawyer, M.G. and Dadds, M.R. (2019). A national child mental health literacy initiative is needed to reduce childhood mental health disorders. *Australian & New Zealand Journal of Psychiatry*, 53(4), 286–290.

Wagner, A.W. (2019). Personal communication to the authors.

Whitehead, M. (2010). *Physical Literacy: Throughout the Lifecourse*. London: Routledge.

Williams, B.J. and Macdonald, D. (2015). Explaining outsourcing in health, sport and physical education, *Sport, Education and Society*, 20(1), 57–72.

Chapter 14

The public policy challenge

Preparing and supporting teacher educators and teachers as change agents and policy entrepreneurs

Jenna R. Lorusso, Suzanne Hargreaves, Andrew Morgan and Hal A. Lawson

Starting with a popular stereotype

Physical educators in many nations do not see themselves as policy actors. One reason stands out: the field has few policy experts. This helps to explain why specialized physical education teacher education (PETE) policy courses and professional development workshops are rare, and also why policy is neglected and stereotypes persist. In the dominant stereotype, policy is the exclusive domain of powerful politicians and specialists in political science, public administration, and educational policy studies. In this view, policy is top-down. Policymakers decide, while principals, head teachers, physical education (PE) teachers, and PETE faculty implement. Incessant policy changes conjure up cynical responses regarding "this year's new thing".

However, the influence between policy and PE/PETE professionals is bi-directional (see Chapter 10). While it is true that public policy is a conduit through which government influences many aspects of our lives (e.g. the inclusion or exclusion of PE as a required school subject), outcomes vary depending upon multiple factors in the complex policy process. One such factor is the way policy is enacted in practice. In this view, teachers, teacher educators, and others invested in PE/PETE programmes are policy actors as they proceed with their work. So are students, whose experiences, optimal and undesirable, may be communicated to powerful political constituencies. For example, as far as PE teachers are concerned, whether one quietly laments a new PE curriculum or enthusiastically enacts it, policy is reinforced. Conversely, teachers may disrupt curricular intentions when they resist and develop their own curricular innovations.

A dual policy rule brings these points home. *Policy influences all practice, and, at the same time, every practice action or inaction is a policy act.* In this view, teachers and teacher educators are not implementation puppets. They can be change agents with the capacity to act strategically and collectively to influence policy in support of their missions to meet students' movement- and health-related needs.

Chapter overview and team approach

In this chapter we address policy stereotypes and the grand challenge we call "policy neglect". Two aspects of this neglect merit immediate attention. One is a lack of awareness regarding the need for, and importance of, policy engagement. The other is a lack of know-how for practical policy engagement.

In response to these needs, we identify key implications of policy neglect and highlight promising opportunities of policy engagement. We provide a primer on the complex policy process and detail a practical engagement framework for those PE/PETE professionals who aspire to be policy entrepreneurs. A PE/PETE case study provides a practical example. We conclude with a collaborative redesign proposal to prepare and support *all* PE/PETE professionals for policy engagement via sustained, practitioner-centred/-led reflective dialogue, guided by complex policy process theory.

Our author teams' roles influence our perspectives. One of our team members enacts PE policy at a district level in Alberta, Canada (Andrew). Another is leading PE policy at a national level in Scotland (Suzanne). Two others are researching educational and PE/PETE policy at various levels in the United States and Canada respectively (Hal and Jenna). We have structured our analysis in acknowledgement of contextual differences: international, national, state/provincial, and local. Our grand aim is to move PE/PETE from a field that neglects policy to one that prioritizes it.

Appreciating the meaning and significance of public policy

The question of "what is policy?" invites controversy. For the purposes of this chapter, policy can be understood as "any course of action (or inaction) relating to the selection of goals, the definition of values or the allocation of resources" (Olssen *et al.*, 2012, p 71). Public policy specifically references policy that government has set out or engaged with. Emphasis on policy processes, rather than policy itself, is key to understanding this.

A short review of policy neglect

Despite the ubiquitous nature of public policy and its relevance to all PE/PETE professionals, many continue to neglect policy study and advocacy. Popular policy stereotypes appear to be one cause. For example, Penney (2017) has suggested the complexity of policy means that much of it remains "frustratingly opaque" (Penney, 2017, p. 127), and therefore, many do not see themselves as "active [policy] agents" (Penney, 2017, p. 132). Meanwhile, Brown *et al.* (2017) found that PE/PETE stakeholders identified the management of constant policy change as one of the greatest challenges facing initial teacher education and, therefore, the development of policy expertise as a top priority.

Any discussion of policy roles must include references to practical constraints. For example, O'Sullivan (2018, p. 538) raised questions of "who and how to take on these [policy] roles while 'doing the day job'". Similarly, van der Mars (2018, p. 182) suggested that "little time and energy" is left for policy engagement when PE/PETE employment reward structures do not incentivize such work. Ultimately, when policy engagement is largely left to volunteerism, impacts and outcomes vary (Thorburn, 2017).

Exploring implications of policy neglect

Policy neglect in PE/PETE has implications for programme quality, equity and survival. If scalable improvements are to be made in PE/PETE, policy expertise is needed. Penney (2017), for example, has emphasized professional responsibility for curriculum reform and contended that "understanding more about curriculum reform 'as policy' ... is a critical prerequisite to challenging the status quo" (Penney, 2017, p. 131). Likewise, O'Sullivan (2018) and van der Mars (2018) have argued that, without PE/PETE's collective involvement in the broader public policy space around teacher education (e.g. education, sport, health), the work of PETE faculty will have limited impact, and the status of PE/PETE will remain the same.

As curriculums become ever-more crowded to ensure students learn the knowledge, skills, and attitudes required in the twenty-first century, who will ensure PE/PETE is relevant and advocate that it has an important place? Who will advocate for teachers? For teacher educators? These questions indicate that policy expertise and advocacy serve professional self-interests.

The possibilities of policy engagement: starting with awareness

In contrast to the potentially dire consequences of policy neglect are the promising possibilities of policy engagement. Awareness comes first. PE/PETE professionals must first become alert to the importance of policy. Key moments of awareness shared by our team may aid readers to expand their own awareness, commitments, and actions.

JENNA: In 2010, a long-awaited provincial HPE [Health and Physical Education] curriculum revision was repealed for political reasons after pressure from small, but policy-savvy, religious interest groups. The new curriculum had been set to introduce important contemporary sexual health content, such as sexting. This repeal lasted five years, leaving students to experience a curriculum that had been in place for approximately 20 years. Through this dramatic and unsettling political event, I came to better appreciate the impact of policy's political nature on educational change and that, without policy-adept HPE advocates, the quality of our subject area would continue to be determined by outsiders.

HAL: As I set out to read Michael Lipsky's (1980) book on the front-line work of human service professionals in public sector bureaucracies, I wondered whether Lipsky, a policy wonk, would have anything important to say about front-line practice. Then I discovered Lipsky's main claim: front-line practice is policy in action. This was a game-changer. I began to realize all that policy entailed, especially its inseparability from practice. My newly-discovered and still-developing policy framework provided better ways to evaluate sub-optimal practices and programmes in schools and universities. As policy became more prominent in my work, the consequences of policy neglect also became more apparent. I became a student of policy.

SUZANNE: When I was seconded from school PE to Scotland's national improvement agency [Education Scotland], I entered excitedly with sleeves rolled up, ready to get stuck in affecting change via curriculum reform. I quickly learned that policy is a complex business. As I came face-to-face with teacher resistance to new policy, the agency of teachers as policy actors became clear to me in ways it had not been during my own teaching career. I needed to learn how to work within the complexity. I came to understand that listening, negotiation, context, and relationships matter hugely in the policy process.

ANDREW: During a secondment from school PE to the provincial Ministry of Education, I was offered the once-in-a-career opportunity to contribute to shaping the future provincial HPE programme of study. My four years at the Ministry were a rich professional experience but emphasized to me the significant gaps that can exist between policy development and implementation. The need for, and promise of, carefully considered implementation strategies that extend all the way to regional and classrooms levels became wildly apparent.

What can be learned from these stories? None of us set out to become "policy people". None of us were trained in the PE/PETE realm for policy work. We all had many (often negative) misconceptions about what policy was or was not, and who may or may not be involved and how so. Then, serendipitously, diverse happenings brought each of us to different realizations about the promise and possibility in policy (e.g. its centrality to change, its connection to practice, the agency of teachers, and the importance of contextual enactment).

We propose that we are not unique in this regard because the PE/PETE system has few requirements and programme provisions to help professionals develop such an awareness. What can be done? The remainder of this chapter provides one perspective. We describe how others might become equipped to see themselves as active agents in the policy process. We also suggest how they might develop practical strategies for complex engagement in their host context.

Developing policy know-how

The complexity of policy engagement

Engagement in policy depends on knowledge of the policy process. This process is complicated, as Penney and Evans (2005, p. 35) have noted, "the complexities of policy are as difficult to describe as they are to adequately explain."

The policy process is nonlinear, contested, and dynamic

Understanding begins with abandoning romantic assumptions of "'evidence-based policymaking' in which we expect policymakers to produce 'rational' decisions in a policy cycle, with predictable, linear stages" (Cairney, 2018, p. 4). In reality, policymakers can only realistically attend to a fraction of the issues brought to their attention. The few proposals that make it to the top of the agenda do so via a combination of "rational" evidence consideration and "irrational" judgements such as gut feelings and deep-seated beliefs (Cairney *et al.*, 2016, p. 399). Furthermore, contextual forces often conspire against entirely new policies. Instead, one or more existing policies typically are targeted for reform (Peters, 2018). None of this work is easy.

The policy process is a contested, political struggle over conflicting values with unpredictable outcomes. Viewed in this way, "policy is socially constructed, mediated and 'flows' within and between agencies, individuals, sites and fields of practice in complex social systems" (Penney and Evans, 2005, p. 24). Policy thus is best conceptualized as a dynamic process. There are no firm boundaries between making, implementing, and enacting policy (Ozga, 2000).

The policy process is multi-directional, contextual, and crowded

Central to an understanding of a group's or individual's role/agency in the policy process is recognition that multiple groups are involved in policymaking. Although public policy may be officially passed by government, it is heavily influenced by the individuals who deliver it at the "street level" (Lipsky, 1980). Street level professionals include teachers and teacher educators.

Similarly, just as policies shape contexts, contextual factors shape policies (Braun *et al.*, 2011). This inescapable reality tempers enthusiasm for cross-context policy transfers.

Adding to this complexity is the crowded nature of policy arenas. In PE's case, the interests of stakeholders in sport, education and health, individually and collectively, influence policymaking (Houlihan and Green, 2006). Competing constituencies, with their respective goals and preferences, create policy tensions and dilemmas as well as sometimes-hidden opportunities for policy coalitions (Lawson, 2017).

An approach for complex policy engagement: policy entrepreneurship

How then do we engage in the complex policy process? While there are no simple answers, policy process theories offer useful frameworks (Weible and Cairney, 2018). The idea of policy entrepreneurship is one key concept. It signals the agency of teachers and teacher educators as political actors.

Policy entrepreneurship is based in the theory of Multiple Streams Analysis (MSA). MSA is concerned with how policy problems and solutions get on the agenda, emphasizing the actions of advocates (including policy entrepreneurs) in this process (Kingdon, 1984). Three related conditions are key: (a) how the policy problem is defined; (b) how the policy solution is framed; and (c) the political circumstances as the policy is considered (Cairney, 2018).

In a MSA view, dramatic policy change is a rare event. It happens only when the three streams of problem definition, policy solution, and politics, come together at a critical moment in a window of opportunity. Policy entrepreneurship actions are central to making this happen.

Which policy entrepreneurship actions can PE/PETE professionals learn to perform? One such action to navigate the problem stream is to tell a compelling story to capture the audience's attention, emphasizing how this story fits with the policy stream(s) under discussion (Cairney, 2018). Here, entrepreneurship involves being a problem-broker or agenda-setter, elevating a problem or way of thinking/talking about a problem (Knaggård, 2015). By focusing attention on a particular problem with a clear problem definition, evidence can then be used to reduce uncertainty (Cairney, 2018). This requires identifying the biases of the audience and correspondingly curating the evidence to produce a succinct and persuasive story that combines facts *and* values, and also promises a practical policy solution (Cairney, 2018).

To navigate the policy stream, effective policy entrepreneurship requires the foresight and dedication to produce "feasible solutions in anticipation of attention to problems" (Cairney, 2018, p. 2). Timing is key. While attention to a policy problem may come and go rather suddenly, the development and acceptance of a policy solution is rather slow. For example, PE-related coalitions must be built, various actors form and reform the policy, policy is adjusted to meet criteria for survival (e.g. logistically feasible, politically acceptable, reasonably budgeted), and "policy specialists with established views [become] 'softened up' to new ideas" (Cairney, 2011, p. 235).

Effectively navigating the politics stream requires strategic adjustment to the particulars of one's given political context (Cairney, 2018). This involves understanding that certain changes in political factors (e.g. elections, changes in government, interest group activity, swings in public opinion) can create favourable conditions whereby things that were not possible before might now be, and vice versa (Mintrom and Vergari, 1996). In large political systems, entrepreneurship actions might best be suited (or limited) to taking a well-defined policy solution and *chasing* a policy problem or political change (e.g. like a surfer catching a wave). In contrast, smaller systems might allow opportunity to *create* a policy problem or *instigate* a political change (Cairney, 2018).

Ultimately, the concept of policy entrepreneurship "gives greater weight to agency, suggests a greater degree of residual randomness in the policy process and identifies the importance of opportunism and the effective exploitation of policy windows" (Houlihan and Green, 2006, p. 80). Policy entrepreneurship is about key microlevel political actions (Mintrom and Vergari, 1996). These actions are not the exclusive territory of those in particular formal roles, thus, it is more relevant to speak of policy entrepreneur*ship* than it is of policy entrepreneurs. Policy entrepreneurship can be taken up by those who wish to be change agents in their particular context and scope by using their power, persistence, good fortune, and knowledge of the policy process in an attempt to advance an agenda (Cairney, 2011).

Policy entrepreneurship in PE/PETE

The value of policy entrepreneurship as a framework for policy engagement has been recognized by some PE/PETE leaders. For example, Gladwin *et al.* (2008) used MSA to investigate the acceptance of a daily physical activity policy and the rejection of a walk-to-school proposal by the provincial government in Alberta, Canada. Critical to the acceptance and rejection of the proposals was the ability or inability to reduce ambiguity about the policy problem and solution, and the presence or absence of policy entrepreneurship actions, respectively.

Similarly, Houlihan and Green (2006) examined the changing status of school sport and PE in England through the policy process theories of MSA and the Advocacy Coalition Framework. They concluded that MSA was the more "illuminating" (Houlihan and Green, 2006, p. 73) and "plausible" (Houlihan and Green, 2006, p. 89) way to understand policy change as their findings reflected the impact individuals can make in the policy process, and importantly, their interactions with, and adjustments to, the particulars of the political context.

Examples of policy entrepreneurship in the PE/PETE literature primarily focus on analysis rather than strategies for action. Therefore, in the following sections, we provide a brief case from Suzanne's professional experience and highlight the practical policy entrepreneurship strategies she used to achieve policy change.

Suzanne's policy entrepreneurship: PE and Scotland's Curriculum for Excellence

Curriculum for Excellence (CfE), Scotland's national curriculum released in 2010, launched PE into a new prioritized role in the nation's schools. The new curriculum reflected Scotland's ambition for more children to be more active, more often. CfE involved a target to increase curricular PE time to two hours/ periods per week, and in 2012 a two-year, £5.8 million investment (£2.4 million from Education Scotland and £3.4 million from sportscotland) was provided to support the meeting of this target. Outcome monitoring was to be facilitated through Scotland's annual "Healthy Lifestyle Survey", with additional scrutiny provided by external academic researchers.

I had the privilege of being assigned lead responsibility for this national PE programme. As part of a wider political, social, and cultural system, I recognized I couldn't operate in isolation. I needed to enlist the support of credible, well-respected colleagues from all system levels. I ultimately formed a multi-sectoral network of teachers, school senior management, government civil servants, teacher educators, and health/sport stakeholders. Together, and with a clear and shared understanding of the transformation agenda, these national advocates and local champions worked to change the hearts and minds of key stakeholders across the system in service of achieving the two-hours/periods per week target.

The funding package allowed for the placement of key people at national and local levels to drive the agenda and make change quickly. By the end of the funding period in 2014, 99 per cent of schools were meeting the target, up considerably from just 5 per cent of schools in 2006. This impressive new figure created a groundswell of support, signalling the funding had achieved its outcome, at least quantifiably. However, learners' activity time was just part of the outcome chain. Significant work remained on improving the quality of the learning experience. Meanwhile, the existing funding was ending.

I recognized that a potential opportunity lay in this previously-described groundswell of political support. I aimed to elevate "the PE problem" and provide a specialized way of thinking and communicating about it as more than just an issue of quantity, but also of quality. I relied on the quantitative survey evidence of schools now meeting the PE target, as well as the qualitative evidence from the external academic research report about the need for improved quality. I used this evidence together to paint a picture whereby PE was meeting some of the Scottish Government's national outcomes for children and youth as I advocated for more funding to meet others. I was committed to addressing the long-term implications of this change agenda to ensure sustainability beyond the funding phase. Fortunately, the Scottish Government agreed a further £5.8 million (£2.4 million from Education Scotland and £3.4 million from sportscotland). Clearly, trust had been built in the collective responsibility to improve PE.

In the process, I and my colleagues learned evaluation must be a centrepiece in policy implementation, to be prepared to demonstrate (or not!) whether funding improved outcomes when the opportunity arises. I also learned that careful selection of policy advocates is critical to success. Advocates must have credibility across the system to influence the hearts and minds of key stakeholders who, for good reasons, may not be in a position to join the revolution. Key people must be brought to the table when decisions are being made. When these stakeholders cannot make it, or worse, are not invited, tensions arise and preventable impediments develop. I found that policy enactment works best when it is "with teachers in situ". Such a collaborative approach addresses front-line delivery challenges, enables mutually beneficial solutions, and facilitates teachers' readiness and commitments. We learn together as we implement, evaluate, and improve policy innovations.

Learning from Suzanne's entrepreneurship strategies

There is much to learn from how Suzanne navigated the complex convergence of streams. In terms of the problem stream, Suzanne and her team told a clear and compelling story to capture the government's attention. She played the role of problem-broker and elevated one aspect of the problem over others – that is, the need to ensure the *quality* of PE provision over quantity. She did this by appealing to the feasibility and impact biases of policymakers through both quantitative evidence of past success and qualitative evidence of need.

In terms of the politics and policy streams, Suzanne and her team recognized they were working within a large political system and thus that it would be more realistic for them to chase, rather than instigate, political change. They identified the closing of the original funding period as a potential window of opportunity to exploit and worked to have a well-developed policy solution ready by that time.

Fundamental to all of these strategic actions was Suzanne and her team's knowledge of the policy process as well as their real and perceived agency to intervene in that process. Without policy expertise, their actions would not have been as effective. Without these colleagues' sense of agency, this would not have happened at all.

Moving from policy neglect to prioritization

To move PE/PETE from a field that neglects policy to one that prioritizes it in service of better outcomes for students, teachers, and teacher educators, we suggest a two-part agenda; (a) developing a thorough understanding of the practical strategies involved in complex policy engagement, and (b) determining how to prepare and support teachers and teacher educators to undertake such engagement.

Our proposal for pursuing this agenda takes its lead from public policy researchers who have addressed the practical challenge of preparation and support for complex policy engagement (Cairney, 2015). We suggest progress necessitates sustained collaborations with key stakeholders from various spheres of the system (i.e. teachers, teacher educators, policymakers, policy developers, researchers, and scholarly and professional associations), with operational guidance provided by complex policy process frameworks. This approach involves movement from high-altitude academic-led discussions of policy complexity to practitioner-centred and -led discussions facilitated by reflexivity (Cairney, 2015). This recommended practice focus is not at the expense of policy theory and research. Rather, it entails tapping into personal narratives of working with policy when thinking about new, complex policy process theories.

Reflective learning occurs when diverse groups "work together to make sense of theories and empirical studies, primarily by relating them to lived, professional experience" (Cairney, 2015, p. 34). Through such reflective policy dialogue, groups organize for collective action, gaining influence and impacts few individuals could achieve in isolation. Such diverse collaboration may, for example, result in the development of toolkits that promote a common language and mutually beneficial goals (Cairney, 2015). Because PE/PETE crosses policy boundaries for health, sport and education, policy engagement depends on boundary-crossing leaders who have an understanding of the political, social, and cultural context and can harness expertise and political will to bring about change.

Complex policy process frameworks offer important guidance. They ensure inherited assumptions and routine ways of dealing with policy are continuously evaluated. Structured properly, these evaluations enable reflective learning and facilitate future agenda-setting, for example, fresh determinations of policy goals, advocacy mechanisms and outcomes.

Policy toolkits are needed. They translate theory to action, and they are developed through interpersonal negotiations in host contexts such as states/provinces, nations, and international alliances. PE/PETE policy experts need to take charge.

The sustained nature of collective action formations, known variously as coalitions, collaborations, and partnerships, are key to ensuring toolkits are adopted and enacted. Such ongoing interactions "may produce new ways of thinking – using the literature's insights as the way to begin a conversation; to turn abstract concepts into meaningful conclusions" (Cairney, 2015, p. 33).

One vision for how this might be carried out is within those groups with collaborative professional relationships for continuous professional development already in place (see Chapter 13). Where PETE faculty and PE teachers already collaborate on practice-based research projects, there are opportunities to recruit other policy actors (e.g. policy developers, policymakers, and representatives from scholarly and professional associations from across education, sport and health sectors). Importantly, this work would take place in schools and surrounding communities with preparation provided in universities.

Partnerships among governmental agencies, schools, and universities are an important facilitator for the policy work that lies ahead. Partnerships are boundary-bridging and gap-filling mechanisms, and they have the potential to empower teachers and teacher educators. Policy leadership develops as teachers, teacher educators, and their allies negotiate the political, social, and cultural systems in their respective host contexts.

Epilogue

Our author team's experience constructing this chapter is evidence that engaging individuals from across policy spheres in sustained, theory-guided reflection can be powerfully generative, i.e. new knowledge and understanding are created as prior knowledge is shared and used. Everyone learns and gains more expertise.

This dynamic approach combats policy neglect and prepares colleagues for the future because policy agendas are always changing.

Our team's approach may benefit others. Our writing team consisted of individuals working in different policy roles (i.e. teacher, teacher educator, policy developer, policy researcher), contexts (i.e. Canada, Scotland, the United States), and scales (e.g. district, provincial/state, national). We communicated regularly over a six-month period via videoconference and email. We became a community of practice as we shared and discussed: (a) stories of our initial and continuing motivations for our policy work; (b) details about what our policy engagement looks like on a daily basis; (c) our hopes for what the broader PE/PETE field might come to appreciate about policy; and (d) how the policy process theory of MSA, and its notion of policy entrepreneurship, applied to our professional practice.

Our team formation and developmental process serve as a miniature example of collective policy engagement and offers insight into the productive potential impacts of such work. For example, we: (a) explored our differences and discovered contradictions (e.g. some team members were more interested in policy enactment than advocacy, or vice versa, depending upon how privileged a place PE/PETE currently held in their policy context); (b) had our assumptions challenged (e.g. how best to unpack and interpret PE policy processes); (c) realized narrative privileges (e.g. coming to appreciate that we may view a particular policy differently because we are "in the know" by virtue of our privileged positions); (d) generated enthusiasm (e.g. becoming motivated by our team members' various stories of policy success); and (e) illuminated new ways of thinking about, understanding, and approaching our policy work (e.g. becoming aware of terminology in policy theories that better describe the policy actions we had already been carrying out in practice). Our rich experience of this developmental process signals the promise of such collaborative redesign models of school programmes and teacher education – and with a special priority for public policy.

References

Braun, A., Ball, S.J., Maguire, M. and Hoskins, K. (2011). Taking context seriously: Towards explaining policy enactments in the secondary school. *Discourse: Studies in the Cultural Politics of Education*, 32(4), 585–596.

Brown, R., Williams, B., Pendergast, D., Reynolds, J., Enright, E., Hay, S., Rossi, T., Usher, W. and Whatman, S. (2017). Communique: Queensland Health and Physical Education Initial Teacher Education Summit 2017. Available at: https://plhub.griffith.edu.au/u/lib/mob/20180509112445_0e59c6f3162132344/hpesummitcommunique2017.pdf (accessed 1 August 2018)

Cairney, P. (2011). *Understanding Public Policy: Theories and Issues*. London: Palgrave Macmillan.

Cairney, P. (2015). How can policy theory have an impact on policymaking? The role of theory-led academic–practitioner discussions. *Teaching Public Administration*, 33(1), 22–39

Cairney, P. (2018). Three habits of successful policy entrepreneurs. *Policy & Politics*, 46(2), 199–215.

Cairney, P., Oliver, K. and Wellstead, A. (2016). To bridge the divide between evidence and policy: reduce ambiguity as much as uncertainty. *Public Administration Review*, 76(3), 399–402.

Gladwin, C.P., Church, J. and Plotnikoff, R.C. (2008). Public policy processes and getting physical activity into Alberta's urban schools. *Canadian Journal of Public Health*, 99(4), 332–338.

Houlihan, B. and Green, M. (2006). The changing status of school sport and physical education: explaining policy change. *Sport, Education and Society*, 11(1), 73–92.

Kingdon, J. (1984). *Agendas, Alternatives and Public Policies*. New York: Harper Collins.

Knaggård, Å. (2015). The Multiple Streams Framework and the problem broker. *European Journal of Political Research*, 54(3), 450–465.

Lawson, H.A. (2017). Reproductive, reformist, and transformative socialization. In K.A.R. Richards and K.L. Gaudreault (eds), *New Perspectives on Teacher Socialization in Physical Education*. London: Routledge, pp. 243–261.

Lipsky, M. (1980). *Street-Level Bureaucracy*. New York: Russell Sage Foundation.

Mintrom, M. and Vergari, S. (1996). Advocacy coalitions, policy entrepreneurs, and policy change. *Policy Studies Journal*, 24(3), 420–434.

Olssen, M., Codd, J.A. and O'Neill, A.M. (2012). *Education Policy: Globalization, Citizenship and Democracy*. London: Sage.

O'Sullivan, M. (2018). PETE Academics as public intellectuals and activists in a global teacher education context. *Physical Education and Sport Pedagogy*, 23(5), 536–543.

Ozga, J. (2000). *Policy Research in Educational Settings: Contested Terrain*. Philadelphia: Open University Press.

Penney, D. (2017). Policy and possibilities. In C.D. Ennis (ed.), *Routledge Handbook of Physical Education Pedagogies*. London: Routledge, pp. 131–142.

Penney, D. and Evans, J. (2005). Policy, power and politics in physical education. In K. Green and K. Hardman (eds), *Physical Education: Essential Issues*. London: Sage, pp. 21–38.

Peters, B.G. (2018). *Policy Problems and Policy Design*. Cheltenham: Edward Elgar.

Thorburn, M. (2017). "When an old cricketer leaves the crease": bittersweet reflections on examination awards in physical education. *Sport, Education and Society*, 24(4), 1–11.

van der Mars, H. (2018). Policy development in physical education… The last best chance? *Quest*, 70(2), 169–190.

Weible, C.M. and Cairney, P. (2018). Practical lessons from policy theories. *Policy & Politics*, 46(2), 183–197.

Chapter 15

Learning to plan and planning to learn during turbulent times

Hal A. Lawson

Nations everywhere are experiencing turbulent times. Rapid, dramatic societal changes associated with globalization are implicated. Three examples launch this chapter (UNESCO, 2019). All are consequential for school physical education (PE), subject-specific teacher education (PETE), and schools.

Unprecedented numbers of people are "on the move", as evidenced in two migration patterns, (1) intra-nation movement from rural areas to cities, and (2) international re-location. These patterns can be viewed in two ways: moving to take advantage of perceived opportunities (e.g. parent/guardian employment); and moving to escape poverty, social exclusion, and ethnic conflict. Both patterns produce divided family systems, so named because some members are left behind. Both usher in ethnic and cultural diversity, posing challenges to schools' missions to serve as guardians of cultural traditions and assimilation mechanisms.

At the same time, multiple forces associated with the global economy are impacting every nation's schools, which helps to explain why education-oriented economists have gained importance. They emphasize "human capital development", i.e. the knowledge, skills, abilities and other important attributes such as health and well-being that are needed to produce goods, services and new ideas. For example, the service-oriented economies of advanced industrial nations (e.g. the USA, UK, Australia) require a workforce with post-secondary education, while so-called developing economies (e.g. Indonesia, Viet Nam, Thailand) require labour for assembly line production.

Meanwhile, digital age technologies, a defining feature of globalization, are catalysts for pervasive change. For example, cell phones and "wearables" (e.g. computer-like wristwatches; heart-rate monitoring devices) facilitate "anytime, anywhere, anyone learning" and self-directed physical activity monitoring. As learning becomes boundaryless, two distinctions gain prominence. Education systems are not the same as school systems, and teaching is not the same as learning. Every school subject and teacher education programme will be impacted.

These changes implicate others, and together they signal turbulent times. All recommend SWOT analyses – scans aimed at internal and external strengths, weaknesses, opportunities – as emphasized in Chapter 1.

Turbulent times bring formidable challenges and offer timely opportunities. Either way, leaders need to take notice and get ready for a shift from an enduring focus on implementation. Everywhere schools and education systems are being redesigned, signalling that PE professionals must learn to plan evidence-based programmes that are fit for purpose in these new school designs. Because few colleagues will succeed the first time, everyone must also plan to learn.

This dual framework for learning to plan and planning to learn enables leaders to address each of the grand challenges described in previous chapters. It also holds promise for a more complicated challenge. During turbulent times, leaders must learn how to simultaneously address many challenges.

Internationally-oriented books such as this one provide leadership preparation to the extent that they emphasize such cutting-edge issues, provide innovative frameworks, feature promising programmes and practices, and facilitate proactive planning. Mindful of the constant pressures to work locally, they also invite PE readers-as-leaders to take stock of developments elsewhere in the world. These PE-focused international comparisons mirror the efforts of each nation's leaders who may rely on international comparisons on academic achievement tests (e.g. PISA) and study school systems in high achieving nations (e.g. Finland).

The previous chapters offer the same potential, and readers are invited to evaluate them in this way. Have leaders in designated nations figured out what to prioritize and do? What are the implications for PE and PETE in my nation? What are the implications for school systems? What are the implications for higher education, particularly PETE? For public policy?

More poignantly: can PE teachers and PETE faculty reasonably be expected to anticipate and respond alone to all of these grand challenges? Who are the allies? What other professions appear to be the best partners? Public health? Sport science? Kinesiology? School reformers? Private-sector providers and competitors? All of these groups?

Getting started: learning from other exemplars

An exemplar is an established, justifiable model for PE practice, PETE programmes, and policy. Nearly every chapter in this book describes, recommends, or implicates at least one exemplar. Like consumer products, the best exemplars often have the equivalent of warranties. They have been tested, and there is evidence of their effectiveness (Lawson, 2018).

Exemplars are inherently attractive when author/advocates describe and promote them. Predictably, PE professionals may experience a nearly-irresistible temptation to imitate what colleagues in other places have prioritized and done. Some even may target the wholesale transport of models developed, evaluated, and disseminated in other places.

In fact, cross-border borrowing has been evident for some time. For example, advocates for specialized PE models, such as sport education, teaching personal and social responsibility, and teaching games for understanding, have developed international networks, which enable preferred models to travel. This pattern is known as technology transfer.

All such efforts to transport a specialized model for PE and PETE from a sender nation to a new nation can be viewed as examples of globalization. All are based on important assumptions. First and foremost: the surrounding context – national, regional, state/provincial, local – does not matter. Other assumptions follow suit. The host nation's public policy configuration (education, sport, health) doesn't matter; the particularities of each nation's school systems are inconsequential; PETE programmes can and should prepare future teachers in nearly identical ways; customized professional development programmes for experienced teachers are available and teachers welcome them; and children are more or less the same everywhere.

Readers should take stock of this cluster of assumptions. Assess their validity and evaluate their practical relevance during turbulent times.

One conclusion merits consideration. However attractive the success stories in other parts of the world may be, the risks and dangers associated with uncritical, cross-border technology transfer merit attention.

What, then, should readers prioritize and do? Two alternatives offer guidance.

Cross-border lesson-drawing

International-comparative experts recommend taking stock of contextual differences – national, regional, state/provincial, and local. They also recommend preserving national and local uniqueness in the face of globalization's homogenizing forces.

A formal process called lesson-drawing offers guidance (e.g. Rose, 1993; Schön and Rein, 1994). Two mains assumptions introduce it. Direct technology transfer from one nation to another is fraught with risks and dangers. On the other hand, it is foolhardy to be insular.

Lesson-drawing advocates claim that it offers a happy medium between wholesale transfer and isolation. Six interacting phases lend structure (Lawson, 2018; Rose, 1993).

- Searching experience across time, space and place to find a policy, strategy, programme or practice that appears to solve a particular problem or meet a prioritized need.
- Developing a model or a theory of change, i.e. specifying the relationships between the policies/programmes/strategies and the desirable outcomes they help to achieve.
- Adapting the lesson to the home context, searching for supportive research evidence and making the model explicit, testable, justifiable and adaptable.
- Developing a context-sensitive, implementation framework, emphasizing consequential roles for leaders. Should they make it happen, help it happen or let it happen?

- Developing tailor-made evaluation frameworks, founded on a review of implementation requirements and proceeding with an understanding of the contextual variability.
- Embedding evaluations in the implementation process and expecting to adapt, learn, generate new knowledge, and improve during the redesign journey.

Readers are encouraged to use this lesson-drawing framework to reflect on the preceding chapters. It is a way to benefit from international innovations by bringing the lessons learned to one's host context(s) – nation, region, state/province, local community.

Criteria for programme transportability

Cautions against wholesale technology transfers of school PE and PETE programmes do not rule out the strategic borrowing of policies, models and strategies developed in international contexts. Eleven criteria offer guidance (Lawson, 2001; Rose, 1993).

- The fewer the number of unique programme elements, the more transferable the PE or PETE programme.
- The simpler the cause-and-effect structure of the programme, the more transferable the programme.
- The more substitutable the institutions of PE programme delivery (e.g. schools, community agencies), the more transferable the programme.
- The more substitutable the institutions of PETE programme delivery (e.g. universities, technical institutes, professional development agencies), the more transferable the programme.
- The greater the correspondence between cultural traditions (e.g. ethno-sports, cultural norms for participation), the more transferable the programme.
- The fewer companion changes required (e.g. policy change), the more transferable the programme.
- The greater the correspondence between student, school and community characteristics, the more transferable the programme.
- The greater the congruity between policymakers' values, the more transferable the programme.
- The greater the equivalence of governmental resource allocations, the more transferable the programme.
- The greater the correspondence between governmental policies and accountability mechanisms in the two nations, the more transferable the programme.
- The greater the correspondence between PE's occupational socialization mechanisms, the more transferable the programme (Lawson, 2019a).

Readers can employ these criteria alongside lesson-drawing principles as they evaluate previous chapters and get ready for the planning that lies ahead, but with a reminder. To the extent that some PE and PETE outcomes are sub-optimal, planning for a more desirable future is a practical necessity because the profession's future depends on its members' ability to achieve desirable outcomes for young people, equitably and at scale (Lawson, 2018).

Two strategies for futures-oriented planning

A twentieth century management guru, Peter Drucker, emphasized that planning for the future requires a theory of planned abandonment (Drucker, 2008). It begins with the following question: "If we hadn't inherited it, would we do it this way?"

Macdonald and her colleagues (2018) offer a second strategy. "Rely on the forecasting advanced by experts known as futures-scholars." Macdonald *et al.* present Australian futurists' projections of life and living in the middle decades of the twenty-first century – when today's school-aged children will be adults. These authors also describe recommended changes in PE, health education, and schools overall. The main takeaway: if educators are to prepare youngsters for the world of tomorrow, prerequisite changes must be made in schools today.

These two strategies are like bookends. One emphasizes what to stop doing (Drucker), while the other helps to identify innovation priorities in order to prepare for a desirable future (Macdonald *et al.*, 2018). Together these frameworks serve as a reminder that a futures-oriented planning agenda is not "out with the old, in with the new". Justifiable twentieth-century inheritances are maintained and perhaps strengthened while leaders emphasize twin competencies for adaptive planning and non-stop learning. Everyone involved in and associated with the PE system must take notice, gain preparation, mobilize support, and get started.

Evaluating the inherited PE system

This book features the two core elements of the system: school programmes and teacher education. Like systems frameworks (e.g. Lawson, 2019b), the editors and chapter authors emphasize the relationship between PE and PETE because changes in one (e.g. school PE) influence and are influenced by the other (e.g. PETE).

School–higher education partnership proposals structured to facilitate simultaneous learning, improvement and redesign follow suit (Lawson, 2018). A solid rationale supports this dual approach. When school PE programmes are changed without companion adaptations in PETE, every new teacher must be retrained. Alternatively, change PETE without companion changes in school programmes, and new teachers may experience reality shocks, which cause them to give up what they acquired in previous PETE programmes.

Other undesirable outcomes follow when PE and PETE programmes are disconnected, and there are no formal mechanisms for teachers and teacher educators to plan, learn, generate new knowledge, and improve. Isolation is the enemy of improvement (Elmore, 2008).

An expansive view of the PE system

Isolation has another important meaning as planning for the future commences. Are PE teachers and PETE faculty the only components in what can be called the PE system? If not, what is missing, and who else needs to be involved?

A companion analysis addresses these two questions (Lawson, 2019b). Other key components in the PE system include public policy, PETE doctoral programmes, kinesiology and sport science, and public health. These additional systems components are justifiable to the extent that, (1) all influence, and are influenced by, the two-component relationship between PE and PETE; (2) all exert influence on physical activity and sport programmes for children and youths, whether in schools, youth sports programmes, or child- and youth-serving community organizations; and (3) all are implicated in planning for, and analyses of, the social determinants of paediatric health and well-being, including efforts aimed at physically active lifestyles that stretch into adulthood.

Blurred PE visions in some nations

This expanded view of the PE system may be especially relevant and useful in nations exhibiting three characteristics. First: school PE programmes are routinely conflated with physical activity programmes, extending to public policy standards that specify only activity minutes per day/week without accountability requirements for learning-focused outcomes. Although physical activity participation priorities and learning priorities are potentially like opposite sides of the same coin, their ideal relationship gets muddled in some nations.

Second: PE is broadly defined, so much so that it escapes the confines of a required school subject. Here, PE translates to physical activity opportunities provided by community organizations, sport clubs, and afterschool programmes. These school-community configurations eliminate some of the requirements for PETE (e.g. teacher certification) as well as requirements for the conduct of PE programmes (e.g. grading students in conformity with the sorting machine apparatus of industrial age schools).

Third: PE teachers and teacher educators in some nations confront mixed expectations and requirements from three policy sectors: education, sport and health (Lawson, 2017). Conflicting programme aims and competing programme models are normative, and both teachers and teacher educators may get caught in policy and practice cross-fires. It follows that outcomes for young people and their PE teachers are mixed and inconsistent, in part because leaders for school systems lack understanding of PE's rhyme and reason.

Summary reflections on previous chapters

An expansive view of the PE system and alternative institutional arrangements for PE, PETE, PETE doctoral programmes, public policy, and relations with kinesiology, sport science, and public health can be brought to bear on evaluations of the previous chapters. Overall the chapter authors focus on the inherited model of a school. Authors' language preferences tend to be school-centred. For example, they describe priorities for "students" instead of talking about young people, youths and "kids". They emphasize teaching methods and curriculum – pedagogy – at the expense of public health discourses and physical activity interventions (Lawson, 2018).

All in all, the weighty influence of the inherited version of the school is omnipresent, extending to PE and PETE traditions. Drucker's question is relevant: if we hadn't inherited these versions of PE and PETE, would we prioritize and implement them in these ways?

New designs for new times

One such inheritance is an implicit model for what a school is, encompasses, prioritizes and accomplishes. Notwithstanding international differences, "school" has standardized meanings, starting with academic learning and achievement in specialized subjects and necessitating specialist teachers with postsecondary education credentials. International testing regimes such as PISA and reciprocity agreements in hiring teachers (e.g. a teacher prepared in Ireland has received training suitable practice for Canada) are indicators of significant homogenization. There are others.

Inherited assumptions

Consider the main assumptions for "school". For example: (1) all students will arrive regularly, on-time, and they will be ready and able to learn; (2) most students will remain in the same school and school system; (3) site-based teams consisting of educators and hand-picked parents pick the reform priorities for each academic year; (4) planning focuses on the school day and privileges academic learning and achievement; (5) the school's student support professionals and special educators are able to meet the needs of the limited number of students assigned to them; (6) teachers, usually working alone, are responsible for student engagement and classroom management; and (7) after school ends, students return to home environments supportive of homework completion and healthy development.

This inherited model can be characterized as walled-in and building-centred; restricted to the school day; focused primarily on academic learning and achievement; and with evaluation and accountability systems predicated on the assumption that teachers "can do it all, alone". Implicit distinctions between "academic subjects" and "non-academic subjects" remain, and they have not been kind to PE teachers and their working conditions. In fact, inherited, sub-optimal conditions help to explain why some teachers have struggled to achieve equitable outcomes at scale for the young people in their charge (Lawson, 2018), and they also explain why some teachers change schools and leave the profession.

Alternative school designs

Turbulent times generated by rapid, dramatic social change have been instrumental in the development of new models for what a school is, prioritizes, and does. While priorities for academic learning and achievement remain, departures from the inherited twentieth century model are visible in many nations. Some feature digital technologies, including bridge-building mechanisms between schools, homes and community technology centres. Others are sponsored by private sector entities (e.g. charter schools; community technology centres). Yet others respond to place-based, school-clustered poverty, social exclusion, and social isolation, including community schools, community learning centres, extended services schools, and multi-service schools (Lawson and van Veen, 2016).

All such alternative school models, like the turbulent public policy environments that surround them, present both challenges and opportunities. In theory, these models provide affordances for several justifiable PE/PETE models, each of which is customized for an alternative kind of school.

Consequential planning choices start with ones regarding the parameters of specialization, both in PETE and school programmes, extending to whether and how PETE faculty should prepare novice teachers to serve as change agents. There are no easy answers because competing constituencies with diverse goals are the norm for PE and schools (Lawson, 2017).

Blending three twenty-first century models

Educators worldwide are asking and addressing generative planning questions about schools' missions, goals, operational structures and desired outcomes. Their efforts often commence with recognition of the changing condition of communities, families and children. Examples include the rise of single-parent, mother-headed families; place-based poverty, social exclusion and social isolation; and the challenges and opportunities associated with culturally-diverse immigrant children. At the same time, educators have learned that no longer is it safe to assume that all children will attend school regularly, arrive on time, and be ready to engage, learn, achieve and succeed.

It also has become apparent that teachers, working alone in classrooms, gymnasia, playing fields, art and music studios, and other school facilities cannot be successful without additional assistance, support and resources. Timely questions are being raised about teachers' preparation, roles, responsibilities and accountabilities, and there are no easy answers.

Generic, probing questions about schools give rise to subject-specific questions regarding PE teachers and programmes as well as about other special subjects such as art, music, drama, and dance. As evidence grows about these subjects' potential contributions to child/adolescent development and academic engagement (e.g. Tomporowski and Pesce, in press), opportunities abound to consider these subjects' redesign together. This futures-oriented work requires planning beyond the school's confines because community organizations routinely offer opportunities for instruction and participation.

In all of these special subjects, there is no reason to hold firm on the idea that all instruction, learning and participation are bounded by the school's walls and timetables. Certified teachers are not the only experts.

Two developing models for what a school is, prioritizes, and does, offer opportunities for PE's redesign.

Digital age learning systems

Digital age learning systems usher in the first set of opportunities, alternatively called "challenges". These systems present alternatives to the inherited model for teaching-instruction orchestrated and controlled by specialist teachers. No longer is it assumed that all learning is attributable to teachers. However, it is assumed that teachers have pivotal roles to play in preparing students to learn how to learn, nearly anytime and anywhere. Ultimately, learning systems, both assisted and self-directed, are as important as teaching systems. Armour and colleagues provide examples in Chapter 9.

Children's identity development

The second set of questions is founded on perceived needs to provide identity-related supports and life skills guidance to young people. This broad pedagogy is gaining traction as educators seek better ways to attract and engage young people, particularly as their families change. In this new framework, learning is not merely directed at knowledge, skills, attitudes and behaviours. *Educators assume shared responsibilities for students' identity development.* The foundational assumption is noteworthy: students' life plans and choices are keys to attendance, engagement, learning and success.

Consider young peoples' perspectives. Why stay in school and strive to succeed if there is no tangible reward? Why engage in PE if there are no perceived benefits, both immediate and long-term? Are physical activity, sport and health-enhancing lifestyle choices merely behaviours that I adopt, or are they defining features of who I am and wish to become?

These questions introduce educators' importance in helping students envision, and strive to achieve their envisioned, "possible selves", i.e. what they wish to be and become. Typically visions of possible selves develop in tandem with companion visions of "avoidant selves" – for example, a sedentary, obese person who smokes cigarettes.

In both cases – possible selves and avoidant selves – identity-development is the driver, and the guiding theory is identity-based motivation theory (Oyersman, 2015). This theory and its practical applications offer opportunities for teachers to engage, assist, and support young people in new and better ways (e.g. Oliver *et al.*, Chapter 8). "Want-to motives" co-constructed with students substitute for

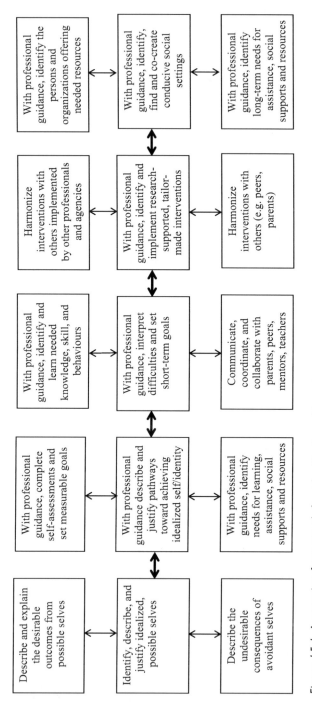

Figure 15.1 A practice framework for identity-based learning.

teacher-directed "have-to motives". Motivational congruence develops between teachers and students as they plan together.

Where PE and PETE are concerned, this new approach mixes conventional pedagogy, learning systems, and identity development systems. Figure 15.1 presents a PE practice framework. It builds on, but also transcends what many PE teachers have learned to call "exercise prescription". It prepares students for future learning in whatever physical activity and sporting pursuits they value.

Comparing and contrasting three models

Table 15.1 presents these three models: teaching-instruction, learning systems, and identity development systems. They are not mutually exclusive. Elements of all three are already evident in new school designs planned and implemented during turbulent times. Perhaps their main contribution is signalled in the title for this chapter. They signal that PE professionals must learn to plan and plan to learn during turbulent times.

Conclusion

Together, this book's chapters are like essential pieces of a giant jigsaw puzzle. Unfortunately, there is no clear picture on the top of the puzzle box, and there is no reason to believe that a one best puzzle design will be fit for purpose everywhere in the world. While this unavoidable situation poses challenges to PE professionals seeking to adopt and implement a "one best system", it also illuminates a twenty-first century agenda named "planning to learn and learning to plan". A PE profession accustomed to merely borrowing and implementing models and strategies developed elsewhere needs to get ready for futures-oriented planning, particularly innovations that prepare students for today's and tomorrow's turbulent times.

International and comparative analyses such as this book's chapters provide resources and guidance. They also offer opportunities for lesson-drawing and justifiable technology transfer.

Meanwhile, teachers, teacher educators, policy leaders, and specialists from related fields (e.g. kinesiology, sport science, public health) offer specialized expertise and contributions. Unfortunately, in some nations they are not aligned. They may even work at cross-purposes.

Imagine how much more child advocates might accomplish if they planned and learned together. Collective action strategies promise better outcomes for teachers, teacher educators, schools, families and communities, realizing a promise that standalone schools and their specialized subject matter configurations cannot keep. As planning shifts from isolated schools to education systems, including fresh priorities for learning systems and young people's identity development, opportunities for innovative school-community partnerships and interprofessional collaboration grow. Young people will benefit, and so will PE teachers whose working conditions in inherited school designs are sub-optimal. Other benefits will follow as PE leaders learn to plan and plan to learn during turbulent times.

Table 15.1 A comparison of programmes for instruction, learning and identity development

	Instruction	Learning	Identity development
Primary target(s)	Individual students in the context of groups (classes)	Individuals and groups	Individuals, peer groups, parents, family systems, communities
Locus of expertise	The instructor, teacher, trainer	Teachers and peers with expertise	Distributed among significant others and variable over time
The curriculum	Pre-packaged curricula with a clear beginning and end; and with predetermined measurable outcomes amenable to examination	Learning opportunities indexed against twenty-first century skills provided to individuals, groups, and teams in a variety of settings	Connecting physically active, health-enhancing lifestyles with possible and avoidant selves, emphasizing pathways to achieve idealized selves
Primary materials	Teacher-developed and controlled sports, games, and exercise/fitness regimens	Structured problem-solving tools and protocols; web resources; e-resources	Structured problem-solving tools and protocols; web resources; community assessment data
Curriculum design challenge	Make the curriculum 'teacher- and trainer proof'	Ensure authentic assessments and best learning practices to achieve desired outcomes	Authentic participation in one or more health-enhancing communities of practice
Key problem(s)	Student/trainee resistance and lack of engagement; large, heterogeneous classes, lack of differentiated instruction; elitism and gender biases; teacher role stress and conflict	Preparing expert learning facilitators; creating and connecting supportive settings; engaging, empowering, and retaining reluctant learners	Countering sedentary and unhealthy lifestyles among significant others; providing psychological safety for learning about embodiment; personalizing interventions
Temporal orientation	Bracketed by the hours/time schedules of schooling	Bridges in-school and out-of-school time	Framed by life course health development theory and bridging in-school and out-of-school-time via connections to peer networks, family ecologies, and community characteristics

	Instruction	Learning	Identity development
Power relations	Asymmetrical: professional knows best	Power shifting: continuous recalibration as learners progress and develop mastery	Power sharing: young people are afforded agency, voice and choice
View of the child/youth	Student	Student and learner	Children and youths
Teacher/coach/leader needs	Student behavioural compliance and management; whole group engagement strategies; devising defensible evaluation and grading plans	Acquiring and learning new theories, models, strategies, protocols, and tools for extended, expanded, accelerated, and connected learning, including digital portfolio development that encompasses students' activity profiles	Developing clinical-counselling expertise focused on young people's embodiment and physical literacy; person-centred interventions that are tailor-made for identifiable sub-populations of young people
Accountability structures	Involuntary and external: rule-based and procedures-oriented	Mixed and improvement-oriented: results- and performance-based	Primarily voluntary with shared accountability among teachers, young people, parents and community leaders
Formidable constraints and barriers	The logic of the industrial age school, especially conformity to the model for core academic subjects	The reluctance of teachers to view students as 'developing experts', and ability to learn from them as curriculum and instruction are planned and implemented	The institutionalized apparatus for PE in schools; the current design of teacher education programmes; inherited roles of PETE and PE professionals
Orientation to place and local contexts	Place- and context-insensitive: norms of generalizability and transferability emphasize replication and standardization	Place- and context-dependent, including priorities for place-based learning and pedagogies	Place- and context-dependent with special priorities for school–family–community partnerships for active lifestyles
Role of local community leader	Indirect: provide resources, assistance, and support	Direct, active facilitation of learning and participation during out-of-school time; firm connections to in-school time and learning	Direct: specialist people and mechanisms for cross-boundary collaboration, cemented by organizational partnerships among schools, youth sports organizations, and youth development agencies

References

Drucker, P.F. (2008). *The Essential Drucker: The Best Sixty years of Peter Drucker's Essential Writings on Management*. New York: Collins Business Essentials.

Elmore, R. (2008). *School Reform from The Inside Out*. Cambridge, MA: Harvard Education Press.

Lawson, H.A. (2001). Globalization, flows of culture and people, and new century frameworks for family-centered policies, practices, and development. In K. Briar-Lawson, H.A. Lawson, and C.B. Hennon with A. Jones (eds.), *Family-centered Policies and Practices: International Implications*. New York: Columbia University Press, 338–376.

Lawson, H.A. (2017). Reproductive, reformist, and transformative socialization. In K.A.R. Richards and K.L. Gaudreault (eds), *New Perspectives on Teacher Socialization in Physical Education*. New York: Routledge, pp. 243–261.

Lawson, H.A. (2018). *Redesigning Physical Education: An Equity Agenda in Which Every Child Matters*. London: Routledge.

Lawson, H.A. (2019a). Social determinants of the physical education system. *Quest*. doi: 10.1080/00336297.2019.1632214

Lawson, H.A. (2019b). The physical education system as a consequential social determinant. *Quest*. doi:10.1080/00336297.2019.1627224

Lawson, H.A. and Van Veen, D. (eds) (2016). *Developing Community Schools, Community Learning Centers, Extended-Service, and Multi-Service Schools: International Exemplars for Practice, Policy, and Research*. The Hague, NL: Springer International.

Macdonald, D., McCuaig, L. and Enright, E. (2018). Re-visioning the Australian curriculum for health and physical education. In H.A. Lawson (ed.), *Redesigning Physical Education: An Equity Agenda in Which Every Child Matters*. London: Routledge, pp. 195–205.

Oyersman, D. (2015). *Pathways to Success through Identity-Based Motivation*. New York: Oxford University Press.

Rose, R. (1993). *Lesson-Drawing in Public Policy: A Guide to Learning across Time and Space*. Washington, DC: CQ Press.

Schön, D.A. and Rein, M. (1994). *Frame Reflection: Toward the Resolution of Intractable Policy Controversies*. New York: Basic Books.

Tomporowski, P. and Pesce, C. (In press). Exercise, sports, and performance arts benefit cognition via a common process. *Psychological Bulletin*.

United Nations Educational, Scientific, and Cultural Organisation (2019). *Migration, Displacement, and Education: Building Bridges, Not Walls*. Global Education Monitoring Report 2019. Paris: Author. Retrieved from: https://unesdoc.unesco.org/ark:/48223/pf0000265866/PDF/265866eng.pdf.multi

Chapter 16

Developing commitments and capacity to learn with, and from, each other

Ann MacPhail

The intention of this book is to generate a scholarly forum for strategic planning, proactive leadership, and adaptive designs to shape more desirable futures for physical education (PE), physical education teacher education (PETE), teachers, children and youth, and schools and communities. "Grand challenges" are identified and presented in each chapter (Chapters 2 through 14) in a bid to capture illuminating dramatic, and somewhat variable, changes underway in nations around the world. Chapter authors were encouraged to propose collective action strategies in response to each grand challenge on how best to respond (e.g. via reform and improvement strategies) as well as whether, and how, to assume leadership for bold redesign strategies.

Author teams were asked to propose a collaborative, relevant future research and development agenda for a specialized grand challenge. Analysis of their respective chapters yields five components in a shared agenda:

1   the most effective ways to justify and advocate for PE as well as providing evidence of student learning in PE;
2   an improved and sustained shared collaboration, with enhanced responsibility, alignment and coherence across PETE, policy makers and PE spaces in schools in a bid to ultimately support young people's physical activity, sport and health-related needs;
3   the extension of collaboration beyond subject-specific PE to encourage PE/PETE stakeholders to be involved in deeper connections across school and community, working towards a strong integrated educational system;
4   professional development configurations that provide a shared space for all stakeholder groups and prioritize career-long adaptive competence; and
5   inter- and multi-disciplinary connections that will encourage effective "boundary spanning", nationally and internationally, across and external to PE/PETE.

While each chapter explores a specific grand challenge, they collectively represent the complex ecologies of PE and PETE that arise when conversations arise in response to specific "grand challenges" for PE/PETE across numerous associated stakeholders and differing context and cultures. Each writing team was tasked with presenting a chapter that incorporates professional partnerships in favour of positioning separate experiences. Authors self-identified across a range of "professions", including as a consultant for career transitions, curriculum manager, education officer, pedagogical coordinator, PhD candidate, professional practice fellow, professor, programme manager, school teacher, teacher educator and university instructor. It should also be noted that while individuals identified currently occupying one position, a number of contributors have transitioned within, and across, stakeholder groups during their professional career. Indeed, some contributors work in a "third space", e.g. a curriculum manager working between schools and universities.

The complement of authors represents individuals residing in different jurisdictions and includes Australia, Belgium, Canada, Ireland, Japan, the Kingdom of Saudi Arabia, New Zealand, Sweden, the UK (England and Scotland) and the US. Such an impressive collection of individuals encourages us to consider who the "actors" in PE/PETE are and how to most effectively ensure their respective voices are appropriately represented. Critical contributions of partnerships and professional cultures are the main threads throughout this concluding chapter.

Twenty-first century thinking and global themes

The sub-title of the book, "Collaborative redesign for the twenty-first century", deliberately draws attention to the importance of considering twenty-first century challenges and generating new considerations and thinking related to what needs to be different in schools if young people are to be well prepared for life in the knowledge age. Twenty-first century thinking and the associated drive for "twenty-first century skills", such as teamwork, critical thinking and technology literacy (Bellanca and Brandt, 2010), are required to attend to global themes.

Important global themes emphasized in the previous chapters include: (1) social, economic, political and digital transformations; (2) the increasing drive for accountability, performativity and achievement outcomes; and (3) the diversity of contexts in which we each operate and how, in turn, we effectively address diversity. It is evident that traditions and culture mediate all such global imperatives. We are each therefore encouraged to consider the extent to which the collective action strategy suggested in response to each "grand challenge" is scalable to our specific context. Directions on how best to critically consider this are captured in the lesson-drawing framework and criteria for programme transportability shared in Chapter 15.

It is important to acknowledge the intensification of the above-noted global themes via a Global Education Reform Movement. This movement is founded on a neoliberal educational reform orthodoxy within many education systems throughout the world. Sahlberg (2016) notes five globally common features of education policies and reform principles: (i) *standardization of education*; (ii) *focus on core subjects* in school; (iii) *the search for low-risk ways of reaching learning goals*; (iv) *use of corporate management models* as a main driver of improvement, and (v) adoption of *test-based accountability policies* for schools.

The chapters of this book have, to differing extents, challenged this prevailing neo-liberal agenda. While distinctive responses are evident in chapters, the impact of globalization reveals a similarity in the responses across chapters. Proposals such as culturally responsive teaching and constructive pedagogies are considered to respond more appropriately to diversity (see Chapters 8 and 9) and are central to collective action strategies. Many chapters suggest how established teachers and beginning teachers can be supported in making necessary changes for diverse learners and contexts to optimize learning for all.

"Mind the (collaboration) 'gap'"

This concluding chapter builds on a point shared in the exit section of Chapter 15 – namely, PE and PETE stakeholders (i.e. teachers, students, schools, teacher educators, pre-service teachers (PSTs), government agencies, policymakers, communities) are challenged to plan and learn together with the intention of delivering collective action strategies. There continues to be a need for greater coordination between researchers, policymakers and practitioners (The Royal Society/The British Academy, 2018).

A main premise and intention of this book that aligns with this challenge, and underpins the focus of this concluding chapter, was clear from the start of the book,

> The bottom line remains and can no longer be ignored and denied. There is a significant gap between recommended practices and policies and what happens in the day-to-day realities of schools. To address this, we need to stop working in isolation and work with, and learn from, each other, while remaining mindful of systematic differences visible nationally and internationally. […] allows for a shared understanding on why we have set such an agenda and encourages enactment through ongoing learning and capacity building.
>
> (Chapter 1)

Chapter 15 aids the reader in considering how they go about determining the extent to which what they have read in the preceding chapters relates to their own context, whether that be local, state, regional or national. Taking a different, but complementary, stance, this final chapter's focus is on exploring the process by which we have, and can, most effectively work with, and learn from, each other as close to the inception of an idea/the identification of a "grand challenge" as possible.

Equitable accountability

How best can all PE/PETE stakeholders (whoever is deemed to be relevant stakeholders under the specific circumstance) be held accountable for determining an international framework for strategic planning, proactive leadership, and adaptive designs. Equitable accountability means that all relevant PE/PETE stakeholders be legitimized as contributors from the beginning discussions of what this book has termed "grand challenges". Two questions arise.

First, have the chapters of this book provided space where a range of PE/PETE stakeholders authentically contributed to considering the specific grand challenge and, in turn, agreed what the related collective action project should be? An affirmative response to this question would suggest that including a range of PE/PETE stakeholders is likely to encourage the involvement of those responsible for confronting how best to respond to the specific grand challenge, those likely to be directly affected by the specific grand challenge (and therefore able to accurately determine the respective ongoing needs and demands) as well as those expected to assume leadership for bold redesign strategies (an intention noted in Chapters 1 and 11). This situation supports the notion of "meeting spaces between settings" (Chapter 6) and "shared occupational space" (see Chapter 11).

Second, are there instances where it is the case that the work that lies ahead on completion of the chapters by specific PE/PETE stakeholders, and starts now, is a collective action project that requires additional stakeholders to be identified and included for successful delivery of the project? An affirmative response to this question might imply there is a rational argument for specific PE/PETE stakeholders initially working in isolation from other stakeholders in addressing a grand challenge. Once the groundwork has been completed by the specific PE/PETE stakeholders then the "collective action project" is shared with other stakeholders. This situation alerts us to considering the extent to which it is important that those stakeholders completing the "groundwork" acknowledge what they do know as well as what they do not know about the circumstances surrounding the grand challenge.

There are of course other ways in which different stakeholders' views can be captured and represented other than from being involved in the production of a book chapter. For example, it is clear from reading Chapter 9 that the authors have drawn on their research with a wide range of stakeholders, including young people, care-experienced youth, academic leaders and practitioners. The important word here is "with". That is, they have worked "with" (rather than "on") a wide range of stakeholders, conveying a level of respect and integrity, in capturing and representing views. Indeed, there are likely to be instances when this is the preferred means of capturing views (from the perspective of those looking to capture the views as well as those providing the views) rather than a more formal and potentially greater commitment to a writing project, such as a book chapter.

Three considerations for working with, and learning from, each other

1 Roles, responsibilities and weakening boundaries

There is no denying the centrality of teachers (Stenhouse, 1981) and students (Fielding, 2001) as active agents in any collective action strategy with the intent of making progress in meeting the physical activity, sport and health-related needs of children and youth worldwide. Teachers' perspectives relate to the reality of the complex, multi-layered contexts in which they work, referred to as an ecosystem of structures, cultures, practices and policies (Godfrey and Brown, 2019) (see Chapter 5). An understanding of young people and their experiences and perspectives should be central to any consideration of how best to support their physical activity, sport and health-related needs, while instilling a sense of empowerment (see Chapters 8 and 9).

Different and complementary roles and responsibilities

The roles and responsibilities of a range of stakeholder groups can be different and complementary (see Chapter 10). The principle of complementary expertise (Locke, 2017) is important, acknowledging that stakeholders/partners bring different kinds of expertise and all have something to offer. However, the challenge resides in putting that discourse into practice through those stakeholders who may be more privileged than others (Chapter 8), and inviting, and working with, different but complementary stakeholders to determine collective action strategies. In working towards this, it is prudent to establish the essential roles and responsibilities of all PE/PETE stakeholder categories in planning for, and delivering, collective action strategies and also the extent to which such roles and responsibilities are mutually exclusive, or not.

Ecosystem of research informed practice

There is widespread agreement that effective teaching draws on research to inform professional practice. This includes teachers being assisted in accessing research, learning how to read research, applying research to practice and, most recently, gaining skills and guidance in conducting research into, and to inform, their own practice. Cain (2019) shares an ecosystem that views research informed practice at the policy level (exosystem level), at the practising teacher level (mesosystemic level) and during initial teacher education (microsystemic level). At the exosystem level, government policy encourages development of school–university partnerships so that university research expertise is available to schools. At the mesosystemic level, experienced teachers are encouraged to engage with/in research, both for their own professional development and to support initial teacher education. At the microsystemic level, PSTs are encouraged to read research about these areas and to use their reading to plan, implement and evaluate improvements in their own practice. Elements of this ecosystem are captured in Chapters 12 and 14.

Scholar-practitioner and practitioner-scholar roles

The roles of scholar and practitioner are not mutually exclusive, with an increasing number of practitioners doing scholarly work, and an increasing number of scholars also engaged in policy and practice (De Wit, 2016). Consequently, this challenges the boundaries between those who are primarily responsible for delivering PE/PETE and those primarily responsible for studying/researching PE/PETE. There is a need to support the professional journey experienced by those wishing to become a practitioner-scholar as well as a scholar-practitioner. In turn, this will hopefully result in making explicit the links between theory/research and practice (Chapter 12) and finding alternative ways to close the multiple theory/research–practice gaps that restrict the growth of knowledge in the PE/PETE field (Chapter 9). There is a growing interest in long-term collaborations between practitioners and researchers which are organized to investigate problems of practice and solutions for improving educational practice. Such collaborations have been termed "research-practice partnerships" (Coburn and Penuel, 2016).

The practitioner-scholar role continues to gain support across many jurisdictions that stipulate teacher education programmes are required to provide sufficient space in the programme to prepare PSTs for the role of "teacher as researcher"/research-engaged practice (The Teaching Council, 2017). This has subsequently led to a strong emphasis on collaboration between teachers and research activities that strengthens the links between research, policy and practice (see Chapters 11, 12 and 14). Ways that research can contribute to programmes of teacher education have been previously documented (BERA/RSA, 2014). Indeed, it has been suggested that if we are to support schools in becoming enquiry-based learning organizations, that evaluation criteria are designed around how schools engage in research and use research evidence to inform their practice (Ehren, 2019).

The development of the scholar-practitioner is encouraged by supporting collaboration between teachers and other stakeholders in education, enhanced in some instances by joint funding opportunities (see Chapter 14). This trend is increasingly evident across international funding agency calls (e.g. Erasmus+) that require funding to support education, training, youth and sport and which are contingent on academic institutes working in partnership with schools, training agencies, community organizations, national government agencies, etc. This, in turn, supports a strengthening of (professional) community–university practitioner–scholar and scholar–practitioner partnerships. Indeed, key objectives of the 2011 founding of the *Research in Sport Pedagogy Network* of the European Educational Research Association were to stimulate research collaborations across national boundaries and to develop strong consortia that can bid for research grants. It would appear timely to revisit and act on these key objectives.

It was explicit in some of the preceding chapters that receiving recognition for the work undertaken as a practitioner-scholar or scholar-practitioner is crucial to developing the related capacities within the PE/PETE profession (see Chapters 6 and 11). University-based teacher educators need to be able to support teachers to respond to changes, while simultaneously meeting the expectations associated with their university roles (Cowie and Cooper, 2018). Building academic support structures in higher education for practitioner scholarship (Chapters 11 and 12) and enhancing opportunities for practitioners to develop their research knowledge and skills (Chapters 4 and 12) are considered essential in providing recognition to practitioner research and scholarship.

2 Support structures and networking as effective practice

Much has been written about professional learning communities (see Chapter 13). While attention has tended to focus on catering for communities that service a specific group of stakeholder (e.g. teachers or teacher educators), less attention has been focused on the notion of collective professional learning communities that deliberately set out to provide a supportive and safe space for multiple groups of stakeholders.

Professional learning community for multiple stakeholders

The communities of learning supported by the New Zealand government initiative, *Investing in Educational Success*, include school leaders, educators and professional development providers who aim to help students achieve their full potential (McNae and Cowie, 2017). Shared goals or achievement challenges are agreed and the learning communities then work with students, parents and communities to achieve these challenges. One would anticipate that, related to the premise of this book, such collaboration and sharing of expertise could only enhance the intent of making progress in meeting the physical activity, sport and health-related needs of children and youth worldwide. In turn, such collaboration and sharing of expertise could result in personal empowerment, allowing individual and collective stakeholders to gain a growing sense of identifying with something bigger than the individual self, and which enhances the self's sense of meaningfulness (Locke, 2017).

Networking as a collective strategy

In order to consider the most effective way to approach the evolution of professional learning communities, networking as an effective practice is a compelling consideration. As Groundwater-Smith (2017) explains, networking

> is not a practice that treats others as a means to an end, but rather builds in a reciprocity that will bring benefits to those with whom a networker engages. It requires consummate skill and sensitivity […] enthusiasm, generosity, trustworthiness, commitment, approachability and sincerity […] a sense of responsibility that will enable each party to share and interrogate information.
>
> (Groundwater-Smith, 2017, p. xx)

Social networking (face-to-face and online) as a form of professional support for novice and experienced teachers has gained popularity, acknowledging the continued prevalence of networked social platforms such as Facebook, LinkedIn, Skype and Twitter. To be a "networked teacher" it is suggested that a teacher understands the theory and research behind social networks and puts this knowledge into action (Baker-Doyle, 2011). Goodyear *et al.* (2014) explored how social media operated as a communicative space, external to the physical site of an emerging community of practice that supported physical education teachers' professional learning and their subsequent longer term changing practice.

It is important to acknowledge that there is no guarantee that similar groups of stakeholders not involved in the professional learning communities would arrive at, and support, the specific collective action strategy. However, if, in becoming aware of the collective action strategy, they become excited about how best to solve the grand challenge from their perspective, and in turn identify an alternative collective action strategy, this would be a worthwhile achievement.

True partnership and communication across PE/PETE

It is the concept of effective partnerships that will determine the "readiness" of PE/PETE to work together on collective action strategies with the intent of making progress in meeting the physical activity, sport and health-related needs of children and youth worldwide. The increasing need for professions (primarily through evidence-based practice/academic research) to feed policy and practice in the field heightens the necessity for PE/PETE stakeholders to consider how best to work in partnership (see Chapters 2 and 12) and how best to communicate their shared message. A frequent message that arises across the complement of chapters is the (un)intentional partnership that exists between PE and PETE. That is, changes in one influence, and are influenced by, the other.

Learning from, and negotiating, partnerships

In a true partnership, knowledge is multi-perspectival, acknowledging that no one person or organization has a monopoly on the knowledge required for wise decision-making (Locke, 2017). As Western (2019) warns,

> Researchers who want to partner deeply need to listen to properly understand a problem as partners define it, and to understand their partners' needs and constraints. Taking these considerations seriously enables researchers to tap into real-world expertise – taking what we know, but modifying it for new problems.
>
> (Western, 2019, p. 28)

A challenge to understanding others' considerations is negotiating the most effective mode and style of communication that allows stakeholders' perspectives and expertise to be captured, as we move towards agreeing a collective action strategy. The lead authors of a selection of the preceding chapters shared that it was most effective for them to arrange phone or Skype calls with co-authors in order to capture specific stakeholders' perspectives rather than rely on all co-authors solely contributing in writing to the development of a chapter. In some instances this added to the complexity of stakeholder partnerships as regards finding mutually suitable times and modes through which to communicate.

Strategies for communicating productively

Another communication challenge is to develop strategies for communicating productively with those we hope will use our research (e.g. teachers, academic colleagues, national and international policy communities). It is no longer feasible to rely on traditional forms of dissemination that tend to target specific stakeholders, e.g. written reports with restrictive access to policymakers, publications for paid academic subscribers. Social networks (e.g. blogs, websites, Twitter) are increasing the exposure of information, becoming places where stakeholders can connect with others with similar interests, access and discuss research as well as share their expertise and perspectives. This requires interrogating the motives for social media posts beyond what could be considered "self-promotion". Indeed, social networks have the potential to produce more connected educational research communities across multiple stakeholders than perhaps more traditional/dated practices. The participation of all stakeholders in the dissemination of collective action strategies offers an increased likelihood that findings are expressed in a language, and in ways and formats, that the respective peer group of stakeholders will understand (Cowie, 2017).

Are we ready to engage with collective action strategies?

To what extent is PE/PETE ready to engage with collective action strategies from an individual, collective and infrastructural perspective? This includes considering PE/PETE may not yet be in a place where stakeholders and/or infrastructures allow for the development of collective action strategies.

Determining and appreciating "space" and "flexibility"

In working predominantly with the chapter lead authors and discussing the realities of working with, and learning from, colleagues operating in other stakeholder groups, it became evident that the notion of "space" and "flexibility" occupied much of our conversations. The range of co-authors are aligned with many different affiliations, whether it be higher education institutes, research centres, schools or curriculum agencies. More specifically, on a daily basis, the space they occupy includes predominantly an office, a laboratory, school gymnasiums or meeting rooms. Working across these spaces has, for some authors, heightened the acknowledgement of how busy we all are in working hard in different ways in order to fulfil the different expectations of our respective roles and responsibilities. It is also evident that the spaces some stakeholders occupy allow for a greater level of flexibility, not only in the working day but also in terms of determining, to some extent, what specific areas they invest their energies in (e.g. higher education institutes). It is imperative that those who are more privileged with space and flexibility consider how to effectively encourage and support ways in which to work with, and learn from, colleagues operating in other stakeholder groups.

Advocating for shared recognition

In some instances, there is minimal recognition for some stakeholder populations to commit to working with others under the auspices of working towards collective action strategies for (physical) education. It is therefore essential that those of us wishing to be involved in such work educate those responsible for recognition within the specific stakeholder fields to the necessity and value of working with those operating at different levels of the education system. The impact of this would be enhanced if members across stakeholder fields (e.g. a PE teacher, physical education teacher educator and curriculum manager) were to join together in advocating for shared recognition. It needs to be made clear that this type of operation is necessary if we are to successfully justify and advocate for school PE (Chapter 2) and provide evidence on the learning that takes place in school PE (Chapter 2, 3, 4 and 5). This positioning needs to be aligned with considering the most effective way in which such work complements, and contributes to, already recognized practices and infrastructures.

Acknowledging the "privileged"

Returning to "networking as effective practice", it is likely that, dependent on the "grand challenge", there will be a more privileged group of stakeholders (see Chapter 8) who already have some expertise related to the grand challenge and/or have inhabited a space where they have experienced the reality of the grand challenge. In such instances, it is prudent that such groups of stakeholders are responsible for establishing, enacting and sustaining partnership work. In doing so, there needs to be an acknowledgement that different groups of stakeholders/partners are not always equally involved and the implications of the project for their day-to-day interactions and agendas are not the same (Cowie and McNae, 2017).

For numerous co-authors (predominantly PE teachers, education officers, professional practice fellows/instructors and programme managers), this was the first time they had been approached by "colleagues" residing in other stakeholder groups, far less asked if they would be willing to join a team and work towards a collective action strategy. This resulted in the identification of talented and committed individuals who, while less confident about their abilities to be involved in what in essence was a writing project, could not be faulted on the level of experience, expertise and passion they possess with respect to the specific grand challenge. Indeed, in some chapters we explicitly hear from these individuals (see Chapters 2, 7, 11 and 14).

For other co-authors (predominantly those working in higher academic institutes), this provided the first, or rare, opportunity for them to write with different stakeholder(s). In talking with some of the lead authors, this led to them gaining a new respect for, and appreciation of, the recognition of possibilities that arises in undertaking such collaborative work. This is evident when reading epilogues that some of the chapter teams have chosen to include (see Chapters 4, 7, 8, 11 and 14).

Conclusion

A main premise of this book is to acknowledge that we need to stop working in isolation and work with, and learn from, each other, while remaining mindful of systematic differences visible nationally and internationally. Lead authors have chosen various ways, and extents, in which to address this, including working with colleagues across different jurisdictions, working with colleagues with differing experiences and perspectives (and across different jurisdictions), as well as identifying representation from different stakeholder populations in a bid to represent a multi-layered response to the grand challenge. An extension to the conversation is in considering working with specialists from the related fields of kinesiology, sport science and public health (for example) (see Chapters 6 and 15). That is, to what extent can (and should) PE professionals consider serving as boundary spanners (see Chapter 6) across interdisciplinary, as well as multidisciplinary, networks/sub-specialties (Lawson, 2009).

The dual challenge set for the chapters in this book has been to consider a specific grand challenge and which reflective stakeholders to work with, and learn from, in proposing a collective action strategy. This has resulted in writing teams considering the "added value" of including authors with whom they may not have previously worked. In instances where such individuals agreed to be included, it was evident that this posed numerous challenges to the collective writing team with respect to considering what was to be prioritized in the chapter and how best to capture the multiple positions inhabited by the chapter contributors.

This pushed us to consider options, ideas and perspectives outside our usual/daily "zone" and recognize that we do not always know everything there is to know, as well as acknowledge that we do not know what we do not know. This sharing of space was new (and uncomfortable) for some contributors and heightened the extent to which we each consider (regardless of our affiliation with a specific group of stakeholders) our interest and ability to act as "critical friends" within, and across, stakeholder groups. That is, how best do we ensure that the "starting point" and subsequent conversation related to a grand challenge encapsulates a level of inclusiveness that allows for flexibility and freedom in determining where different stakeholder energies are best invested? How can we ensure that such investment results in high quality and high equity of provision? It might only be in considering these questions that we can legitimately make progress in establishing an evidence base through international collaboration and transnational and comparative research (informed by the authors of each chapter and summarized at the start of this chapter) that shifts our thinking on how to most effectively meet the physical activity, sport and health-related needs of children and youth worldwide.

References

Baker-Doyle, K.J. (2011). *The Networked Teacher: How New Teachers Build Social Networks for Professional Support*. New York: Teachers College Press.

Bellanca, J. and Brandt, R. (eds) (2010). *21st Century Skills. Rethinking How Students Learn*. Bloomington, IN: Solution Tree Press.

British Educational Research Association/Royal Society for the Encouragement of the Arts, Manufacturing and Commerce (2014). *The Role of Research in Teacher Education: Reviewing the Evidence*. London: BERA/RSA.

Cain, T. (2019). Research-informed initial teacher education. In D. Godfrey and C. Brown (eds), *An Ecosystem for Research-engaged Schools*. Abingdon, Oxon: Routledge, pp. 123–137.

Coburn, C.E. and Penuel, W.R. (2016). Research-practice partnerships in education: outcomes, dynamics, and open questions. *Educational Researcher*, 45(1), 48–54.

Cowie, B. (2017). Introduction: partnership as knowledge building and exchange among stakeholders. In R. McNae and B. Cowie (eds), *Realising Innovative Partnerships in Educational Research*. Rotterdam: Sense, pp. 117–121.

Cowie, B. and Cooper, B. (2018). Looking for synergies to meet the challenges of teacher education. In C. Wyatt-Smith and L. Adie (eds), *Innovation and Accountability in Teacher Education*. Singapore: Springer, pp. 187–200.

Cowie, B. and McNae, R. (2017). Partnership research: a relational practice. In R. McNae and B. Cowie (eds), *Realising Innovative Partnerships in Educational Research*. Rotterdam: Sense, pp. xvii–xxi.

De Wit, H. (2016). Foreword. In B. Streitwieser and A.C. Ogden (eds), *International Higher Education's Scholar-Practitioners*. Oxford: Symposium Books, pp. 9–12.

Ehren, M. (2019). Accountability structures that support school self-evaluation, enquiry and learning. In D. Godfrey and C. Brown (eds), *An Ecosystem for Research-engaged Schools*. Abingdon, Oxon: Routledge, pp. 41–55.

Fielding, M. (2001). Students as radical agents of change. *Journal of Educational Change*, 2(2), 123–141.

Godfrey, D. and Brown, C. (eds) (2019). *An Ecosystem for Research-engaged Schools*. Abingdon, Oxon: Routledge.

Goodyear, V.A., Casey, A. and Kirk, D. (2014). Tweet me, message me, like me: using social media to facilitate pedagogical change within an emerging community of practice. *Sport, Education and Society*, 19(7), 927–943.

Groundwater-Smith, S. (2017). Partnerships, networks and learning in educational research: contested practices. In R. McNae and B. Cowie (eds), *Realising Innovative Partnerships in Educational Research*. Rotterdam: Sense, pp. xvii–xxi.

Lawson, H.A. (2009). Paradigms, exemplars and social change. *Sport, Education and Society*, 14(1), 97–119.

Locke, T. (2017). Community partnerships creating spaces for democratising enterprise. In R. McNae and B. Cowie (eds), *Realising Innovative Partnerships in Educational Research*. Rotterdam: Sense, pp. 191–196.

McNae, R. and Cowie, B. (2017). Elaborating local research agendas. In R. McNae and B. Cowie (eds), *Realising Innovative Partnerships in Educational Research*. Rotterdam: Sense, pp. ix–xv.

Sahlberg, P. (2016). The global educational reform movement and its impact on schooling. In K. Mundy, A. Green, B. Lingard and A. Verger (eds), *The Handbook of Global Education Policy*. Chichester, UK: Wiley-Blackwell, pp. 128–144.

Stenhouse, L. (1981). What counts as research? *British Journal of Educational Studies*, 29(2), 103–114.

The Royal Society/The British Academy (2018). *Harnessing Educational Research*. London: The Royal Society.

The Teaching Council (2017). *Initial Teacher Education: Criteria and Guidelines for Programme Providers*. Maynooth: The Teaching Council.

Western, M. (2019). Listen to "lay experts". *Times Higher Education*, No. 2, 404, p. 28.

Index

Cain, T. 183
Cambodia, curriculum aims in 62
Canada, policy in 159
Capel, S. 135, 137
care-experienced young people (CEYP) 96–7
Casey, A. 120, 132
Centers for Disease Control and Prevention (CDC) 52, 128
co-authoring reports 145
Coll, R. 107
collaboration "gap" 181–2
collaboration within school districts 47–9
collaborative approach to curriculum development see school curriculum challenge
collaborative approach to policy making 160–1, 162
Collaborative for Academic, Social, and Emotional Learning (CASEL) 50–1
collaborative leadership 65–6
collaborative learning 100
collaborative professional development 119, 120, 121–3, 147–8
collaborative/shared research: and digital challenge 96–8, 99; in doctoral programmes 122–3; in Ireland 20; long-term 184; in New Zealand 19; recommendations for 55–6; and sensorimotor control concepts 66
collective action projects 182
collective action strategies 175, 181–2, 186, 187–9
colonialism 6
communication challenges 186–7
community leaders, role of in different learning/teaching models 177
community organizations 170, 173
community sports 61, 170
competing programme models 170
competition in PE 89
complementary expertise 183
conflicting programme aims 170
constraints and barriers in different learning/teaching models 177
constructivist-oriented curricula 75, 77
content descriptions 24
content knowledge of teachers 146, 148
contexts, importance of: in CPD 120; in curriculum development and enactment 106, 107, 108, 109; in finding solutions

3; minimized in handbooks 1; in policy making 157, 158; in student-centred inquiry 87; in technology transfer 167; in using research 129
continuing professional development (CPD) 141–52; and accountability 144–5; and alignment and coherence 41; and assessment 17; collaborative forms of 119, 120, 121–3, 147–8; and curriculum enactment 109–10, 111; and diversity 19; in Europe 146; importance of 15; incentives for 147, 149; international perspective 145–7; looking ahead 148–50; and the PE teaching profession 143–4, 145; and research 148, 150; in Scotland 147; silos in 123–5, 124; and socialization 118; standards and requirements 143; variability and context-specificity 146–7
continuum for teachers and teacher educators 120, 120–1
Cook-Sather, A. 82, 83
core subjects, focus on 180
corporate management models, use of 180
critical inquiry approaches 50
critical movement theory 141
cross-border learning 4–5, 166–7, 167–8
cultural competence challenge 82–91; Activist Approach 82–5, 88–9; building the foundation 85–6; example of student-centred inquiry 86–8
culture, collaboration as 47–8
curiosity as frame of reference 134, 134
curricular reform, standards-based see standards-based curricular reform challenge
curriculum development see school curriculum challenge; standards-based curricular reform challenge
curriculum, in different learning/teaching models 176
curriculum planning and student centred inquiry 85–6
curriculum reform as policy 155, 156

data collection 129, 137, 137–8
decision-making 51
deficit, avoiding sense of, in tasks for PSTs 134
dialogue between teachers 138